Professional Procedures & Portfolio Development

Taken from:

The Job Searcher's Handbook, Third Edition
by Carolyn R. Robbins

Brand You Marketing: Real People, Real Choices, Fourth Edition
by Michael R. Solomon, Greg W. Marshall, and Elnora W. Stuart, with Liz Harris-Tuck

Career Focus: A Personal Job Search Guide, Third Edition
by Helene Martucci Lamarre

Taken from:

The Job Searcher's Handbook, Third Edition
by Carolyn R. Robbins
Copyright © 2006, 2002, 1997 by Pearson Education, Inc.
Published by Prentice-Hall, Inc.
Upper Saddle River, New Jersey 07458

Brand You Marketing: Real People, Real Choices, Fourth Edition
by Michael R. Solomon, Greg W. Marshall, and Elnora W. Stuart, with Liz Harris-Tuck
Copyright © 2006 by Pearson Education, Inc.
Published by Prentice-Hall, Inc.

Career Focus: A Personal Job Search Guide, Third Edition
by Helene Martucci Lamarre
Copyright © 2006, 1998 by Pearson Education, Inc.
Published by Prentice-Hall, Inc.

This special edition is published in cooperation with Pearson Custom Publishing.

Printed in the United States of America

10 9 8 7 6 5 4

ISBN 0-536-17791-0

2005540119

EM

Please visit our web site at *www.pearsoncustom.com*

PEARSON CUSTOM PUBLISHING
75 Arlington Street, Suite 300, Boston, MA 02116
A Pearson Education Company

Brief Contents

Planning Your Career: The Advantage Is Undeniable   193

How do I develop a career plan? What are my career strengths? How can I find career opportunities in trends?

Creating the Product—You: Identifying Your Benefits   207

How can product layering help you define your strengths? How can you uncover the benefits you have to offer? How can you present a professional package?

What to Know and Do   217

Career Success Skills   223

Contents

3 Organizing, Searching, and Planning   109

Interviewing Made *Almost* Easy   133

Appendix   171

Welcome to Brand You: Creating and Delivering Career Value   185

Planning Your Career: The Advantage Is Undeniable   193

Creating the Product—You: Identifying Your Benefits 207

What to Know and Do 217

Career Success Skills 223

Taking Inventory

A constructive approach to job searching, career
changing, or making any life-altering decision should
begin with self-evaluation. Steven Graber, author of
The Everything Get-a-Job Book, says "One of the
biggest mistakes job seekers make is to start looking
for a job before they're really ready"[1]—and getting
ready begins with an honest self-assessment.

You can increase your chances of getting the job you want and being successful in it by taking the first step, that of honestly appraising who you are, what is important to you, and where you are going. You cannot honestly know what is going to make you happy and successful unless you first do some "inventorying." Therefore, contrary to popular belief, a job search does not begin with a resume; it begins with self-analysis.

Most people resist looking very long and hard at themselves. They are afraid to challenge their self-image and to examine their attitudes. They give very little thought to the context, the fundamentals of job searching, such as "What kind of person am I? What kind of people do I best interact with? Based on my values, what are the most important things I want in a job?" They usually just rationalize any self-evaluation away by saying, "Oh, I know me; I don't need all that stuff. I *know* what I want." However, when they begin to write their resume, they discover that they can't even construct a coherent job objective. In an interview, when asked what is most important to them, they mumble something about a good salary, good benefits, etc. To avoid having this happen to you and to help you succeed in getting the job that is right for you, begin by examining three important areas: your values, attitudes, and goals.

Personal Values: How They Affect Job Choices

What is a "value"? Marsha Sinetar in her book *Do What You Love and the Money Will Follow* describes a value as "something tangible or intangible that we esteem highly like health, truthfulness, beauty, courage, playfulness, self-sufficiency, wealth, and time to spend as we like." How do our values affect the choice of a job? Because you attribute worth, merit, or usefulness to your values, they greatly influence career and job choices. Also, your values change. What was worthwhile to you in earlier jobs may not be that important now, and other things may be more important. So, if you want to make wise choices in job selection, clarifying your values and deciding what's really important to you is a necessary step. Completing this step will help you to be more focused in your job search and to make healthy decisions (without internal conflict) about which job offers to accept and which ones to reject. According to Steven Reiss, Ph.D., in the *Reiss Profile of Fundamental Goals and Motivational Sensitivities*, shared values produce team spirit and cohesiveness in the workplace, whereas, conflicts of values lead to divisiveness and hidden agendas. He believes that "just because somebody can do something doesn't mean they'll be happy doing it. To do well in a career and enjoy life, people need to choose jobs compatible with their enduring strivings."[2]

When clarifying your values and deciding what is important to you, remember that self-evaluation is primarily a "do-it-yourself" project. Friends and family are not the ultimate authority on who you are or what you should do; *you* are the authority on you!

Consider the life of Babe Ruth, one of the all-time greats in American sports. As a boy, Babe was so incorrigible that he was sent to a school of correction for children. His parents gave up on him, and it was apparent to everyone that he was heading for a life of misery and failure. At one point in his life, however, Ruth looked into a mirror and saw a grim image of himself. He saw a young man without a reason to live and without a place to go in life. For the first time, he began to decide what was good and what was not good, and what was important to *Babe Ruth*. Not what was important to his parents, or the school, or his friends, but what was important to *him*. He changed his thinking and set his sights on baseball, and well, the rest is history. He went on to become one of the most legendary figures in the Baseball Hall of Fame.

Sadly, many people go to work each week hating Monday and praying for Friday, so to avoid that pitfall, it's vital that you take the time to assess your values and determine your needs in a job. From the list of personal values that follows, rate each one individually on a scale of 1 to 10, according to how important it is to you in the workplace. Do not *rank* them, that is, choosing only one as a "10," only one as a "9," and so on. They can be all 10s if that is how important they are to you. After you have rated them, go back and complete the statements after each value, then write out how they relate to the job you are seeking. Ask yourself, "How does this value affect my choice of a job?" Describe in detail how and why each one is important.

Personal Values

Rating scale: 1 = least important, 10 = most important

____ 1. *Recognition:* "I feel the most recognized when an employer

_____

_____

_____

_____

____ 2. *Independence:* "A supervisor monitoring what I do

_____

_____

_____

_____

____ 3. *Challenge/Variety:* "I have to be challenged and have variety in my work or

_____

_____

_____

_____

____ 4. *Money/Compensation:* "If I get paid (don't get paid) a salary that's equal to my worth, I

_____

_____

_____

_____

____ 5. *Respect:* "I feel respected in my job when an employer

_____

_____

_____

_____

____ 6. *Honesty:* "If my employer is dishonest, it does/doesn't affect me because

_____

_____

_____

_____

(continued)

PERSONAL VALUES Continued

____ 7. *Personal Pride/Satisfaction:* "My personal pride and satisfaction with my job are derived from

_____

_____

_____

_____

____ 8. *Health:* "My well-being and health are affected on the job

_____

_____

_____

_____

____ 9. *Family:* "My family (those persons most important to me) comes first/second to my job because

_____

_____

_____

_____

____10. *Education:* "It's important/not important that an employer assist me with furthering my education because

_____

_____

_____

_____

If there are other values of importance to you that are not named on these pages, use the space below to list them.

_____

_____

_____

_____

_____

_____

Based on how you rated your values and to get a clearer picture of where your priorities are, both personal and work-related, go to the next few pages. There, you will build your Personal Values Mountain and plot your Personal Values Wheel.

Values Mountain

 Values come in all shapes and colors. Some people divide values up into *Things & Processes*, *Intrapersonal* (things you value inside you), and *Interpersonal* (values between people).

Below are lists of some of those values. Over the next few pages, you will decide which of these values, or other values you add in, are the most important to you.

THINGS & PROCESSES

1. Prefer to work in *clean, orderly environment*.
2. Can tolerate *untidy workplace*.
3. Prefer *strict regulations*.
4. Prefer *low regulations*.
5. *Money/compensation*.
6. *Promotion or advancement*.
7. Prefer *casual wardrobe*.
8. Prefer *traditional wardrobe*.
9. *Slow-paced work* environment.
10. *Fast-paced work* environment.
11. *Task variety*.
12. *Similar tasks* every day.
13. *Like overtime*, more pay.
14. Prefer *time off*, no overtime.
15. *Flexible work schedules*.
16. *Fixed work schedule*.
17. Like to *travel*.
18. Do *not want to travel*.

INTRAPERSONAL VALUES

1. *Honesty* from boss/peers.
2. *Respect* from boss/peers.
3. Like to work with *details*.
4. Like to work with *big picture*.
5. Like to *take work home*.
6. *Leave work at work*.
7. Need to feel sense of *achievement*.
8. Would like a position with *power/status*.
9. Need to feel *personal pride and satisfaction*.
10. Want *recognition* for my work.
11. Like *autonomy*, no supervisor looking over my shoulder.
12. *Health*.
13. *Education and future training* opportunities.

INTERPERSONAL VALUES

1. Prefer to *work in teams*.
2. Prefer to *work alone*.
3. Like to *work directly with customers*.
4. Like to *work indirectly* to support customers.
5. Like to *communicate face-to-face* with others.
6. Prefer to *communicate with messages and e-mail*.
7. Like to *supervise others*.
8. *Don't want responsibility for others*.
9. *Family responsibility*.
10. *Child care*.
11. *Elder care*.

PERSONAL VALUES MOUNTAIN

Look at this example of how to plot the things you value most on your Values Mountain. Then create your own Values Mountain. Place the most important thing on the top of the mountain, the second most important below that, and work your way down the mountain in descending order of priority of values.

Money & Compensation

Respect

Independence

Challenge and Variety in Work

Minimum Supervision

Clear Guidelines and Regulations

Casual Wardrobe

Fast-Paced Work

Time Off

Responsibility

Details

Team Decision Making

No Take-Home Work

Honesty

Family Responsibilities

Clean, Orderly Workplace

PERSONAL VALUES MOUNTAIN

List the things you value in your personal life and professional life. Consider the values listed on pages 4–6. You can also add value items that are not in the previous lists. What is the most important thing in your life? Place it on the top line. What is the next most important thing you value? Place it on the second line from the top and so on, until all the things you value are sorted down the mountain in descending importance.

Giving some thought to what is really important in your life will aid in your career choices. You can further clarify your values by completing a Values Wheel.

PERSONAL VALUES WHEEL

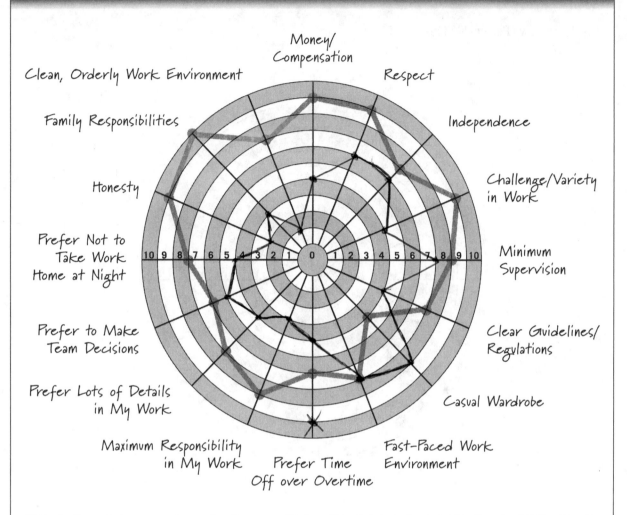

Write in the values you most care for (from your Values Mountain) on the outside of each of the spokes in your Values Wheel. Score each of these values from 0–10 based on how well you feel that value is now being met. Placing a dot on the 0 ring means that that value is not being met at all. A dot on the 5 ring means that you are satisfying that value about half of the time. A dot on the 10 ring means you are very satisfied, and it couldn't be better.

Connect the dots to form a graphic display of how well your values are being currently met. The short spokes of your graph indicate a desire for them to be better. When you begin your job search, you might ask yourself the question, "Will these values be better or worse at this new job?" This graph tells you what you are truly looking for in a career. Our productivity in the workplace is the greatest when many of our values are met.

PERSONAL VALUES WHEEL

Create your own Personal Values Wheel.

Attitude

W hat exactly is meant by "attitude"? How do you define it? Well, Webster's definition is that an **attitude** is "a manner, disposition, feeling, position, etc. toward a person or thing." The relationship between your values and your attitude is that a value, an idea or belief you hold to be true, arouses an emotional response. That emotional response creates an attitude either for or against certain things. For example, if you value exercise and believe that it is the only way to be healthy, your attitude toward those who exercise will be that they are healthy and those who do not are unhealthy. Obviously, this could be a faulty assumption based simply on your attitude; therefore, it is wise to examine the attitudes you've acquired. Is it possible that they are based on some faulty thinking?

Since you began to acquire your attitudes as a child and have continued to add to them throughout your life, they are deeply ingrained, and you may not even be aware of how they are affecting your life and your career. What is your attitude most of the time? Positive or negative? Do you believe good things are ahead for you? Or do you think, "Oh, this is too good to be true; I just know it can't last." If you find that your general outlook on life is one of doubt and trepidation, you may wish to examine your attitudes. By the way, not only is your attitude important because of its effect on your job search, it is vital to your health. Did you know that five minutes of negative thinking discourages your body for 24 hours?

James E. Challenger, president of Challenger, Gray & Christmas, Inc., an outplacement firm, says, "Job seekers with negative or self-centered attitudes end up prolonging the (job) search."[3]

Peter Thompson, a psychologist in Littleton, Colorado, who owns a consulting service specializing in personnel and personality assessments, speaks about attitude in the employee selection process.

> When an applicant satisfies the minimum entrance qualifications, what sets the mediocre apart from the stellar? . . . As elementary as it sounds, an optimistic attitude is fundamental to a successful business. Optimistic people see the potential and good in any situation or person. An optimistic employee is not necessarily smarter, nor does she possess super-human qualities. Rather, it is her outlook and positive perceptions which allow her *basic skills* [italics mine] to be utilized more effectively.[4]

While it is true that you cannot control outside things such as the weather, the economy, or what others do, you can control your own attitude. Research studies show that the persons most likely to succeed in life believe that they have control over their destinies, whereas "losers" feel that luck is what determines their accomplishments in life and that they are powerless to do anything about it. Which are you? If you have been unsuccessful in getting or keeping the job you really want, is it possible your attitude had something to do with this? If you are serious about examining inner attitudes, the following suggestions may help you to do so.

1. *Change your thinking.* Try to become aware of your negative attitudes and make a conscious effort to change them. Your mind can hold only one thought at a time, and since there is nothing to be gained by thinking negative, think positive.
2. *Accept yourself and others.* Don't criticize or belittle; we all have weaknesses and strengths. Self-acceptance comes first. Until you master that, you will not be able to accept others.
3. Above all, *believe that good things do happen* and that there is an abundance of everything you desire. Remember, it's your choice. You can remain a slave to negative attitudes that limit your ability to take advantage of the wonderful opportunities and jobs waiting for you, or you can decide now to begin thinking and doing positive thoughts and actions.
4. Keep this thought in mind: *It is our attitude toward life that determines life's attitude toward us.*

To determine what your attitude is today, take the following attitude quiz.

HOW'S YOUR ATTITUDE?

To discover what kind of attitude you have at present, answer the 15 questions below as **honestly** as possible, using the following scoring system:

Heartily Agree	Agree	Neutral	Slightly Disagree	Disagree
5	4	3	2	1

5 1. I take time to admire flowers or something pretty both at work and at home.

4 2. I think my fortunes will increase and life will be much better for me next year.

2 3. I hate to work closely with people; I prefer to work alone and be responsible for my own work.

4 4. I think the mores, values, and work ethics of this nation are deteriorating quickly.

5 5. Employers look for people not only for their skills but also for their ability to deal effectively with others and contribute to the company's growth.

1 6. I have the right to hold a grudge against people who have wronged me.

1 7. I believe it is a waste of time to set goals because things change so fast, it doesn't do any good to set them.

4 8. When there are abrupt changes at work, I freely support them and look for ways to take advantage of these changes.

1 9. It really isn't important whether I get along with others because I'm really good at what I do.

2 10. When someone informs me that I have made an error or done something wrong, I know they are just trying to put me down and build themselves up.

5 11. I frequently compliment and recognize my peers for the good work they do.

5 12. A wise person admits to mistakes.

3 13. When I think back on my life, I see more mistakes and failures than I see successes.

4 14. The way in which I think about my job makes me very productive.

2 15. If I have had a lot of problems in previous jobs, it was because people just didn't understand me.

Scoring: Reverse score questions 3, 4, 6, 7, 9, 10, 13, and 15 as shown below:

Heartily Agree	=	1
Agree	=	2
Neutral	=	3
Slightly Disagree	=	4
Disagree	=	5

(continued)

HOW'S YOUR ATTITUDE? Continued

For the remaining questions (1, 2, 5, 8, 11, 12, and 14), give them the point value according to the scoring table at the beginning of this exercise. Total your points.

If you scored . . .

65 or over	Great attitude!
60–64	Excellent attitude. Very positive thinker!
55–59	Good attitude. Your thinking is somewhat positive.
50–54	Fair, you are half and half. Sometimes your attitude is good, sometimes it isn't up to par.
49 and below	Don't send out your resume until you have practiced positive thinking.

If you scored 49 or below, ask yourself, "Is this the kind of attitude that will help me to get the job I want and to keep it?" Probably not! Reread the previous page, then begin to practice the four suggestions for positive thinking.

Interests, Wants, and Needs

During the job search, you will need to create a resume and be able to sell yourself to employers by describing who you are and what you can do for them. You also need to know what you want so that you can make the correct decision as to which job is right for you. If you can't identify what you truly want, you will probably settle for what you *think is possible* rather than what you *truthfully desire*. The following exercises will help you prepare for these decisions.

For additional assistance in assessing your career interests, you can go to the website www.ZDNet.com, key in "Interest Inventory Downloads," and download a self-scoring Interest Inventory program. By answering a series of questions regarding general job activities and work situations and then ranking their importance to you, you can create a list of general job classifications rated according to how well you would be suited to each one. This program also explores how interests and personality preferences fit with the tasks needed to perform in many professional occupations. Another tried and proven online testing program, self-scoring Strong Interest Explorer, is accessible by keying in www.psychometrics.com. This test measures interests in a broad range of occupations and work and leisure activities, as well as how they are similar to the interests of people successfully employed in a wide range of occupations.

WHAT DO I WANT?

For each list, rank the items according to how important they are to you, using a scale of 1–10, 1 being the least important and 10 being the most important.

What Do I Want for Myself? (your own personal wants and needs)

3 1. Popularity   8 6. Honors, awards, recognition

7 2. Wealth   2 7. One special person in my life

4 3. Nice figure, physique   5 8. Privacy

6 4. Good friends   1 9. A family

9 5. Reputation as a good person, intellectual, and hard worker   10 10. Good health

What Do I Want from My Job/Career? (aim for the most nearly ideal)

7 1. Status, position   8 6. Nice office, work environment

9 2. First-rate salary   5 7. Responsibility, challenge

10 3. Personal satisfaction   1 8. Variety

3 6 4. Friendly coworkers   4 9 9. Opportunity to advance

6 5. Fair, equitable boss   2 10. Top benefits package

What Do I Want for My Future? (5, 10, or 15 years from now)

8 1. Further education, training   9 6. A nice, modern home

3 2. New activities, interests to pursue   6 7. Money to travel, explore

4 3. Personal and emotional growth   2 8. All the latest tech gadgets

7 4. The highest position in my field   1 9. An expensive, late-model car

5 5. Retirement/semi-retirement to do the things listed below   10 10. Good health

What Do I Like to Do in My Leisure Time? (some of these also relate to the workplace)

3 1. Watch TV   6 6. Read

2 2. Sports, as a participant   7 7. Go to movies

1 3. Write poetry, stories   10 8. Travel, camping

9 4. Do yard work, gardening   8 9. Try new things

4 5. Do crafts, art work   5 10. Sleep

PRIORITIES CHART

Select your top five personal desires and top five professional desires. They can be from any of the four areas, and some may even overlap from personal into professional and vice versa. Award them the same points as you did on the previous page. Your scores should give you a good idea of where your top priorities lie and give you a direction as to what kinds of companies and positions you should look for that would offer you the kind of personal and professional environment you need in order to be successful and happy.

PERSONAL	POINTS
1. Good Health	10
2. Reputation as good person, intellectual, hardworker	9
3. Honors, awards, recognition	8
4. Wealth	7
5. Good friends	6
Total	40

PROFESSIONAL	POINTS
1. Personal Satisfaction	10
2. First rate Salary	9
3. Nice office, work environment	8
4. Status, position	7
5. Fair, equitable boss	6
Total	40

Donovan J McCarvel
April 15, 2008
Professional
Port.

WHO AM I?

Answer the questions below to discover the things you honestly enjoy and those that you are especially good at.

1. In all areas of my life, what things do I do really well? In what areas am I most competent?

   Great listener & insightful person. Listening to other people discuss their opinions on key issues &/or problems. I then give my opinion & insight. If they choose to use the information, fine. If not, their loss. I'm a compassionate person that believes in integrity, responsibility, accountability, & fairness

2. At this time, what is the highest position in my field for which I believe I could qualify?

   The highest position which I could qualify would be PCB Test Technician. I do not have the work experience & degree to get into management yet.

3. What things am I doing now or have I done in the past that were the most enjoyable or rewarding to me? (These do not have to be job-related; they can be from any area of your life.)

   I enjoy interacting with others to get matters of opinion. This in turn enables me to understand different aspects of life which to me are many stepping stones to good wisdom & compassion

4. If I had an Aladdin's lamp and had three wishes, who would I be, what would I be doing, and with whom would I be doing it? (Have some fun with this; who knows, dreams do come true!)

   I would be President of the United States of America. I would be rectifying all the mistakes this country has made with its people, business dealings, immigration & foreign affairs. I would team up with the most savvy individuals that are committed to correcting these follies

5. What are the things that people most often compliment me on?

   Most ppl. compliment me on my charisma, personality, eyes & intelligence.

(continued)

W HO AM I? Continued

6. In my opinion, what has been my greatest accomplishment? What abilities, both technical and personal, do I possess that enabled me to accomplish it? (List all the abilities that you can think of, as you're going to use these in an exercise later.)

Maintaining my sanity despite being knocked down time at time again. My perserverance a my ability to adapt with changes quickly coupled with patients a compassion have led me to being a well-rounded, but stable individual.

7. Using the space below or a separate piece of paper, imagine your ideal day and write it out in complete and vivid detail. Describe colors, places, feelings, exact amounts, etc. Let your imagination run free; don't let your doubts about what is possible get in the way. Albert Einstein said, "Imagination is more important than knowledge." Remember, everything that exists today once began as an idea in someone's mind. All our modern technology in business, in the home, and in entertainment came from someone who believed there was a better way to live. Who's to say that what you imagine can't become a reality?

Waking up to a beautiful morning. Going to the kitchen to make coffee in my 600,000 house. Checking my messages a emails. I look up at the clock, it is 8:30 so I decide to see if the morning paper has come. Checking out the stock market. I then go back inside to study reports a findings. I then make several phone calls to help clear the air a respond with several e-mails. I look up a it is now about noon. I go to the local park, know for its beauty of flowers & wild life, I walk around for a while. I take several important phone calls a go back to the great outdoors. After a couple hours I decide to head home a make up a grocery list to fix tonight's dinner. I go the store, pick up the ingredients needed to make Beef Strogonoff a head home. I fix dinner, eat a clean up. It is about 530 pm. so I decide to take one last walk around my garden in my rear yard a even sit back for a while. I double check my messages a emails. Later I decide to go out with friends a we cruise around, have dinner again a go to a local club. Around 10:30 I leave to head home an check to see how "My Business" did for the day.

INVENTORYING YOUR STRENGTHS

Mark an X beside those strengths that describe you as you are now. Then circle the 10 that are *most like you.* When you finish, you will have a list of specific items for selling yourself on paper and in the interview, and also for completing the Marketing Appraisal at the end of this chapter.

Academic X	Courageous X	Honest X	Outgoing	Sincere X
Accurate X	Creative	Humorous	Painstaking	Sociable
Active	Curious	Idealistic	Patient X	Spontaneous
Adaptable X	Daring	Imaginative	Peaceable	Spunky
Adventurous	Deliberate	Independent	Persevering X	Stable X
Affectionate X	Democratic	Individualized	Pleasant	Steady
Aggressive X	Dependable	Industrious	Poised	Strong X
Alert	Determined	Informal	Polite X	Strong-minded X
Ambitious X	Dignified	Ingenious	Practical	Sympathetic X
Artistic	Discreet	Intellectual X	Precise	Tactful X
Assertive X	Dominant	Intelligent X	Progressive	Teachable X
Attractive X	Eager	Inventive	Prudent	Tenacious X
Bold	Easygoing X	Kind X	Purposeful	Thorough
Broadminded X	Efficient X	Leisurely	Quick X	Thoughtful
Businesslike X	Emotional	Lighthearted	Quiet X	Tolerant X
Calm X	Energetic X	Likable X	Rational X	Tough X
Capable	Enterprising X	Logical	Realistic X	Trusting
Careful	Enthusiastic X	Loyal	Reasonable X	Trustworthy X
Cautious X	Fair-minded X	Mature X	Reflective	Unaffected
Charming X	Farsighted	Methodical X	Relaxed	Unassuming
Cheerful	Firm	Meticulous X	Reliable X	Understanding X
Clear-thinking X	Flexible X	Mild	Reserved	Unexcitable
Clever X	Forceful	Moderate	Resourceful X	Uninhibited
Competent X	Formal	Modest X	Responsible X	Verbal
Competitive X	Frank	Natural	Retiring	Versatile X
Confident X	Friendly X	Obliging	Robust	Warm X
Conscientious	Generous X	Open-minded X	Self-confident X	Wholesome
Conservative	Gentle X	Opportunistic	Sensible X	Wise X
Considerate X	Good-natured X	Optimistic X	Sensitive	Witty
Cool	Healthy X	Organized X	Serious X	Zany
Cooperative X	Helpful X	Original	Sharp-witted X	

SKILLS AND ABILITIES ASSESSMENT

This is an opportunity for you to assess all your abilities, your marketable skills (technical, educational, personal), and your achievements. Don't leave anything out; even though you might believe it isn't significant, you may discover an employer who is looking for that particular skill, ability, or expertise.

1. List all your personal qualities and characteristics, such as dependability, enthusiasm, honesty, high energy level, tact, cooperativeness, punctuality, and sense of humor.

_____

_____

_____

_____

2. List all your marketable skills that are work-related, such as leadership, ability to learn quickly and retain what you learn, effectiveness at prioritizing, innovation, and investigative and problem-solving skills.

_____

_____

_____

_____

3. List your vocational and educational skills. Examples: computer programming and networking; computer maintenance and repair; office technology; service-related skills such as hospitality, medical, and accounting; and mechanical or drawing skills.

_____

_____

_____

_____

4. List all your accomplishments: personal, educational, and job-related. A high grade point average, scholarships earned, honors, improvements in the workplace that you've created, promotions, volunteer work, and community service are all achievements that can sell an employer on your value to them and help you net a job offer.

_____

_____

_____

_____

SKILLS AND ABILITIES WHEEL

Ability to Learn Quickly

15 Years In-Depth Experience in the Field

Effective at Prioritizing

Technical Writing or Business Correspondence

Tact

Excellent Skill at Resolving Conflicts Between Employees

Dependability

Innovation. Ability to Create New Solutions

10 9 8 7 6 5 4 3 2 1   0   1 2 3 4 5 6 7 8 9 10

Honesty

High Energy Level

Installation of Computer Software Programs

Multitask Orientation

Ability to Get Others to Follow Directions

Ability to Learn New Systems and Techniques with Minimum Training and Supervision

Punctuality

Specialized Training in Excel and Word

A skill is a thing that you do well. An ability is the power to do something without necessarily having the skills to do it. In the job search process, you must have a clear idea of what skills and abilities you have to offer an employer. Review the Strengths exercise as well as the Skills and Abilities Assessment, and decide which of them to place on your wheel.

While we all have skill sets and abilities, not all of them are at their peak. Pick the skills and abilities you feel you possess and place them on the spokes of your Skills and Abilities Wheel. Rate your skills and abilities on a 0–10 scale. Of course 0 means you are not capable of performing that skill without constant supervision or have no ability in this area but are willing to learn. A score of 5 means you could do the job half the time or have a 50 percent chance of success if given an opportunity. A score of 10 means you feel confident to apply that skill with minimum or no supervision or feel confident that given an opportunity, your abilities would almost guarantee you success.

See the example above. The short spokes are the areas that could be improved in the future to make yourself more marketable. The long spokes represent what you can sell immediately.

S KILLS AND ABILITIES WHEEL

The completed Skills and Abilities Wheel is your sales program in an interview. The long spokes will be your first features to sell an employer. The next longest spokes will be sold as additional skills and abilities that can be brought up to speed with brief training. The lowest spokes are areas you would like to improve to be more competitive.

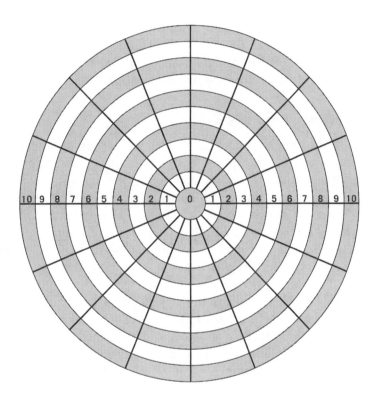

Success Through Goal Setting

N ow that you've taken the steps to inventory your interests, needs, and wants, and have defined your strengths, skills, and abilities, you're ready for the final step to finalize your package for success. Success often begins with a commitment to self-improvement through goal setting. It's remarkable how few persons are aware of this, and they live their lives "putting up with" situations that are not to their liking rather than being motivated to change them. Little do they realize that goal setting is the means by which all things are possible. Setting goals will give you the pattern for opportunity, add aim to your energy, focus your talents, and even structure your time.

Inside every successful person, you will find an avid goal-setter. In a study at Yale University, 20 questions were asked of graduating seniors. Three had to do with goals: Have you set goals? Have you written them down? Do you have a plan to accomplish them? Only 3 percent answered yes to those three questions. Twenty years later, surviving members of that class participated in another study. The 3 percent who had said yes to goals were more happily married, more successful, had a better family life, and had better health than their non–goal-oriented classmates.

If you want to be successful and acquire those things you selected on the previous pages as your priorities, defining your goals and making a written plan for achieving them is absolutely necessary. Why do they have to be written? you ask. Well, at any given moment, you can be consciously aware of only about 30 to 40 percent of what's in your mind. If your goals are only "in your head," they are likely to stay there! You can stay focused and organized only by writing your goals out. Otherwise, you get hung up in day-to-day frustrations and problems, and you run the risk of missing out on opportunities that come your way.

Guidelines for Setting Goals

The basic principles and techniques for setting and achieving your goals are actually quite simple. Maybe that's why so many people don't do it; they are looking for something that is tedious and difficult. Is it possible that we believe if something comes easily, it probably isn't worth much? This is not always true.

When setting your goals, keep in mind that you need to set short-term goals: those you want to acquire in, say, a month to six months or maybe even in a week. These are followed by long-term goals, things you want to happen in one, three, or five years, maybe longer. If you set only long-term goals, your focus is too far in the future; you need a plan that will break those long-term goals down into more manageable blocks of time. For example, your long-term goal might be to be employed with the company of your choice making a top-notch salary and on your way to an excellent promotion. How exactly are you going to obtain that long-term goal? You must set short-term goals to reach in the interim. What *specifically* are you going to do to get that job? Obviously, your first short-term goal would be to do some research to find out just where that kind of job exists. What skills and abilities does it require? Your immediate goal might be to learn where this information could be found. The second short-term goal would be to assess your skills and abilities to determine if you qualify for that kind of position. As you can see, many short-term goals need to be set and achieved before you can work on the long-term goal. The more you break your long-term goals down into smaller tasks and increments of time, the more successful you'll be in obtaining them.

A good goal statement should answer the three following questions:

1. *What* is going to happen?
2. *When* is it going to happen?
3. *How* is it going to happen?

Below are seven basic steps to assist you in setting well-defined, specific, and clearly stated goals.

1. *State your goal specifically and completely so that you know exactly what it is that you desire.* The more detailed your goal statement, the better you will be able to visualize yourself actually having or doing what it is that you want. It's a fact:

Most people spend more time planning their vacations than they do planning their careers or their lives. You must plan for your future; you have to live there!

2. *Set dates for your short-term and long-term goals.* Even if they have to be revised later, setting them will keep you from the "plague of procrastination." Caution: Don't let yourself get caught in a trap of feeling that you're a failure if you don't make those deadlines! If you miss a goal, simply evaluate where you are at the time and set new dates. You can't always know what is going to happen in the future.

3. *Goals should be realistic and reachable, but don't be afraid to strive for something that seems a bit out of reach.* If you are really determined and really want this goal, then set preliminary, short-term goals. Assess your lack of knowledge or expertise, then plan a method for acquiring any skills you lack. Goals that are set too low are not really goals at all; they don't motivate you and could be a sign that you are insecure, that you're "playing it safe." On the other hand, goals that are too high or unrealistic can destroy your enthusiasm and self-confidence when you fail to achieve them. Above all, don't give up if you don't succeed on your first attempt. How many attempts did it take you to learn to ride a bike, drive a car, or program your computer? Did you give up after the first or second try?

4. *Goals must be measurable.* This is why you set short-term goals. How will you know where you are in terms of acquiring your long-term goal if you don't set benchmarks or yardsticks to measure your progress toward that ultimate goal? For instance, if your long-term goal is to get a job in six months, the one that you've dreamed of and worked hard toward acquiring the skills for, what would be the first thing you must do? What would you need to do this week, next week, and so on? Let's say that you know that you must market your resume to at least 20 to 30 firms before getting an interview, and that the interviewing process can take up to several weeks or a few months. What do you think your time frame for your short-term goals would be in order to get that job in six months?

5. *Make certain that your goals are* your very own *goals, not things someone else wants for you.* If a goal is not yours, you won't be committed to it. All too often, parents, spouses, lovers, and those you admire exert an unknowing influence over your choices in life. Setting goals to please *them* won't work.

6. *Have fun!* As the bumper sticker reads, "Life is a game to be played, not a puzzle to be solved." In order to keep a balance in your life and take setbacks with a positive attitude, you need to have a good sense of humor. People will want to be around you if you're pleasant and enjoyable. Also, if attaining your goals means "all work and no play," you may feel overwhelmed and give up.

7. *It's very important that you identify your internal roadblocks, self-imposed barriers that could cause you to self-sabotage no matter how good your plans are.* The most damaging roadblock is usually right between your ears; it's that thought, that belief that you're not good enough, not capable of accomplishing your goals. You know, the little voice in your head that says, "Who do I think I'm kidding, I'll never make it; there's probably someone else who knows more or does it better than I." I've found that in the majority of my students' goal-setting worksheets, they repeatedly express the idea that they are afraid that they are not "good enough" to acquire the job goal that they described in number 1. Recognize that the internal messages of "I'm not good enough," "He or she is better, smarter, than I" stem from an earlier period in your life when some

uncaring or unthinking person might have been attempting to control you. *These messages are no longer relevant; get rid of them!* Many excellent books currently on the market are designed to help you achieve a healthy sense of self-esteem and promote a comfortable confidence in your abilities. Two examples are *Reality Therapy, Take Effective Control of Your Life* by William Glasser and *Psychology of Success* by Denis Waitley.

Begin today to move in the direction you want to go. First, review the two sample goal-setting worksheets on the following pages. Then, using the blank worksheet on pages 29–30, set your goals for three to six months or a year from now and design plans to achieve them. As a goal-directed person, you will find many doors open for you that otherwise would have been closed. Once you have your goals written out and your plan in place, start visualizing them as already being accomplished. The power of visualization is not to be minimized; it is utilized by major athletes, sports teams, and winners from all walks of life. Visualizing leads to desire, and desire leads to action and belief. You can't hit a target that you can't see! If possible, cut out pictures of what you desire and put them where you'll see them daily. This will help to embed them in your mind and remind you of where you are going. It's also a wonderful cure for procrastination. "It's been proven that an idea, a dream that is consciously and persistently held in the mind, will manifest itself into reality," according to Henry David Thoreau.

One final thought from author Rudyard Kipling: "If you don't get what you want, it's either a sign that you didn't seriously want it or that you tried to bargain over the price."

GOAL-SETTING (SAMPLE)

1. I believe that setting goals is important because:

   goals are the roadmap to your future. They are the motivation behind actions. Without goals, life can be rather aimless and without direction. Direction = accomplishment.

2. My **immediate** job goal (the one I'm seeking now) is (include **specific** details on salary, type of company, location, and any important particulars about the job you plan to attain. The more specific your details, the more easily you can visualize them):

   one that will lend me the opportunity to develop skills that I can use as a foundation for a better job. I will make no less than $15 an hour with a computer firm in Houston, Texas.

3. The main benefits and rewards (both internal and external) that I will receive from reaching this goal are:

   (1) transferable job skills, (2) gaining experience in my field to move up in the company, and (3) the satisfaction that I have accomplished what I planned upon graduation.

4. The roadblocks (internal: faulty thinking, assumptions, etc. and external: lack of skills, training, etc.) that I need to remove to reach my goal are:

   (1) fatigue from juggling an already full schedule, (2) thinking I am not good enough, and (3) that people with more experience are the ones that get the jobs.

5. Actions I am going to take to get rid of these roadblocks are:

   (1) planning my time more efficiently so I can get the rest I need, (2) delegating external responsibilities to my husband and other family members, and (3) reminding myself every day that I do have the skills needed to get this immediate job and that I have other qualities that employers look for such as a good attitude, willingness to learn, and flexibility.

6. The skills and knowledge I need to have to reach my goal (those I have now and those I need to acquire) are:

   (1) the technical knowledge and skills that I'm now learning in college, (2) good time management, and (3) how to sell myself to an employer.

(continued)

GOAL-SETTING (SAMPLE) Continued

7. Individuals, clubs, organizations, and groups that will help me to attain my job goal are:

   (1) my husband and family, (2) my teachers, (3) the trade organizations for computer networking, and (4) most of all, myself by following the steps outlined in this book and advice from others in the field.

8. My action plan (the **specific steps** that I must take to reach the immediate job goal I described in Statement 2) is:

   A. *make out a time-management schedule for work and to meet the needs of my family and children*

   B. *continue to maintain my current positive attitude and GPA*

   C. *create an honest and impeccable resume and cover letter*

   D. *conduct several informational interviews to better prepare myself for interviewing*

   E. *complete the necessary follow-up on leads, interviews, etc.*

   F. _____

   G. _____

I promise myself that I will follow the steps I've outlined above, visualize myself as being already in possession of my goal, and do everything in my power to obtain this goal.

Today's date: _____

Date for the completion of my goal: _____

My signature: _____

After you've completed this form for your immediate job goal, you can use this same outline for writing your personal, financial, or spiritual goals.

GOAL-SETTING (SAMPLE)

1. I believe that setting goals is important because:

   having goals gives you something to strive for, something to motivate you. If you don't set goals for what you want, you have very little control over your life and what you get; you will probably just take whatever comes along

2. My **immediate** job goal (the one I'm seeking now) is (include **specific** details on salary, type of company, location, and any important particulars about the job you plan to attain. The more specific your details, the more easily you can visualize them):

   securing a position in the computer networking field with a small to medium-sized company, one that is progressive and stable. It will be located in the north metro area, and I will be earning a beginning salary of approximately $35,000 a year. Most importantly, I will be happy to go to work every day doing what I enjoy and will not consider it a job.

3. The main benefits and rewards (both internal and external) that I will receive from reaching this goal are:

   I will have a good budget plan and be able to pay my bills plus have money left over to enjoy my life. I will feel good about myself and what I do. Also, I will gain valuable experience so that I can move on to bigger and better things in a few years.

4. The roadblocks (internal: faulty thinking, assumptions, etc. and external: lack of skills, training, etc.) that I need to remove to reach my goal are:

   I don't give myself much credit for my experience and knowledge, and thinking that maybe the job market is not so good out there. I really don't have any external roadblocks except maybe some people who aren't very positive that I think are my friends.

5. Actions I am going to take to get rid of these roadblocks are:

   I will keep telling myself that I do know my stuff, and I'm proving it every day at school. Even if an ad says they want "X" number of years' experience, I will apply for it and prove to them that I am capable of doing what the position requires. I will also try to choose my friends very carefully so that I am not around negative people.

6. The skills and knowledge I need to have to reach my goal (those I have now and those I need to acquire) are:

   the skills I'm learning now, the ones I've acquired from previous jobs such as good work ethics, team playing, and my exceptional ability to stay motivated, determined, and willing to get the job done correctly and on time.

(continued)

GOAL-SETTING (SAMPLE) Continued

7. Individuals, clubs, organizations, and groups that will help me to attain my job goal are:

   (1) the Career Development department here at the college, (2) my reference people, whom I will keep in close touch with, (3) my teachers and people I know who are already in the field, and (4) trade organizations and publications related to my field.

8. My action plan (the **specific steps** that I must take to reach the immediate job goal I described in Statement 2) is:

   A. _I will graduate from college. I need to keep this vision clear; just because I'm almost finished doesn't mean I can slack off now._

   B. _I will prepare my resume and cover letters carefully and honestly so that they will assist me in securing interviews._

   C. _I will visit with the job placement personnel here and follow up on leads they give me._

   D. _I will keep in close touch with them, especially after I graduate._

   E. _I will post my resume and cover letter on the Internet and circulate them to let companies know I'm available and what I can offer them._

   F. _I will go to all interviews and present myself positively and professionally in order to get job offers._

   G. _I will do the proper follow-up on all leads, calls, and interviews._

I promise myself that I will follow the steps I've outlined above, visualize myself as being already in possession of my goal, and do everything in my power to obtain this goal.

Today's date:

Date for the completion of my goal:

My signature:

After you've completed this form for your immediate job goal, you can use this same outline for writing your personal, financial, or spiritual goals.

GOAL-SETTING

1. I believe that setting goals is important because:

   _____

   _____

   _____

2. My **immediate** job goal (the one I'm seeking now) is (include **specific** details on salary, type of company, location, and any important particulars about the job you plan to attain. The more specific your details, the more easily you can visualize them):

   _____

   _____

   _____

3. The main benefits and rewards (both internal and external) that I will receive from reaching this goal are:

   _____

   _____

   _____

4. The roadblocks (internal: faulty thinking, assumptions, etc. and external: lack of skills, training, etc.) that I need to remove to reach my goal are:

   _____

   _____

   _____

5. Actions I am going to take to get rid of these roadblocks are:

   _____

   _____

   _____

   _____

6. The skills and knowledge I need to have to reach my goal (those I have now and those I need to acquire) are:

   _____

   _____

(continued)

GOAL-SETTING Continued

7. Individuals, clubs, organizations, and groups that will help me to attain my job goal are:

_____

_____

_____

8. My action plan (the **specific steps** that I must take to reach the immediate job goal I described in Statement 2) is:

A. _____

_____

B. _____

_____

C. _____

_____

D. _____

_____

E. _____

_____

F. _____

_____

G. _____

_____

I promise myself that I will follow the steps I've outlined above, visualize myself as being already in possession of my goal, and do everything in my power to obtain this goal.

Today's date: _____

Date for the completion of my goal: _____

My signature: _____

After you've completed this form for your immediate job goal, you can use this same outline for writing your personal, financial, or spiritual goals.

Benefits You Can Sell to the Employer

When you are writing your resume and being interviewed, it is not enough to make *generalized* statements to an employer. Making a **generalization** (a statement that implies rather than giving facts, specifics, and information) to a prospective employer is risky unless you back it up with evidence. To convince an employer of your worth, you must give specifics. How do you prove to an employer that you are dependable, flexible, able to cope with technological change, etc.? An effective way of presenting yourself is to prepare some carefully constructed, well-thought-out statements of your abilities with examples that illustrate them. These are called **benefit statements**.

A good benefit statement has three parts: It begins with a statement of your skill, ability, knowledge, etc. It then gives examples of when and where you demonstrated or learned it, in other words, *proof* that you actually have it. The key selling factor of a benefit statement is the third part: informing the employer how and why it will benefit him or her. In order to do this, you must put yourself in the place of the employer. If you were the employer and this were your company, what would help you to be profitable and successful?

The more explicit you can be, the better. Give facts, figures, *quantitative evidence* of your knowledge or experience in the stated area. Don't simply restate the ability that you gave in part one. When you tell employers how your ability will benefit them, remember that the bottom line for all companies is saving time and making money. How could your skill of problem solving, for instance, save them time and money? Try to relate the skill directly to their specialized needs.

In order to write effective benefit statements that will sell you to an employer, you should do some informational interviews and research positions in the *DOT (Dictionary of Occupational Titles)* and the *OOH (Occupational Outlook Handbook)* to get a good idea of the skills and abilities that are required for the position(s) you are seeking. These are explained in Chapter 3.

Below are some examples of benefit statements. Study them so that you can interview skillfully and construct a resume and cover letter that will get you that interview.

Sample Benefit Statements

Skill: I am a detail-oriented person.

Proof: When I was working for United Aviation and in the Marine Corps, I followed step-by-step procedures, schematics, drawings, and prints. I troubleshot and pinpointed problems on systems using schematics. I fabricated parts to the customer's drawings.

Benefit to an employer: I will follow instructions to the detail, thereby saving time by doing things correctly the first time. This is a benefit to any employer, as not following instructions and having to do things over is costly in terms of profit and time.

Skill: I am a dependable person.

Proof: While in the military for four years, I never missed a day. I now work full-time and attend school full-time and still always complete my work duties, assignments, and tasks on time.

Benefit to an employer: He or she can always count on me to be there, to complete the tasks given to me, on time. All in all, I will get the job done and done right.

Skill: I am flexible and adaptable to unscheduled priorities.

Proof: Throughout my career, last-minute things have always come up. A vehicle that goes down that has high priority and needs to be fixed immediately, or a late order that needs to be filled quickly—I am able to adapt quickly and get the job done.

Benefit to an employer: I am able to adapt to different and unplanned schedules, work habits, and policies, and can understand that there are sometimes last-minute things to be completed. Therefore, I will be willing to stay late and work extra hours to get them done.

Skill: I have excellent time-management skills.

Proof: While attending college to obtain my degree and working 50 hours a week for Commnet Cellular as a Senior Systems Engineer, I still carried a 4.0 GPA in school.

Benefit to an employer: This ability will allow me to complete more projects in a timely manner, thereby offering you a more productive workforce and an increase in profits due to your not having to pay overtime.

Skill: I am a stable and dependable person.

Proof: I have been in the workforce for 15 years and have had only two employers. I was in the United States Air Force for eight years and have worked for Commnet Cellular for seven years.

Benefit to an employer: This benefits your company because you will not have to spend time and money training me only to worry about my leaving your company. You would not have to hire a replacement and spend money and time in retraining.

Skill: Leadership is one of my strongest qualities.

Proof: One of my responsibilities at Commnet Cellular was to implement digital technology as an overlay to our analog system. This required coordinating and managing multiple departments to ensure that everything was done. The project was completed one and a half months ahead of schedule.

Benefit to an employer: Leadership is always needed in all progressive companies, and employers want to be satisfied that when they delegate responsibility for a project to someone that that person will be able to coordinate all departments, stimulate cooperative teamwork, and complete the project on time. I can do this.

Skill: I am a very creative and original thinker.

Proof: I have the ability to picture in my mind the design that I am going to make. My house is full of all the designs I created while in school. This is why I chose to become a draftsperson. I was chosen by my instructors in college to mentor and assist other students with their drawings.

Benefit to an employer: Profits are gained from new and repeat customers. I will be able to come up with fresh, new ideas that will be what the customer wants. This will attract new customers and keep them coming back.

Skill: One of my greatest strengths is excellent communication skills. I can express myself clearly, both orally and in writing.

Proof: At Quality Insurance, where I worked for five years, I was responsible for dealing directly with the customers who were filing claims. I was able to assist them, over the phone and in person, in an effective manner by listening carefully and then transcribing the information correctly for the claims adjustors. This saved time and kept the customers happy because their claims were quickly identified and handled.

Benefit to an employer: I believe you would find this skill very useful in your business because listening to the customer and identifying what he or she needs is critical to good business and repeat business.

BENEFIT STATEMENTS

Go back through the previous worksheets that you've completed and choose your major skills and abilities. Write at least five, preferably more, benefit statements of your own. The more you have, the better equipped you'll be to persuade an employer to interview you or to offer you the job.

Skill #1

Proof

Benefit to the employer

Skill #2

Proof

Benefit to the employer

Skill #3

Proof

Benefit to the employer

Use a blank sheet of paper for more benefit statements.

The Bottom Line

he keys to successfully marketing yourself to prospective employers are knowing yourself and what you have to offer, having a definite direction, and showing that you have it. A salesperson would never think of trying to sell a product to a customer without knowing everything there is to know about that product—what it can and cannot do, what its strong and weak points are—and having answers for any questions the customer might raise about that product. It is no different when you are job searching; you are the product *and* the salesperson.

If you have completed the exercises on the preceding pages, you are now ready to summarize your assets and create a personal profile, your "marketing appraisal." Here is an example of what it might look like:

> I have the personal characteristics of honesty, loyalty, reliability, integrity, and sincerity needed for successful and productive job performance in my industry. I am cost-conscious in terms of materials, time, and personnel and am flexible and adaptable in dealing effectively with change in the workplace.
>
> I have a proven record in troubleshooting and problem solving and have been consistently rated a top performer in my job appraisals. I have a positive attitude that is demonstrated by my ability to be a cooperative team player and to work successfully with my coworkers and supervisors.
>
> I am open-minded, perceptive, and diplomatic in my interactions with customers and business clients. I produce accurate and timely work and am ready to be a productive employee for your organization.

In Chapter 2, "The Paper Trail," you will learn how, where, and when to use your marketing appraisal.

NOTES

1. Steven Graber, *The Everything Get-a-Job Book* (Avon, MA: Adams Media, 2000).
2. Steven Reiss, "Reiss Profile of Fundamental Goals and Motivational Sensitivities," [online]. Available at www.reiss.7osu.edu.
3. Carol Kleiman, *Rocky Mountain News*, "Positive Attitude Pays Off in Job Interview," January 27, 1991, Careers Section, 2.
4. "Key Attribute of Employee Is Positive Attitude," *The Denver Post*, January 4, 1998, Sec. J, 5.

MY MARKETING APPRAISAL

(What I Can Offer an Employer)

The Paper Trail

Paperwork is, to a large degree, what a job search
is made of. In any employment market, whether
there's an abundance or scarcity of jobs, it is
imperative that you prepare your paperwork
carefully so that you do not get eliminated in the
first "round." It is highly unlikely that you can
get a job just by visiting a few employers and
having two or three brief interviews. A manager
for professional recruiting and university relations
at General Electric remarked that when
companies are presented with candidates for
a position, they "all look for differences among
applicants to separate the best from the rest.
The first screening that occurs is based on
the paperwork."

CHAPTER

2

Employers rarely receive high quality resumes, even though mid-sized companies accumulate up to 200 of these documents each week. Typical resumes have not been proofread for basic spelling and grammar mistakes—and they include too much data or too little pertinent information. That's why most resumes are left unread, unacknowledged, and eventually discarded. If candidates can't take the time to construct a good piece of writing, then why should the employer waste valuable time considering their qualifications?[1]

Now more than ever, employers are requiring both resumes *and* cover letters. Ninety-five percent of all employment hires begin with the resume. Companies use your paperwork as a screening device to "weed out" the unqualified, and often just to get the "stack" down to a manageable level so that they can get on with the interviewing and get someone on board. If you don't include a cover letter, that alone could disqualify you if the response to an opening is high.

Four documents will be required for your job search:

1. The *resume*, to help you get interviews.
2. The *cover letter*, which not only reinforces what is on the resume but also gives you the opportunity to sell yourself to the employer.
3. The *application form*, which, if not properly completed, could prevent you from getting the job.
4. *Follow-up correspondence*, the thank-you and no-thank-you letters sent after interviews and job offers.

The instructions on the following pages will give you some simple techniques for writing a sound, results-getting resume and cover letter, show you how to complete the application forms correctly, and provide you with samples and suggestions for follow-up correspondence.

Writing an effective resume and cover letter need not be painful. Look at the process as an opportunity to present yourself as a positive, willing, and motivated person who can be an asset to the company of your choice. Creating a positive and personalized tool for marketing yourself to prospective employers can actually be an uplifting experience.

Resume Preparation

The major purpose of the resume is to help you to get interviews. If it does that, it has done its job. If your preparation is substandard and your resume is poorly written, this will diminish your chances of getting interviews and, subsequently, a job. Remember, your resume is your first introduction to the employer; therefore, you must be extremely careful to present your qualifications in the most positive and professional manner. If your resume doesn't pass this initial inspection, you will be "stuck on first base," wondering why you aren't being called for interviews.

Gathering Information

To begin creating a convincing resume, the first thing to do is to gather all your background information and compile it on the blank worksheets provided for you in this chapter. If you already have a fairly recent resume, you can use that as a worksheet, then revise and update your material. Don't worry about organization at this point; just get all the information down so that you have a complete record of your background and qualifications. You'll organize it later. Be sure that you include everything you have done, been a part of, attended, and so on. Many people overlook vital information at this stage, believing it not to be important. Trust me, the item you leave out just might be the one thing that an employer is looking for.

Organizing Your Information

Once you have your background information down on paper, the next step is to organize it. At this point, you want to decide what you are going to include based on the job that you are targeting. As you organize your information, keep in mind that your resume is not an obituary nor is it your life history. Many resumes are discarded because they include too much data, so concentrate on using only relevant information that will interest the employers in your field and encourage them to call you for an interview. Many employers, myself included, have received hundreds of resumes where the applicants just rambled on and on with a total disregard for any pertinence to the position for which they were applying. These are the resumes that get rejected, the ones that are called "pink slip" resumes. Unfortunately, they are so common that Robert Half, head of Robert Half International, a San Francisco–based employment firm, has written a book compiling the many resume blunders he has encountered over the years. Keep in mind that human resource directors say they receive 25 to 100 resumes each week and of those, only 5 percent lead to an interview.

When you have decided on the material that you are going to include, you are ready to choose a format or design. The manner in which you present your information is as important as what you say because it is perceived as part of your professional image. The format you choose should introduce you to an employer in the most favorable light. The following descriptions and the examples in this chapter will help you decide on the style that is best for your individual needs and the job or career you are targeting. Whether you intend to mail, e-mail, or hand-deliver your resume also has a bearing on how you format it.

Resume Styles

 he two basic styles of resumes are the *chronological* and the *functional* formats. All others are variations of these two.

Chronological Format

A **chronological** resume (see Exhibit 2.1) is one that lists your jobs, education, and events in a chronological order. Items are presented "backward," beginning with your present job or school and working back in time. The chronological resume is probably the most common and the easiest to write. It is generally used when you have a very stable and impressive work background

ANN CONNELL

4021 WEST 120TH AVENUE   (303) 541-7866
WESTMINSTER, COLORADO 80235   ACONNELL@AOL.COM

PROFESSIONAL OBJECTIVE

Long-term employment that allows for advancement in both learning potential and professional development within the drafting field. Am open to residential and/or commercial design.

QUALIFICATIONS

CAD Operation—Completed training on "virtual reality" software, invested 300 hours in lab study. Am knowledgeable in AutoCAD 14 and 2000.

Architectural Drafting and Design—Created models and architectural drawings for urban design, also researched applications for federal grants, and made final sketches accompanied by notes and specified dimensions.

Specifications Writing—Rendered directions and explanations of architectural plans for use by contractors and other on-site building personnel, prepared program development reports regarding cost analysis and building code analysis, and assisted with design proposals for low-cost housing for senior citizens.

EMPLOYMENT HISTORY

Gerold Mills Architectural Associates, Littleton, Colorado, 2001–2004
Architect
Was responsible for urban design of large-scale architectural projects and site plans that shaped an urban environment. Created and rendered urban design plans and concepts.

Norwalk Architects, Denver, Colorado, 1996–2001
Began as draftsperson and was promoted to Senior Draftsperson.
CAD and board design plus writing specifications for use by contractors for low-cost housing.

EDUCATION

University of Colorado, Boulder, Colorado, Graduate, Architecture degree, 1999.
Internship with Howdershell Planners, Westminster, Colorado.

Bay Valley Technical Institute, Hays, Kansas, Associate's degree in Architectural Drafting, 1995.

Licensed: State of Colorado
Membership: American Association of Architects

with no major job gaps. One of its advantages is that it enables you to show progression and increasing responsibilities in your job(s).

If you have gaps in your work history, are changing careers, or are not in what many employers view as a "favorable age group," you probably should use the *functional* or *hybrid* format. These styles focus more on skills than on any specific order or dates.

Functional Format

A **functional** resume (see Exhibit 2.2) lists your information under skill headings without necessarily focusing on dates. The main section of a functional resume is titled "Qualifications Summary," "Skills Composite," or something similar. Beneath this heading, you list your specific skills under subtitles such as "Administration," "Technical," "Sales," "Supervisory," "Marketing," and "Computer." Beneath the subtitles are brief descriptions that demonstrate your abilities in those areas. Specific examples and results that you produced are especially important (this is true for all styles of resumes). For example, "Increased sales production by 40 percent," "Reduced employee turnover by 15 percent," "Designed promotional program that resulted in an increase in our customer base from 265 to 345." Begin each statement with an action verb that emphasizes the skill you want to sell. Refer to the list of action verbs on page 64 when you write your skills summary.

Hybrid Format

The **hybrid** style is a combination of the chronological and functional formats (see Exhibit 2.3). As in the functional resume, you list functional, transferable skills that you can offer an employer, but unlike in the chronological style, you can give time periods (number of years rather than dates) for the jobs you've held. When a purely functional resume is used, except in applications for middle and upper management positions, employers sometimes tend to be a little suspicious and assume the applicant may be hiding a lack of skills or experience. Including the number of years of experience helps to keep them from prejudging you for not having shown a chronological job history. I asked my friend Jane Turk, who has been a human resources manager for many years (including seven years as a major recruiter for Martin Marietta in Denver, Colorado), if she would consider only those resumes with dates and reject the ones without. She said, "Of course not. If I see that the applicant has valid skills and experience for the position for which he or she is applying, I will call them for an interview." Giving dates is *essential*, however, when the skills you are selling relate to a field that changes rapidly, such as Internet programming. In this situation employers need to know that your skills and experience are up-to-date.

If you choose the hybrid format, you can include dates of employment under the Employment History heading if you are not fearful of revealing job gaps or your age. Whether to reveal your age can be an important decision. Some employers may subscribe to myths such as "If you're under the age of 25, you're unstable" or "If you're over 55, you are over the hill." According to Robert Lewis in an article in the *AARP Bulletin:*

> What for the most of the 1980s and early 1990s was a shortage of jobs for older workers is becoming a shortage of older workers for jobs … In fact, a just-released Bureau of Labor Statistics (BLS) survey says 55-plus workers are finding new slots faster than people in their 30s and 40s.[2]

MATTHEW ALLEN

2102 West 153rd Avenue, New York, NY 10024
(212) 567-3000, Cell: (212) 340-9080
mallen@evernet.com

OBJECTIVE

A position in the field of Electronics, prefer Satellite/Communications Systems related.
FIVE-YEAR CAREER GOAL: Communications Analysis Management.

SUMMARY OF QUALIFICATIONS

Electronics Applications—*Four years.* Installed, maintained, transferred, and repaired
2-way radios, telecommunications, electronic, and data equipment. Experience with electrical controls, circuit construction and applications.

Computer Applications—*Three years.* Computer programming and microprocessors to
include UNIX and C++ programming.

Mathematics—*Four years.* Performed daily algebraic/geometric and trigonometric calculations with emphasis in Electronic Communications systems.

Teamwork—*Seven years.* Worked on diverse teams in different applications stemming
from military career, electronic employment, and the mechanical aspect of maintenance
repair in the communications industry.

EDUCATION

New York Institute of Electronics, New York, NY, 2004
Associate's degree with double major: Computer Programming and Electronics Emphasis in
programming, microprocessors, electronic applications with enhanced troubleshooting skills.
GPA: 3.9 with Honors. Peer Counselor Team member, Tutor for Algebra, Trigonometry,
and Computer Programming/Assembly. Perfect Attendance.

University of California, Irvine, Irvine, California, 2001
Completed Veterans' Upward-Bound Program with advanced studies in Mathematics,
Science, and English. 120 clock hours.

EMPLOYMENT BACKGROUND

Arrow Electronics, New York, New York

G.I.N. Rentals, Irvine, California

Astech, Division of Electronic Research, Irvine, California

United States Navy, San Diego, California

REFERENCES

Professional references are available upon request

EXHIBIT 2.3   Hybrid resume.

EDWARD F. MARTINEZ

9803 Aspen Road, Thornton, Colorado 80229

(303) 252-9187, Cell: (303) 367-9023, efmartinez@rockynet.net

OBJECTIVE: A position in the medical field, preferably as a Medical Assistant in a free-standing emergency center or a fast-paced medical office.

SKILLS SUMMARY: Training in the processing of insurance claim forms, surgical procedures, EKG and radiology, front and back office procedures, computer applications including DOS, Excel, WordPerfect, Windows, and Medisoft. Typing speed of 55 wpm.

EDUCATION: Parks Junior College, Thornton, Colorado 2004
Associate's degree in Medical Assisting, GPA: 3.9 (4.0)
Internship: University of Colorado Medical Center

University of Northern Colorado, Greeley, Colorado 2002
Completed 100 credit hours in Biology/Human Anatomy and Pre-chiropractic Medicine.

EMPLOYMENT: COMPUTER ROOM ASSISTANT, Parks Junior College
4/04 to present. Data entry, running programs and printing rosters.

JOB COACH, Shafer Rehabilitation Center, Denver, Colorado
12/02–4/04. Helped in the instruction of mentally disabled adults in learning how to work in the community.

VETERINARY ASSISTANT, New Life Center, Fort Collins, Colorado.
1/02–12/02. Front office duties of answering phones, making appointments, billing and filing. Back office responsibilities of assisting in surgery, removing sutures, giving injections, and sterilizing equipment.

ACHIEVEMENTS: Alpha Beta Kappa
Director's List for GPA of 3.5 or above
Perfect Attendance Awards
Colorado State Scholarship recipient

REFERENCES: See attached reference letters.

More older workers (those age 55 and above) are working than ever—a total of 16.6 million last year. The BLS also predicted that by the year 2005, 15 percent of the workforce would be 55 or older.[3] No one in *any age group* need be concerned if he or she presents himself or herself in a positive and enthusiastic manner. Even though discrimination against applicants based on age is illegal, you would be amazed at how many employers disregard this law. Job gaps, as long as they are not extreme and you have justifiable reasons for them, are not as serious as most people think. In my experience, I have found very few people who haven't had some gaps in their work background for various reasons.

Targeted Format

A focused presentation of accomplishments and skill areas directed toward a specific job or career is known as a **targeted resume** (see Exhibit 2.4). This kind of resume may be in the chronological, the functional, or the hybrid format, but the difference is that it includes the actual title of the job or career you are seeking instead of a job objective (discussed in the next section).

The targeted resume looks like any of the other formats, except that it is **more focused** and includes information that is directly related to the targeted job. This format is especially effective when you are especially interested in a specific job and when you need separate resumes for different career paths.

Electronic Format

Whatever style of resume you decide to use—chronological, functional, hybrid, or targeted—an electronic resume is different only in the way it is laid out on the page and in the wording. It is formatted so that you can send it via e-mail or post it on the Internet. Instead of emphasizing your skills and accomplishments with action verbs, you must use nouns as keywords that will be recognized by the employers' software that scans it for matches to the advertised opening. In most cases, employers prefer resumes to be submitted in plain text (also called ASCII text or MS-DOS text). However, this is not to say that your resume will always be received if written in that format. Specific instructions for formatting, printing, and sending all styles of resumes are given later in this chapter (see "The Final Draft").

Points to Remember for All Resumes

Give facts, figures, results, quantitative descriptions.   Employers are not impressed with obscure and vague phrases such as "I am a great problem solver, a hard worker, and detail oriented." Almost all applicants *say* these things but give no proof to support them. Employers see these empty words on hundreds of resumes, and they are meaningless unless you back them up with specific examples. Tell the prospective employer where and when you obtained skills and how long you performed them. When you claim to have an attitude or attribute, such as being "detail oriented" or "a hard worker," give a specific example of a time you demonstrated or were praised for that attribute.

Your resume should be original and have a personality—yours.   Don't be afraid of deviating from the "norm" or of being innovative enough to go beyond the typical ways that people design their resumes. A word of caution, however: Keep in mind that employers in industries other than the arts, communication, or sales are usually

EXHIBIT 2.4   Targeted resume.

DAVID A. WILLIAMS

19271 East Ellen Avenue, Aurora, Colorado 80012   •   (303) 366-6933   •   dawilliams@msn.com

JOB TARGET: PERSONNEL & LABOR RELATIONS SPECIALIST

EDUCATION

UNIVERSITY OF TUCSON, Tucson, Arizona 2004
Bachelor of Arts: Business Administration, Minor in Industrial & Labor Relations, GPA: 3.7/4.0

Phoenix School of Business, Phoenix, Arizona
Completed 24 semester hours in Economics and Labor Relations.

RELATED CAPABILITIES

- Written and Oral Communication Skills
- Research & Development of Labor Policies
- Independent Decision-Making Ability
- Patience and Diplomacy
- Good Judgment

EXPERIENCE

RESEARCH ASSISTANT, 9/2004 to Present
A & M Research Services, Aurora, Colorado
Currently doing market research on the union and labor relations in the supermarket industry.
Design client surveys, interpret research data, and prepare final reports.

PLACEMENT ASSISTANT, 2002 to 9/2004
University of Tucson, Tucson, Arizona
Prepared job lead reports, corresponded with students and client companies. Proficient in
Microsoft Word. Procured job leads for students from telephone cold calling. *Contributed to an
increase in student job placement by 20%.*

PERSONNEL ASSISTANT, 1998 to 2002
U.S. Army, Phoenix, Arizona
Assisted with interviews and paperwork of inductees for job placement. *Acted as a grievance
mediator for enlistees.*

PROFESSIONAL AFFILIATIONS

Member of American Society for Personnel Administration, Aurora, Colorado Chapter,
1998 to present. Chapter Research Coordinator.

GOALS: MBA and Graduate Field Work in Labor Relations.

INTERESTS: The history of unions and the progression of labor contract negotiations.

REFERENCES: Please see attached letters of reference:
- A & M Research Services, R & D Director, George M. Silky.
- University of Tucson, Student Services & Affairs Administration, Dr. Lloyd Burns.
- Additional references will be provided upon request.

a bit conservative and might not be receptive to a very unusual resume, such as one done in hand lettering or one that looks like a page out of a magazine advertisement. In the field of art or design, this kind of resume may be regarded as creative and be well received, while employers in other fields may see it as unprofessional. Always use good judgment and taste, and never lose sight of the professional aspect in presenting your qualifications to the prospective employer. Stay away from cutesy gimmicks and don't get carried away with the unusual or bizarre. Get several persons' opinions, particularly from those already in your field. If your college has a career assistance department, ask for suggestions and advice from those personnel, because they are in touch with the employers who hire, and they know what employers prefer to see on resumes. In addition, if you are writing an electronic resume, be certain to follow the guidelines for that format, including the individual employer's requirements.

Writing the First Draft

As soon as you have compiled all of your background information and have chosen the resume style that is best suited to your job objective, you are ready to begin writing the first draft. Unless it is obvious that your employment history and education are directly related to the position(s) you'll be applying for, you should include a job objective. You do not want to make your reader guess at what you want to do.

Job Objective

The **job objective** is a brief statement telling the employer what type of position you are seeking and always appears at the beginning of the resume, immediately after your name and address. It can also contain a short sentence mentioning your long-term employment goals. Objectives seem to be somewhat difficult for most people to write, as they just don't know where to begin. Often, they either don't say anything meaningful at all or get so wordy that the reader is turned off before even getting into the resume. Other job objectives are so general that they have a "cookie-cutter" look, and the employer suspects that they have been copied from a sample resume. If it appears that the applicant either didn't take the time to construct a coherent job objective or doesn't know what it is that he or she wants to do, the employer may conclude that the applicant lacks initiative.

As you write your objective, keep one idea firmly in mind: "What do I want to do; what is my job goal?" This will help to keep you on track and focused so you avoid rambling. I suggest that you not use words like "challenging" or "rewarding," as they are so overused and abstract that they mean little to the reader. Be very careful of using phrases such as "advancement into management." Management of what? Sales? Production? Administration? Personnel? Computer operations? Vague words only reveal to the employer that you haven't done your research to learn what the career path is for your field or that you *really don't know where you want to be in the future.* Though your objective should be concise, you do want to keep it a little general so as not to disqualify yourself from being considered for related positions that the employer may have open. This is especially important if you are just entering your field and do not have an abundance of experience for the position for which you are applying. Try to avoid using specific job titles unless you are targeting one. In this event, you would probably be better off using a targeted format and wouldn't need an objective.

Your choice of words is important because of the "pictures" they paint for your reader and the assumptions he or she will draw from them. Be certain that the words you use are clear to the reader. To avoid being misunderstood, avoid using abstract words (ones that can be interpreted in different ways). Below are a few examples of different ways to write job objectives. Some of the sample resumes in this chapter also include job objectives.

Banquet Manager with responsibilities in food preparation, purchasing, staff development, and menu planning.

Long-term goal: General Manager of Hotel Operations

Editorial position, preferably within the textbook department of a publishing company.

Communications Specialist preparing news releases, designing and editing brochures, displays, and posters, and executing advertising strategies.

Long-term goal: Director of Public Relations

Researcher/technical writer for a communications company devoted to the advancement of information technology.

A position in physical therapy that involves treatment planning, use of therapeutic modalities, and follow-up care for patients.

To associate with a company in information systems management with software development and systems integration projects.

Seeking full- or part-time employment as instructor in networking administration, electronics, or programming.

Once you've written your job objective, the next step is to decide what information to present first. Many resumes begin with a section titled "Summary of Qualifications" (or some similar appropriate title) that summarizes your skills, up front, for the reader. This saves him or her from having to search through the resume to discover what you have to offer. If you need more information to help you write this part, review the Functional format description given earlier.

The order in which you present your qualifications is critical because you have only about 30 seconds or less to convince your reader that you have what he or she is looking for. When you consider the large number of resumes that employers and human resources people have to read, it's not surprising that they will be scanning by the time they are halfway down the page. So, if you want to be considered for an interview, you had better give them your best shot right up front.

After the summary of qualifications, most resumes give either a section on employment experience or one listing education. If your education is what most qualifies you for the position, present it first. However, if your experience is your best selling point, begin there.

Education Section

Under the heading of Education, include all relevant training you have had, whether it was from a formal institution, on the job, or elsewhere. Now, you're probably thinking, "How the heck do I know what is relevant?" Obviously, anything directly related to the position you are applying for is relevant. In addition, take a look at the functional aspects of the position: It quite possibly requires skills such as the ability to communicate, to handle conflict and stress, to take initiative and action, to think strategically, and almost always, to be flexible. These qualifications may not be stated specifically in the ad or job description, but in today's workplace, they are almost always necessary to the performance of any job. Consequently, if you have training or experience in these kinds of functional skills, they would certainly be relevant.

Begin by listing the name(s) of the institution(s) you attended after high school; high school data is included only if there were awards, courses, or relevant (there's that word again) accomplishments that would reinforce your credibility to perform the job. Naming *all* of the classes you have taken is a needless waste of time and space and very boring to read, so don't do it. Your transcript will provide these details, and employers will request one if they feel it is important. It is necessary only to list areas of concentration or majors with emphasis on certain subjects. Include the city and state where the institution is located; street addresses, phone numbers, and ZIP codes are not given on resumes.

If you attended college and did not graduate, but completed some courses that are—you guessed it—relevant, then include information about the college. By all means, if you do list it, be sure to include what you studied there. An effective way to state this is to give the college name and add "Completed (number) of semester/quarter/clock hours in (course or subject name)." By writing it this way, you don't indicate that you "quit," but that you *completed* a certain number of hours in that subject.

A frequently asked question is whether to include your grade point average (GPA) on your resume. This is definitely optional; however, some employers have told me they like to see it. If you leave it off, an employer might wonder how bad your grades really were, but if it is 3.0 or above, by all means do so. However, if you decide to include it and it is below 3.0, then be sure to explain in your cover letter any extenuating circumstances that prevented you from earning a higher average. Maybe you worked a full-time job while you were in school, or you are a single parent with children to care for; any *valid* situation that may have diverted your efforts to maintain a higher GPA would be credible. This can sometimes be advantageous for you as it shows that you are capable of applying yourself and finishing what you set out to do, regardless of the disadvantages. Another option is to list your major GPA or your average grades for only the classes taken in your major.

In a functional resume, dates of attendance and graduation are usually not given. In all the other styles, dates of attendance are not important, but the date of graduation from school is important if your curriculum was of a technical nature because it indicates that your skills are current. The key is to be consistent in all areas and styles.

Employment History Section

In this part of the resume, there are different rules for the chronological and the functional styles. If the chronological style is the best choice for your background, then list your present or most recent job and continue backward for all jobs that you have decided to include. The big question is, "How far back should I go?" For managerial jobs, limit your experience to 15 years. About 10 years is usually sufficient for tech positions unless positions that you held earlier would give additional proof of your ability to do the job. In this case, rather than filling pages with your employment history, you should probably choose a functional or hybrid resume style. If you are using the chronological style and want to inform the employer of the skills that you acquired in those earlier positions, you can do so by adding a few lines about them in your cover letter or add them under a heading of "Other Experience." Briefly explain and do not include dates. (How to do this is explained in the section "Cover Letters.")

When you are listing your jobs in the chronological format, do not repeat the same job descriptions over and over if you have held several similar positions for different companies. This "parroting" of material is one of the major objections to chronological resumes; it makes them repetitive and often boring to read. Simply name the position(s) you held, briefly describe the duties and responsibilities, then list the companies and dates of employment. If you are using the hybrid format, list the companies, and if you choose, the dates or number of years you were there. (See Exhibit 2.12 on page 72.) Whenever you list a company, if its line of business is not obvious from the name, include a brief description.

When you list dates on your resume, don't worry about weeks and days; round all time spans up or down to a number of months and years. If you were at a job less than six months, think about whether it should even be on the resume. Is it relevant to the position you are now seeking? What do you do if you have held a lot of part-time or contract jobs that were for short periods of time, and they show skills that give proof that you can perform the job you seek? In this case, list the jobs under a subtitle such as "Part-Time Jobs."

If you are a new graduate and need to intensify your experience, show every work experience you've had including internships (paid and unpaid), student jobs, co-op education, and even extracurricular activities. If you've been out of the work-force for a few years as a home manager or on a sabbatical, list transferable skills you gained in volunteer, civic, hobby, and household work.

Things that you *do not* put on your resume in the Employment section are reasons for leaving past jobs, past salaries, and present salary requirements. These items can be discussed in the interview or in the cover letter if the employer has requested them.

Related Professional Experience

Include a section with this title if you have relevant experience that you gained by doing volunteer work or some specialized skill(s) that would be of benefit to the prospective employer. If the experience or training is far removed from your job objective or the requirements of the job for which you are applying, leave it out. For example, if you took a course in underwater basket weaving or belly dancing, leave that out unless it is relevant to the position.

Additional Headings

Anything that you haven't already included but that illustrates your special qualities and enhances your marketability can be stated in a separate section with its own title. Some possible titles are:

Professional Licenses, Certifications

Publications

Professional Organization Memberships

Foreign Languages (be sure to indicate degree of fluency)

Awards, Travel

Personal Information

Except in rare occasions, personal information is no longer required on resumes. Since the inception of the EEOC (Equal Employment Opportunity Commission), it is illegal for any employer to select an employee based on this kind of information.

Only if employers can prove that a job requires specific personal qualifications, can they require that you submit this information. For example, you must be 21 years of age to sell alcohol. Even if personal information is requested, you do not need to put it on your resume. You will provide it later when you have been offered the job. Pictures are used only if requested for certain occupations. Do not list your age, sex, marital status, religion, place of birth, state of health, social security number, or any other information of a personal nature on your resume. Including it simply gives an employer the opportunity to prejudge you or to discriminate against you. If an employer does request personal information prior to a job offer, the request may be illegal. Illegal inquiries of this nature are very sensitive subjects. How to handle this kind of questioning professionally is explained in the section in Chapter 4 on application forms and on interviewing.

References

The section of a resume for references is rapidly becoming a "dinosaur," fading into extinction because of legal controversy concerning a person's right to privacy and because background checks have proved to be sometimes unreliable. Also, at the time an employer is reading your resume, he or she is not interested in your references. Only after the employer has interviewed you and has an interest in hiring you will he or she take the time to call or write for references.

To avoid the risk of lawsuits by former employees who receive poor references, many companies now instruct their employees not to give out any references at all. In most states, recent court cases have expanded employees' rights to sue employers, so employers are very concerned about charges of slander or libel. A study by Ramona Paetzold, management professor at Texas A&M University, and Steven Willborn, law professor at the University of Nebraska, shows that the average award in employer defamation cases is $57,000. Some adversely affected employees have even been awarded settlements of $150,000 to $25 million.[4] No wonder employers are very cautious about giving references for former employees.

Some companies will only verify dates of employment. I'm told by a long-time employee of Qwest that they refer all reference requests to the human resource department, which only verifies dates of employment, position held, and wages. For some positions, however, employers do check motor vehicle or credit records. *MSN Money*, in an article "How Bad Credit Can Cost You a Job," states that "Many employers—including the federal government—routinely scour credit reports on current and prospective employees to help decide who's hired or fired." The article also reports that about 35 percent of the companies surveyed by the Society for Human Resource Management checked credit reports of current or potential employees in 2003, up from the 19 percent in 1996.[5] Increasingly employers are using professional background checkers such as Avert, Inc., which is based in Ft. Collins, Colorado. Avert is a nationwide company with 600 couriers who tap databases in all 3,300 counties in the United States for public information about applicants. This company provides employment screening products (some automated) to facilitate verification of references, social security numbers, criminal records, and credit reports. Employers have learned that this information, however, is only as accurate as the data input because it may not reveal records in counties, cities, or states where the applicant has lived and worked. It may not give a complete account of a prospective applicant.

Despite the success of some employees' lawsuits, you must be aware that you can't sue an employer unless you have proof that the reference information or comment was knowingly false, disclosed for a malicious purpose, or violated your civil rights. To avoid unpleasant surprises, you can check your own references prior to your job search through a company like DRC (Documented Reference Check, Inc., www.badreferences.com), based in Diamond Bar, California. DRC has checked backgrounds for thousands of job seekers nationwide. On the other hand, if it is your credit history you are concerned about, you may want to write to one of the following credit bureaus to get a copy of your credit record. You are entitled to a free copy of your file.

- Equifax, 1-800-685-1111
- EXPERIAN (formerly TRW) offers a credit check monitoring service where membership gives you alerts of changes in your credit history and supplies forms and tips for disputes, 1-888-397-3742
- Trans-Union, National Consumer Disclosure Center, 1-800-916-8800

The Internet offers websites that will check your credit history for free.

If you happen to have a credit history that needs repair, you can write for a free booklet called *Getting Back in the Black* from FTC Public Reference Branch, Rm. 130, Sixth St. & Pennsylvania Avenue N.W., Washington, D.C. 20580. The FTC's Web address is www.ftc.gov. According to the Fair Credit Reporting Act (FCRA), you should also know that an employer needs your permission to run a credit check, so failing to do so is an FCRA violation, and he or she is supposed to tell you if credit information is used against you. *Reality check:* Not all employers are totally honest when it comes to leveling with you.

If you absolutely feel the need to include a Reference section, a short statement such as "References will be provided upon request" is sufficient. However, since everyone knows that you will provide references if asked, this statement is rather pointless (especially if putting it in your resume means adding a second page).

Whether you include a References section on your resume or not, you should always be prepared to supply the names, addresses, e-mail addresses, and phone numbers of at least three or four credible references. Have a reference page, typed and ready, that lists people who can vouch for your character. (See the sample reference list in Exhibit 2.5.) Use the names of professional friends and acquaintances, for example, teachers, clergy, or former employers and coworkers who have known you for at least one to three years. Friends and family members do not qualify as references. **Be sure to notify and ask permission from the people you are listing as references. Send them a copy of your resume so they can have it in front of them when they are providing a reference.**

Although a list of references probably does not belong in your resume, *reference letters* are a different matter. If you have current ones from college professors, former employers, etc., and they are excellent testimony to your skill level and good character, you may wish to attach copies of them to your resume. Letters of commendation about notable volunteer services that you have performed are also worth including. Attach no more than two or three letters. If possible, reproduce them on the same kind of paper you use for your resume and cover letter. (See the sample reference letters in Exhibits 2.6 and 2.7.)

With good reference letters and a list of references that you can hand the employer, you can save yourself and the employer a lot of time and trouble. Alternatively, you may wish to call or write your reference people and ask them to send reference letters directly to the employer.

R EFERENCE PAGE

List your references below—at least three or four professional acquaintances. Have this list available for filling out application forms and for the interview, should the employer request it.

NAME AND TITLE	COMPANY NAME/ADDRESS	TELEPHONE/E-MAIL

EXHIBIT 2.5   Reference list.

JANE BRYANT

REFERENCES

Ms. Mary Kay Brown
Human Resource Director
Canco Manufacturing Company
123 Jewell Street
San Diego, California 92010
(714) 461-8111
kaybrown@canco.com

Mr. Joseph Blue
Owner
Pacific Insurance, Inc.
8917 "G" Street
San Diego, California 92102
(714) 442-0331
joeblue@pacific.com

Mrs. Betty Paige
Instructor
Needmore Union Adult School
1211 Morrison Street
San Diego, California 92022
(714) 579-2810
betty_paige@needmore_union.com

Cynthia Blaine
Supervisor
Avery Structures, Inc.
6945 E. 112th Avenue
Suite 349
Seattle, Washington 98109
(206) 424-8987
cblaine@avery.com

KANE ENGINEERING

40526 N. Industrial Lane, Pasadena, California 90406   (818) 555-1234   www.kane.com

Mr. Gregory Mason
Coronet Co.
8711 W. 14th Street
Pasadena, CA 90401

April 14, 2005

Dear Mr. Mason:

John Reddick has been employed with my company for two years. He is extremely efficient and quick to learn the procedures to keep up with the fast pace we required of him. His ability to comprehend what was needed before my direction allowed me to focus on my own responsibilities. He is customer focused and learned the company's short-term and long-term goals.

John's time working for Kane Engineering was enjoyable and will be an experience of which I will have positive memories.

Sincerely,

John Kane

John Kane
President

KANE ENGINEERING

40526 N. Industrial Lane, Pasadena, California 90406   (818) 555-1234   www.kane.com

April 14, 2005

To Whom It May Concern:

John Reddick's work with me has been far above average. He has been on time and available, allowing me to keep up with the demands of my customers. He has been adaptable and willing to meet any training requirements that we together have recognized as necessary. He has shared new technical advancements in computer networking that he learned through his degree program at Westwood College of Technology. He has many times agreed to work overtime or come in on his days off to cover for other employees.

Sincerely,

John Kane

John Kane
President

P.S. Please feel free to call me at (818) 555-1234 or contact me via e-mail at john_kane@kane.com for any additional information you would like.

The Final Draft

N ow for the fun stuff! When you've done all the detail work of compiling your information, chosen your format, written your first draft (and maybe the second or third?), it is time to write your final draft. Now you organize and rewrite all of this material so that you will have a resume you will be proud to distribute to prospective employers. It's at this point that some people even get an ego stroke when they realize what talented and skilled people they really are. Often, when I prepare resumes for customers and they look at the final draft, they exclaim, "Wow, I didn't realize I had so much to offer!"

As you read the following guidelines, look at the sample resumes on pages 68 through 79. (These resumes are for fictitious applicants, and the information is imaginary. Any resemblance to actual persons is coincidental.)

Completing the Final Draft

The following instructions are appropriate for the majority of hard copy resumes. The rules are different for electronic resumes, which are designed to be scanned by computer into a database. Specific instructions for the electronic format appear later in this chapter.

Stick with basic color choices for paper.   Use standard 8.5 by 11-inch white, ivory, light gray, or light blue paper. For those fields in which color and style are key factors, such as the art and design fields, this rule may be broken. In addition, printers and office supply places offer special paper with backgrounds that are quite unique and pleasant to the eye. Just remember to avoid anything that is extreme. Too many job seekers labor under the false illusion that printing a resume on brightly colored paper will draw attention to it. This may be true, but you want employers to be drawn to your resume because you match what they're looking for, not because the color of the paper hurts their eyes. During my years in career development, I have seen just about every color you can imagine; it didn't help anyone to get an interview.

Use an appealing format and layout.   Type should be spaced so that the resume has an all-around balanced appearance. Double- or triple-space between sections and use spacing sparingly within sections. Margins should be from 1 to 1.5 inches. If you do not have a lot of information and you would have difficulty filling a page, *evenly* increase the size of the margins and the spacing between sections. If you have a little more than would go on one page and rewording or deleting would create confusion for your reader, you can decrease the margins to 1/2 inch. However, when keeping your resume to one page requires that you reduce the white space so much that the page looks messy and crowded, it is better to use wider margins and go to two pages rather than to "cram" it onto one page. Aim for a "picture frame" look and a design that is easy to read.

Keep it concise.   Preferably, resumes should be no longer than two pages, except in special cases where it is necessary to provide additional information required by an employer (e.g., government and education). Many employers say they prefer one-page resumes, but, again, do not condense your resume to one page at the expense of readability.

Make your resume inviting and easy to read.   Highlight important points that you especially want noticed by CAPITALIZING, **bolding,** or <u>underscoring</u>. Don't force your readers to "dig" for the information; they won't.

Control the quality.   Your resume should be typed and saved on a computer and printed out using a printer with letter-quality output. The print should be dark enough and large enough so that it can be read easily. Once you have a master copy that is bright and clear, you can take it to a printer for reproduction. Or you can print out as many copies as you need. Just be certain that the copies you distribute are bright and clear.

Identify subsequent pages.   If your resume is on two pages, place a heading on the second page that includes your name and "Page 2" one to two inches from the top. (Most word processing software programs begin your page at the proper number of lines from the top of the page, so begin where you see the cursor.) Either of the following styles is acceptable:

Larue R. Austin	2	(date, optional)
Larue R. Austin		
Page 2		

After this heading, drop down 2 to 4 lines to continue your resume information.

Always be accurate and never "fudge" or lie.   *U.S. News & World Report* has reported that "a surprising number of applicants are telling whoppers on their resumes." According to the article, Jude M. Werra, a Wisconsin headhunter, "checks the education claims on the 300 or so executive resumes he gets annually. In the first six months of this year, 23 percent of his applicants awarded themselves fictitious degrees, up from 17 percent last year." The article reports that this is happening with applicants from janitors to nurses. Werra says he is puzzled because "you don't need to lie. It's also risky because checking is easier than ever."[6] You are going to have to substantiate your information in the interview and on the application form, so be careful of your claims.

Forgo the title.   A title (such as "Resume" or "Resume of Qualifications") is unnecessary. Your reader is quite aware of what the document is. A little humor here: You don't put "Letter" at the top of your letters, do you?

Keep it flat.   When you mail or drop off your resume to a prospective employer, place it in a 9 × 12- or 10 × 13-inch envelope. If you fold it to fit a smaller envelope, you risk having creases that could blur the print. A resume looks more professional if it has not been folded.

Be extremely cautious of using negatives.   Anything that could be interpreted as criticism, conflict, or hostility should not be on your resume, or anywhere else in the job search, for that matter. Be careful about including information that could cause employers to stereotype you. For example, listing an interest in and expertise with weapons of any kind may project an image that an employer could find unfavorable if you are applying for a job unrelated to gun or weapon use.

Proofread.   Last but not least, before you make any copies, have at least three people proofread your resume, preferably a school counselor or someone in your industry. At least one of these people should have good grammatical skills. If you want to be called for an interview, your resume has to be error-free, smudge-free, visually appealing, and professional.

Completing the Electronic Resume[7]

The final draft of your electronic resume should follow most of the guidelines for conventional resumes. Because it must be scanned and sent via e-mail, however, some special instructions apply. These involve the use of keywords that will be recognized by the employer's database, and preparation in a format that can be electronically transmitted and scanned.

A resume that is to be posted to an employer's online resume template or scanned into a database must be prepared and saved as a text-only document. Text-only documents can contain very little formatting, so they are visually not as appealing as paper resumes. Fonts, bolding, italics, brackets, borders, tables, headers, footers, inconsistent tab layout, and underlining are all off-limits, as these things can make the document difficult for the software to read. Saving your resume in rich-text format (RTF) will preserve all the formatting, but your resume may not be readable by some employers' software. So if you want to get the most responses to your electronic resume, save it as a text-only file.

The organization of an electronic resume is also somewhat different from that of the paper resume. The margin and white-space guidelines are the same, but you shouldn't use centered headings, only flush-left text. Since you can't use bolding or different fonts, type your headings in all capital letters so as to make them stand out. The best fonts to use are Helvetica, Times, Courier, and Arial, and the point size should be no smaller than 12.

If you will e-mail your resume, move your address and phone number to the bottom of the resume. If they are at the top, the computer screen may be taken up with the e-mail header, your return address, date and time, etc. If this is all the employer sees on the first page, he or she might not be inclined to read on. Mary B. Nemnich and Fred E. Jandt, authors of *Cyberspace Job Search Kit*, suggest that you

> put only your name and job title at the top of the resume as a heading rather than waste that first screen with a header and address. The top of your resume is the most critical as your reader should know who you are and what you do within a few seconds of reading your resume. Following the heading, you should write a summary. With only about 20 lines to work with on the first screen, it is imperative that you make a strong, favorable impression in those first few lines . . . . The summary paragraph should contain some of the main keywords that describe your skills. Thus, the first part of your resume will look something like this:

> J. B. Seeker

> Public Relations Specialist

> **Summary**: Talented Public Relations Practitioner with more than 15 years of experience and a proven track record in community and media relations. Excellent writing skills. Facility with desktop publishing, including PageMaker, Quark, and Microsoft Publisher. Familiar with Microsoft Word and Windows. Motivational speaker. Adept at press relations and creative advertising. MA in Communication Studies, PR emphasis.[8]

An important element of an electronic resume is the use of keywords. **Keywords** are specific words that an employer looks for when searching a resume database. Your electronic resume will be scanned to create an electronic representation that can be read into an automatic resume tracking system. The tracking system allows the employer to find resumes that include words indicating specific skills—keywords. Keywords are usually noun forms. To make sure your resume is selected by the tracking system, therefore, use nouns such as *electronics technician*, *computer programmer*, *physical therapy*, *network administration*, *leadership*, *flexibility*, and *teamwork*.

If you used verb forms in your paper resume, change them to noun forms for the electronic version. For example:

Verb forms   *Designed* micro-video components for surgical equipment, *charted* statistical data, *handled* all correspondence with suppliers, and *selected and purchased* parts and materials.

Noun forms   Senior draftsperson, micro-video design, parts and materials purchasing, statistical data charting, and supplier correspondence.

If you are not sure about the keywords that companies are using, go to the classified ads in your local newspapers. Nemnich and Jandt suggest that "a good place to find job descriptions with ideas for keywords is the O*NET, a listing of job titles, descriptions, and needed skills that's available in book form from JIST Publishing, Inc. at www.jist.com and online at www.doleta.gov/programs/onet/onet_hp.htm."[9]

The above instructions for writing the final draft of your electronic resume have been adapted from several online sources such as ResumeDoctor.com, and from Nemnich and Jandt's *Cyberspace Job Search Kit*. More excellent detailed advice for preparing an electronic resume can be found in Chapter 7 of that book.

RESUME CHECKLIST

- ☑ Is your name visibly placed at the top? If it's difficult to pronounce, have you given your reader a phonetic spelling?
- ☑ Have you included your *complete* address(es) and phone numbers (home, cell, pager, work)?
- ☑ Did you remember to include your e-mail address if you have one?
- ☑ If this is an electronic resume, are your address, phone numbers, etc. all on separate lines?
- ☑ Did you sell yourself by showing how you could be of benefit to the employer by listing previous accomplishments?
- ☑ Is your resume no more than two pages in length, or if it is longer, are you certain the page(s) are necessary?
- ☑ Is your text balanced on the page(s)?
- ☑ Is your resume concise, specific, and easy to read?
- ☑ Did you avoid using the first person pronoun: "I," "me," "my"?
- ☑ Does it have information that is not relevant to your job objective? If so, remove it.

- Are your indentations, margins, and columns consistent?
- If this is a traditional resume, did you use action verbs to begin your sentences and phrases, and are your sentences brief, clear, and to the point?
- If this is an electronic resume, did you use nouns rather than verbs to describe your skills and accomplishments?
- Did you show progression, growth, and initiative in the positions you've held?
- Most important, have you had at least three people proof your resume for you?

Functional Skills Inventory

Whether you are writing your resume or selling yourself to an employer in an interview, knowing your functional skills can be an advantage. These are the skills that are required in all fields, positions, and companies. They can often fill in for other areas where you may be lacking. When surveyed, employers will list, as a top priority, basic skills such as reading comprehension and writing ability. At the top of the list is the ability to get along well with others, especially in today's diversified workforce. Another common priority is that a potential employee be able to use sound judgment and possess problem-solving skills. I have heard from numerous employers over the years that they are usually willing to provide some training in technical areas, but they do not have the time to train someone in basic skill areas or to teach an employee how to get along with others. A few years ago, the CEO of Burger King, Jeff Campbell, was asked how important he thought it was to be able to get along well with others. His reply was, "One of the hardest things I have to do is to go to an employee who is working his tail off for you and tell him that I have to let him go because he can't get along with the others in the company."

Being aware and knowledgeable of all your functional skills and using them to sell yourself could make the difference in your being chosen over another applicant who may have more experience or education. So, before you prepare your benefit statements or go to an interview, go through the following list, select the skills you have by placing a checkmark in the circle, and incorporate them into your paperwork. You will have some very useful tools to use when speaking with prospective employers.

ARTISTIC:

- Expressiveness (the ability to use my body to express feelings)
- Operate well in a free, unstructured, unsupervised environment
- Have talent for drawing, drafting, or creative writing
- Musical knowledge or apparel fashioning

ATHLETIC/OUTDOOR/TRAVEL:

- Motor/physical coordination and agility
- Skill in general sports, recreation
- Skills in creating, planning, and organizing outdoor activities, such as traveling, cultivating growing things, or working with animals

DETAIL/FOLLOW-THROUGH:

- Ability to follow detailed instructions
- Expert at getting things done
- Skilled at making arrangements for events and processes
- Responsible (consistently tackle and complete tasks ahead of time)
- Good at processing information, classifying, and clerical tasks

DEVELOPING/PLANNING/ORGANIZING/MANAGING:

- Use a systematic approach to goal setting
- Can establish effective priorities
- Adept at policy making, designing projects, organizing others
- Ability to bring people together in cooperative efforts
- Can schedule, assign, supervise others in their work
- Experienced in monitoring others' output
- Good in areas of maintenance and evaluating

INFLUENCING/PERSUADING:

- Able to develop rapport/trust
- Expertise in reasoning persuasively and developing thoughts
- Ability to sell ideas or products
- Recruiter of talent or leadership
- Can arbitrate/mediate between contending parties

INSTRUCTING/INTERPRETING/GUIDING:

- Able to teach and promote a learning environment and convey enthusiasm
- Competent at giving advice
- Encourage and help people to make their own discoveries
- Can counsel and facilitate groups
- Competent trainer

INTUITIVE/INNOVATIVE:

- Highly imaginative, inventive, creative, perceptive, and innovative
- Willing to experiment with new approaches
- Can visualize relationships between apparently unrelated factors
- Show sound judgment
- Derive things from other ideas
- Adaptable
- Can visualize in three dimensions
- Show foresight
- Can recognize obsolescence

LANGUAGE/READING/WRITING/SPEAKING:

- Am an avid reader
- Can edit accurately and compose and communicate with clarity
- Can systematically explain concepts
- Possess verbal/written skills in foreign languages
- Ability to describe people, places, concepts, or things
- Skill in promotional and technical writing

LEADERSHIP:

- Competent in taking managed risks
- Can plan for and effect change
- Unwilling to automatically accept status quo
- Possess excellent decision-making skills
- Can lead others with constructive criticism and feedback
- Ability to guide and chair meetings and groups

NUMERICAL/FINANCIAL/ACCOUNTING:

- Can perform rapid computations in my head or on a calculator
- Can design budgets and manage accounts
- Adept at cost analysis
- Extremely economical
- Bookkeeping/accounting skills
- Can correctly solve statistical problems

OBSERVATION/LEARNING/PROBLEM SOLVING:

- Highly observant of people, data, and things
- Adept at troubleshooting
- Can listen carefully
- Am perceptive, learn quickly, and retain what I learn
- Able to assess situations and problems accurately and provide effective solutions

PERFORMING:

- Can demonstrate products, procedures, systems
- Can perform before groups and stimulate enthusiasm, with a flair for showmanship
- Play musical instruments
- Can make people laugh
- Acting ability
- Adept at various sports
- Able to conduct and direct affairs/ceremonies

RELATIONSHIPS:

○ Ability to meet people easily and interact freely with strangers

○ Treat people with consideration, politeness, and respect

○ Aware of others' needs and feelings

○ Able to listen to others' points of view with an open mind

○ Relate to all people regardless of sex, creed, or race

RESEARCH/INVESTIGATION/ANALYSIS:

○ Ability to survey, interview, and examine critically and effectively

○ Can perceive and define cause and effect relationships

○ Define problems, choose and evaluate options

○ Review and evaluate choices/options

TIPS ON WORDING

- Avoid the use of personal pronouns such as "I," "me," or "my." The subject of your sentences is obviously you, so it is redundant to use these pronouns repeatedly. Begin your sentences with action verbs, or in the electronic resume, use nouns to describe your qualifications.

- Use an outline format with short sentences; even sentence fragments are permissible if they are otherwise grammatically correct and they make sense.

- Focus on your accomplishments and what you can do for the employer, not on wordy, lengthy descriptions of job duties.

- Avoid abbreviations, especially if they might be misunderstood. Use only those that are universally known. Those used in addresses are permissible, but they look more professional when they are spelled out. Even the two-letter abbreviations for states should not be used on your resume unless you need to conserve space.

- Avoid jargon whenever possible. Your readers may not be familiar with it; furthermore, it might insult them.

- Refer to specific projects and responsibilities with words that describe measurable (quantifiable) results.

- Include information on extracurricular activities that illustrate your qualities such as leadership, teamwork, or the ability to save time or money (major concerns of all businesses).

- Write in the past tense, except for current jobs and activities.

- Skip formal wording; it may give the reader the impression that you are rigid and stuffy or, worse, pretentious.

- Give brief descriptions of any organizations or awards you have mentioned and any acronyms you have used that are not common knowledge.

NOUN FORMS (For Use in Electronic Resumes)

Accountant	Electrician	Language	Programmer	Surveyor
Administration	Electronics	Management	Publications	Teacher
Advertising	Engineer	Marketing	Public Relations	Team Leader
Analyst	Entrepreneur	Mathematics	Public Speaking	Teamwork
Animation	Experience	Manager	Purchaser	Technician
Assembly	Finances	Microprocessor	Radiology	Therapist
Award	Function	Narration	Rehabilitation	Trainer
Bookkeeper	Graphic Designer	Negotiation	Repairer	Transcription
Communication	Honors	Network	Research	Vendor
Corporate	Injection	Network Information	Sales	Writer
Customer Relations	Interface Design	Officer	Service	
Director	Internship	Operating System	Specialist	
Draftsperson	Intuition	Pathologist	Supervisor	
Editor	Investigation	Personnel	Surgery	

VERB FORMS (For Use in Printed Resumes)

Achieved	Designed	Financed	Moderated	Processed	Sorted
Administrated	Determined	Formulated	Monitored	Programmed	Succeeded
Allocated	Developed	Generated	Motivated	Promoted	Summarized
Analyzed	Diagnosed	Governed	Negotiated	Proposed	Supervised
Approved	Directed	Identified	Operated	Proved	Supplied
Arranged	Discovered	Illustrated	Ordered	Provided	Supported
Assembled	Dispensed	Implemented	Organized	Recruited	Surveyed
Assisted	Distributed	Indexed	Originated	Reduced	Systematized
Attained	Earned	Initiated	Performed	Reorganized	Tested
Compiled	Engineered	Innovated	Persuaded	Reported	Trained
Completed	Established	Installed	Piloted	Researched	Transformed
Composed	Evaluated	Integrated	Pioneered	Resolved	Troubleshot
Computed	Executed	Invented	Planned	Revised	Unified
Controlled	Expanded	Investigated	Prepared	Scheduled	Updated
Coordinated	Expedited	Led	Presented	Served	Upgraded
Created	Experienced	Maintained	Presided	Simplified	Verified
Demonstrated	Facilitated	Managed	Problem-solved	Solved	

R ESUME WORKSHEET

Continue items on a separate sheet if necessary.

Name: _____

Address: _____

City   State   ZIP Code

Phone _____

Work   Home   Cell/Pager

E-mail Address(es) _____

Career Objective or Position Sought (may or may not be included)

_____

_____

Summary of Skills

List: 1. Specific things you can do.

2. Specific equipment with which you are familiar or skilled.

3. Skills gained in employment, schooling, volunteer activities, or freelance work.

BE SPECIFIC!

_____
_____
_____
_____
_____
_____
_____
_____

Other Achievements: GPA, attendance in college (if good), awards, certificates, etc.

_____
_____
_____

(continued)

RESUME WORKSHEET Continued

Education

Most recent college attended

City, State (no ZIP code)

Graduation Date

Degree received (or hours completed)

Other Schools, Colleges, Trade, Votech, Certificates, etc. (Include high school

only if you took courses that are current and relevant to your objective.)

City, State

Graduation date

Degree received or hours completed

Employment Background

Present (or most recent) Job Title

Name of Company

Location

City	State

Dates Worked

Responsibilities

Second Job Title

Name of Company

Location

City	State

Dates Worked

Responsibilities

(continued)

RESUME WORKSHEET Continued

Third Job Title _____

Name of Company _____

Location _____
                                              City   State

Dates Worked _____

Responsibilities _____

_____

_____

_____

Fourth Job Title _____

Name of Company _____

Location _____
                                              City   State

Dates Worked _____

Responsibilities _____

_____

_____

_____

Military (optional: If experience shows relevant skills, include it)

Branch of Service\Location(s) _____

_____

_____

Skills Acquired: _____

_____

_____

_____

_____

Below list special schools, awards, certificates, volunteer work, etc.

_____

_____

_____

JOHN E. JONES

11567 East 17th Street, Spokane, Washington 01435

(509) 555-4587 (Please leave message)

johnjones95@aol.com

SUMMARY OF QUALIFICATIONS

Eight years' experience as a Surveyor. Proficiency, knowledge, and strengths in the following areas: Surveying, Field Engineering, Mapping, Drafting, Blueprinting, Supervision, Training, Customer Relations. Roads/Bridges: Commercial & Residential.

SUMMARY OF EXPERIENCE

Currently work as an independent contractor doing surveying and drafting for some firms in the Spokane area. Contracts include boundaries, commercial, heavy construction, and topographic jobs.

2002–2005   **Avery Structures, Inc.,** Spokane, WA
            Party Chief on large construction jobs. Responsible for surveying and drafting.

2000–2002   **Centennial Engineering,** Seattle, WA
            Party Chief for survey team in the construction of bridges and roads. Responsible for calculations and drafting on all phases of the jobs.

1998–2000   **J.R. Developers,** Tacoma, WA
            Party Chief completing all survey work on the subdivisions.

1994–1998   **Al Messahaq/Aramco,** Saudi Arabia
            Party Chief on all project work in Geodetic Control, roads and highways, in addition to plant layout.

EDUCATION

ITT Technical Institute, Spokane, Washington, 2000
2000 Hours in Map Drafting

Spokane School of Surveying & Mapping, Seattle, Washington, 1994
Certificate for 1600-hour program in Surveying and Mapping.

REFERENCES

Will be provided upon request.

EXHIBIT 2.9   Functional resume.

JOHN E. JONES

11567 East 17th Street, Spokane, Washington 01435
(509) 555-4587 (Please leave message)
johnjones95@aol.com

OBJECTIVE

A position in Computer Operations with progressively expanding responsibilities leading to an appointment to Systems Analyst

EDUCATION

Spokane Technical Institute, Spokane, Washington
672-hour course in Computer Programming & Operations. State Certified. Graduated with honors. GPA: 3.67

Washington State University, Seattle, Washington
Completed 15 semester hours in Computer Science, including mastering Fortran.

Seattle School of Surveying & Mapping, Seattle, Washington
Certificate, 1600-hour program in Surveying & Mapping.

ITT Technical Institute, Spokane, Washington
Map Drafting (2000 hours).

PROFESSIONAL EXPERIENCE

Computer Computations/Data Processing
Involved in all aspects of data retrieval from computations to design to the finished product in the land surveying industry.

Mathematical
Performed daily algebraic and trigonometric calculations.

Teamwork
Worked cooperatively and effectively in fast-paced, demanding environment with all members of surveying crew, and interacted with various executive key personnel.

EMPLOYMENT HISTORY

Party Chief position for the following companies:
- Avery Structures, Inc., Spokane, Washington
- Centennial Engineering, Seattle, Washington
- J.R. Developers, Tacoma, Washington
- Al Messahaq/ARAMCO, Saudi Arabia

JOHN E. JONES

11567 East 17th Street, Spokane, Washington 01435
(509) 555-4587 (Please leave message)
johnjones95@aol.com

OBJECTIVE

A position in Data Processing, preferably in Computer Operations or Programming. Five-Year Career Goal: Systems Analysis Management

SUMMARY OF QUALIFICATIONS

COMPUTER SCIENCE, OPERATIONS & PROGRAMMING—Two years Computer Programming with emphasis in the following languages, software and operating systems: BASIC, FORTRAN, COBOL, MS-DOS, EXCEL, DBASE III, SPF/PC, IBM OS/VS, JCL and CICS.

COMPUTER COMPUTATIONS/DATA PROCESSING—*Eight years.* Involved in all aspects of data retrieval from computations to design.

MATHEMATICAL—*Five years.* Performed daily algebraic and trigonometric calculations.

TEAMWORK—*Eight years.* Effectively and cooperatively worked in a fast-paced, demanding environment with all members of a surveying crew, and interacted with various executive key personnel.

ADDITIONAL QUALIFICATIONS—Demonstrated ability to "debug" programs written by others. Developed training and instructional materials for software packages. Designed, set up and operated PC-based database for record keeping.

EDUCATION

SPOKANE TECHNICAL INSTITUTE, Spokane, Washington 2005
672-hour course in Computer Programming and Operations. State certified. Graduated with Honors. GPA: 3.67

WASHINGTON STATE UNIVERSITY, Seattle, Washington 2004
Completed 15 semester hours in Computer Science which included courses in Computer Networking.

SEATTLE SCHOOL OF SURVEYING & MAPPING, Seattle, Washington 2001
Certificate for 1600-hour program.

EMPLOYMENT BACKGROUND

Party Chief for the following companies:
Avery Structures, Inc., Spokane, Washington, 2002–2005
Centennial Engineering, Seattle, Washington, 2000–2002
J.R. Developers, Tacoma, Washington, 1998–2000
Al Messahaq/ARAMCO, Saudi Arabia, 1994–1998

REFERENCES

Professional references will be provided upon request.

EXHIBIT 2.11   Functional resume.

Mary C. Barnes

5343 Van Nuys Boulevard, Van Nuys, CA 91401   (318) 555-1354, mcbarnes@yahoo.com

OBJECTIVE

A position with an advertising agency where a sense of responsibility, an ability to work as a team member in groups, and marketing and communication skills are assets.

MAJOR WORK EXPERIENCE

Administrative Management

Hired, trained, and supervised data processing staff of ten. Managed office for national software development firm. In one year, reduced employee turnover in data processing department by 10%.

Public Relations

Prepared press releases and worked with media, brought regional recognition to new software program. Planned and coordinated monthly sales seminars and semi-annual conventions.

Advertising/Promotional

Designed and administrated newspaper, radio, and poster distribution for the introduction of new company programs and for the establishment of area sales centers.

Communication/Writing

Accurately reported sales activities to regional headquarters for all local sales/service centers. Created, edited, and printed revision of sales procedure manual, which directly contributed to a 25% increase in software sales.

EDUCATION

California State University, Los Angeles, CA
Bachelor of Science degree in Business Administration, minor in Computer Science.

Computer Learning Center, Los Angeles, CA
Completed 900-hour course in Data Processing.

REFERENCES

Professional references available upon request.

Pamela J. Smith

904 East 42nd Street   (303) 555-6332
Longmont, Colorado 80397   pjsmith@mci2005.com

OBJECTIVE

A position in the Hotel/Motel industry, preferably in Room Division Management. Five-Year Goal: Resident Manager

SUMMARY OF QUALIFICATIONS

ACCOUNTING—*Two Years.* Knowledge of basic fundamentals and hospitality accounting.

KEYBOARDING—*Two Years.* Earned an "A" in my classes with typing speed of over 50 words per minute in college and high school.

TEAMWORK—Through working experience, involved in teamwork in all positions.

COMMUNICATION—*One Year.* Answering phones, dealing with customers and problem solving at A-Advanced Communications Answering Service. Learned how to communicate with all kinds of people in many diverse situations.

EDUCATION

WESTWOOD COLLEGE OF TECHNOLOGY, Denver, Colorado. Earned Associate's degree in Hospitality Management. Major courses included accounting, supervision, purchasing, front office procedures, sanitation, professional communications and law.

THOMPSON VALLEY HIGH SCHOOL—Earned diploma; completed all major subjects such as English, algebra, accounting, and science.

EMPLOYMENT BACKGROUND

Marriott Hotel, Fort Collins, Colorado. *Public Attendant*, 2002–Present

A-Advanced Communications Answering Service, Denver, Colorado. *Telephone Operator*, 2001–2002

Boyers Donuts, Loveland, Colorado. *Cashier/Counter Help*, 1997–2001

Myers Floor Covering, Lakewood, Colorado. *Sales Help*, 1996–1997

Rocky Mountain Chiropractic Center, Denver, Colorado. *Phone Sales*, 1995–1996

REFERENCES

Available upon request

EXHIBIT 2.13   Hybrid resume.

Dale Merriman

2230 Hayes Street, Dallas, Texas 75234   (214) 555-8965 dmerriman@earthlink.net

Objective

A long-term computer-aided drafting position with an architectural firm that values attention to detail, teamwork, and good communication skills.

Long-Term Goals

Management in a Drafting and Design firm and continued education resulting in the acquisition of an architect's license.

Education

Dallas School of Drafting & Design, Dallas, Texas
Associate's degree in Architectural Drafting, Graduate: 2005

Vrain Valley High School, Arlington, Texas
Graduate: 1992. Completed four semesters of basic drafting and design.

Employment History

Repair Order Booker/General Office, *Miner Lincoln Mercury*
Dallas, Texas. 7/03 to present

Service Advisor/Dispatcher for the following companies:
Glenn Taylor Ford, Dallas, Texas 8/97–6/03
Dallas Hyundai Daihatsu, Arlington, Texas 3/95–7/97
ATC Nissan, Arlington, Texas 1/92–2/95

Summary of Qualifications

Computer-Aided Drafting
Certified in AutoCAD. Experience with 2D, 3D, AutoLISP, and AutoCAD MNU.

Teamwork, Quality Control, Time Management
Seven years as team leader for four to fifteen technicians organizing, assigning and ensuring timely and proper completion of automotive repairs within estimated cost.

Attention to Detail, Organization, Administration
Seven years controlling all aspects of as many as 60 different jobs in any given day. Details included initial contact with customers to determine needed services, estimation of cost for those services, and sales of the services to customers both on the phone and in person. Acquired parts and assigned personnel to complete repairs in the time promised to customer.

Mary Groetken *(Gret'ken)*

633 North La Brea Avenue   (213) 555-4122
Los Angeles, California 90036   marygroetken@pacbell.com

Objective: A position as a Medical Transcriptionist, preferably in Radiology or Pathology.

Summary of Qualifications

Computer Applications

Working knowledge of Life 70, CICS, WordPerfect, Quattro Pro, Excel, MS-DOS, and Medisoft if installed on IBM-compatible hardware.

Mathematical/Accounting

Processed payments from customers and adjusted financial records.

Quality Control

Was responsible for checking accuracy and quality of work done by others and then returning errors to workers for corrections.

Communication

Responded to telephone calls and letters, then supplied required information to customers.

Training

Trained other employees for various positions. Also was responsible for writing procedures for employee training manuals.

Teamwork

Have diverse experience working with department managers, supervisors, fellow employees, and customers.

Education

Los Angeles College of Medical Transcription, Los Angeles, California.

Graduate: 2005, Associate's degree in Medical Transcription.

Awards: Director's List (GPA of 3.7 and above), Perfect Attendance.

Courses: Advanced Medical Terminology, Advanced Transcription (Radiology, Pathology, Cardiology, Gastrointestinal, Orthopedics), Computer Applications (MS-DOS, WordPerfect, Medisoft, and Excel).

Employment History

Self-Employed, Los Angeles, California. Three years, managed mail distribution business.

National Farmer's Insurance Company, Long Beach, California
Ten years in the following positions: Endorsement Specialist, Customer Service, Quality Control, Cash Control, Utility and Filing.

EXHIBIT 2.15   Hybrid resume.

Norman Stevenson

50126 Road 24, South Bend, Indiana 46515   (219) 555-1122 • ns3421@juno.com

OBJECTIVE

A position in the Mechanical Drafting field with an emphasis on Computer-Aided drafting and the potential for advancement into design and development.

EDUCATION

Associate's degree in Mechanical Engineering, Indianapolis, IN
ETI Technical Institute, Graduate: 2005

Courses in the following areas:

Mechanical Drafting: Machine Design, Dimensioning and Tolerancing, Manufacturing Processes, Fasteners, Power Transmission, Descriptive Geometry, Piping, Wiring Schematics.

CAD (AutoCAD): Basic and advanced drawing, layers, blocks, attributes, 3D wireframe and surfacing, solid modeling, AutoLISP programming, designing menus, MS-DOS, batch files.

Math & Design: Algebra, trigonometry, machine design (statics and strengths of materials).

PROFESSIONAL PROFILE

- Experience in Mechanical Drafting and Design
- Leadership qualities: Served as Vice President on Board of Directors for Farmland Co-op, Fort Wayne, Indiana.
- Able to complete projects under pressure, maintained high grade point average at ETI Technical Institute and successfully operated my own farming business.

RELATED EXPERIENCE

Successfully developed conceptual design of equipment trailers. Redesigned various farm equipment; also designed and built a champion stock car.

EMPLOYMENT HISTORY

Owner/Operator—Stevenson Farms, South Bend, Indiana 1999–2005
Board of Directors—Farmland Co-op, South Bend, Indiana 1994–1999

ACADEMIC HONORS

Honors student with GPA of 3.88/4.0
Dean's list of Scholastic Excellence: 2003–2004
National Honor Society, Alpha Beta Kappa: 2004

EDNA L. WYCLIFF

4589 North Hillside, Topeka, Kansas 66609

(316) 555-9022

ednawycliff@yahoo.com

Education

WICHITA TECHNICAL COLLEGE
Automotive Technician
Associate's degree, 2004

KANSAS STATE UNIVERSITY
Completed 3 years of Industrial
Technology: Plastics & Metals Technology
and Fabrication, Electronics, Computer
Drafting, Physics and Mechanics of Materials.

Summary of Skills

Equipment: Alignment Racks, Scopes,
VAT 40-60, Brake Lathes, Valve Grinding
Equipment, Turning Lathes, Mills,
Welding Equipment, Fork Lifts.

Computer: ACAD, WordPerfect,
Macintosh, TWIN, Basic, Al-Data Automotive.
Type 45 wpm.

Automotive Repair Skills:

ASE Certified, Engine Repair,
Brakes, Suspensions and
Steering, Air Conditioning and Heating.

Special Accomplishments

State of Kansas Emissions,
Technician's License

Honor Society—four years

All-Conference Honorable Mention—
Basketball
State Qualifier—Pole Vault

Work Experience

*Emissions technician, bottom
tech, upper bay tech, sales*
Phillips 66 Fast Lube,
Wichita, Kansas 9/04 to present

*General merchandise clerk,
floor care, shelf stocker,
checker, order writer*
Safeway Stores, Topeka, Kansas
8/02 to 9/04

*All-purpose clerk, stocker,
checker, order writer*
Beavers Market, Topeka, Kansas
11/97 to 8/02

*Field applicator, field scout
and advisor, warehouse supervisor*
Morley Ag Services, Topeka, Kansas
5/95 to 11/97

References

Provided upon request.

Phillips 66,
Fast Lube Training Certificate

Future Business Leaders
of America—two years

EXHIBIT 2.17   Hybrid resume.

Joyce Challenger

27932 Cactus Lane   (520) 555-2760
Tucson, Arizona 85719   joycechallenger@azrepublic.net

OBJECTIVE

To work in the computer networking field where the ability to work as a team member, a sense of responsibility, and excellent communication skills are assets.

EDUCATION

Associate of Applied Science degree in Computer Networking
Arizona Technical Institute, Phoenix, Arizona
Graduate: 2005
Associate of Science degree, Northeastern College, Villanova, PA
Graduate: 1999

SUMMARY OF QUALIFICATIONS

- **Operating Systems:** DOS, UNIX/LINUX, NetWare, Windows NT Server

- **Implementing and Supporting the Functions and Administration of Network Information Systems:** Included planning, configuring and installing file server, work station, and print server in the local area environment.

- **Networks:** Peer-to-peer and server-based network connections using NetBEUI, IPX/SPX, and TCP/IP transport protocols.

ADDITIONAL SKILLS

- Microsoft Word, Excel, Access, PowerPoint, Windows, Technical Writing

AWARDS

Alpha Beta Kappa   •   Dean's List for Academic Excellence   •   3.9 GPA

EMPLOYMENT HISTORY

Office Edge Training Center, Tucson, AZ, current position
Green Valley Mountain School, Tucson, AZ, 2001–2004
Better Homes & Gardens Real Estate, Phoenix, AZ, 1998–2001
Interlink Products Corporation, Villanova, PA 1995–1998

NAME: JEAN KRAMER

JOB TITLE: INSTRUCTOR OF ENGLISH AND CAREER DEVELOPMENT

SKILLS SUMMARY

[Summarize your strongest skills and strengths using keywords—nouns, not verbs.]

Classroom and workshop instruction, communication: oral and written, job search skills, counseling, student and client job placement, newsletter production and design, special events coordination, tutor: vocabulary and English as a second language (ESL), owner/manager of career counseling and job placement business, Microsoft Word, Excel, Powerpoint, WordPerfect, Pagemaker.

JEAN KRAMER

jkramer@gpcom.net

(303) 555-6968

Note: *Street address omitted due to privacy concerns*

JOB OBJECTIVE *[State your immediate job goal and long-term goals if you wish.]*

Instructor of Career Development and/or English Grammar and Composition

EXPERIENCE   *[List jobs held that support the position desired, beginning with present or most recent and working in reverse order.]*

Westwood College of Technology, Denver, Colorado. 2000–Present
Instructor/Job Search Skills Counselor
English Grammar and Composition, Job Search Skills, Human Relations, Psychology, Technical Writing.

Control Data Institute, Denver, Colorado. 1996–2000
Student Services Administrator
Career Development instruction, part-time and full-time employment for students, coordination with financial aid and admissions departments to ensure student success and graduate placement, public relations events for the college.

Denver Technical College, Denver, Colorado. 1991–1996
College Student Placement Director and Instructor
Career Development and Job Search Skills design and instruction, small business management and marketing instruction, full- and part-time employment for students, instructor hiring and training.

[page 1]

EXHIBIT 2.18   Electronic resume template. Continued

EDUCATION   *[List all relevant education, naming colleges, locations, and degrees and majors; include on-the-job training if it relates to your objective.]*

University of Colorado at Denver, Denver, Colorado
Master of Arts degree in English, minor in Secondary Education

University of California at Long Beach, Long Beach, California
Adjunct Professor Training in Vocabulary and English as a Second Language

Black Hills State College, Spearfish, South Dakota
Training in Methods and Techniques for Student Success

[OPTIONAL HEADINGS]

SPECIALIZED TRAINING *[those not covered in education section]*

Numerous workshops, seminars, and instructor training for career development, classroom instructor methods and techniques, business management, and student retention.

HONORS/AWARDS *[job-related are especially noteworthy]*

Employee of the Term, Westwood College of Technology, 2002

Teacher of the Year nomination, Association of Post-Secondary Schools and Colleges, 2000

Outstanding Student Advisor award, Denver Institute of Technology, 1995–1996

PUBLICATIONS *[if any; give name of publication, title, and date]*

REFERENCES
[Stating that your references will be provided is not necessary as employers will ask for them when and if they need them. Do not list your references on your resume.]

[page 2]

Cover Letters

Despite the fact that your resume is an excellent summary of your skills and experience, it doesn't always tell prospective employers everything they need to know. Many times they have to interpret the resume to determine what they believe could be of value to their organization. The purpose of a cover letter is to assist them in this and to communicate a specific personal message about how you can be an asset to their company. It helps to generate interest in you as a prospective employee and affords you the opportunity to sell yourself. As stated earlier, not including a cover letter could be reason enough for some employers to put your resume aside. Obviously, if they receive enough resumes *with* cover letters, yours could be screened out for that alone.

During the 25 plus years that I've been involved in career development, I have found that of all the paperwork associated with job searching, cover letters give job searchers the most difficulty. They get as far as the heading of the letter and just don't seem to know where to go from there. Does this sound familiar? Do you have difficulty knowing what to put in a cover letter? The principles of writing all letters may help you. Those principles apply to cover letters as well.

The guidelines in this section will help you write a cover letter. Included are the definition of a cover letter, when to use it, instructions for writing the letter, and how to convert one letter template into all the cover letters you'll need in your job search. So, to begin, I need to explain just what a cover letter is.

A cover letter is a short letter, consisting of a few paragraphs, that is attached to (covers) your resume. It identifies the position for which you are applying (if you are writing for a known opening) and directs the reader to take note of relevant items in your resume. It can also point out important strengths, skills, or experience, either to emphasize items on your resume or to add information that is not included in the resume. It gives you the opportunity to establish and reinforce your suitability to the job for which you are applying. You should use the language common to your field to indicate your knowledge and expertise in that area. Tailor your language to your reader, in other words, if you are a graphic designer writing to another designer, you can use the trade language, but if writing to a human resources person, you may want to use everyday terms. Just don't "overkill"—you don't want to sound pretentious (stuffy, formal, or know-it-all). Write in a conversational tone (contractions are used in conversation so it is acceptable to use them) as if you were speaking to the person face-to-face; however, always use correct grammar. Always end the letter with a request for an interview. If you are writing to a company in a distant city to which you will be traveling, give your reader the date of your arrival and say that you will call for a time that is convenient for him or her to meet with you. If possible, include a phone number in that city where you may be contacted.

When Do You Use a Cover Letter?

If you have heard that you send a cover letter only when you *mail* a resume, please forget that. A cover letter should *always* be attached to your resume. I can think of only one instance when you probably wouldn't need one: when you are handing your resume to the interviewer at the same time you are being interviewed. In this situation, you can personally explain and enhance what is on the resume, and a cover letter probably is not necessary. For all other times, whether mailing, faxing, e-mailing, or dropping off your resume, I highly recommend that you use a cover letter. Why? First, the fact that you took the time and effort to write it could make the difference between your getting an invitation to interview or being screened out. Second, its enclosure is an act of courtesy and a sign of a serious, professional approach to job searching. Finally, the cover letter affords you that extra opportunity to sell yourself to a prospective employer.

Guidelines for Constructing the Letter

The opening. If possible, always address your letter to a specific person. Your intent is to make a personal connection with the reader. Use directories, newspaper ads, locate the company's website on the Internet, or just pick up the phone and call to ask for the appropriate person's name if you don't already have it. If you are just not able to get a name, address the letter to the head of the department, the person who would be in charge of the position for which you are applying. For example, "Senior Network Administrator," "Technical Supervisor," "Manager of Administrative Support," or "Director of Nursing." Instead of the usual salutation ("Dear Mr. Jones:"), use a subject line such as "Attention: Associate Editor." *Never* address a letter to "Sir or Madam," "Hiring Executive," or "To Whom It May Concern." Address it to "Human Resources" only if you've been directed to do so. The first persons to know of openings in any department are those who are in charge of the department. Sometimes, human resource departments are the last to know of a job opening within their company. If they are not aware of any openings when your letter and resume reach them, they may file or ignore your paperwork.

The first paragraph. Begin your first paragraph with the purpose of the letter: *why* you are writing. State the position for which you are applying (or, if no known opening exists, the position for which you qualify). If you are writing from a referral, tell the reader who referred you. Explain why the company is attractive to you as a potential employer, but make it brief. At the end of the first paragraph, be sure to give your reader a lead-in sentence to the next paragraph. Don't leap into the next paragraph without letting your reader know where you are going. This is called a **transitional sentence**, and it prepares the reader for what's to follow. You can see an example of a good lead-in sentence to the second paragraph in the cover letter sample in Exhibit 2.23. *I am confident that upon review of my qualifications, you will find that I am a strong candidate for your next available opening.*

As my resume indicates, I have just completed a program at the American Trades Institute specializing in Heating, Ventilation, Air Conditioning, and Refrigeration. Some sample opening paragraphs appear in the following box.

The second and third paragraphs. In the second and third paragraphs, state the qualifications you have for the position. Now is the time to sell yourself to the employer. Why should the employer select you to interview? Remember, you are of interest to a potential employer only because of your possible value to them, not because you want a job. Establish your value by referring to and expanding on your resume. *Relate your qualifications to their needs.* In any selling situation, you make the sale (i.e., get the job) because you find a need and fill it. In order to do this in your cover letter, you must first have done your research and know something about the company to which you are applying. The most valuable message you can convey to an employer is that you know the company well enough to know what its needs are and how you can help fill those needs. (See Chapter 3 to learn how to research companies.)

SAMPLE OPENING PARAGRAPHS

1. Enclosed is my application for the position of Graphic Arts Designer for which you advertised in the *Denver Post* on Sunday, June 5, 2005.

2. Mr. Barry Elwood, my computer teacher at Westwood College of Technology, recommended I contact you about the possibility of openings for Medical Assistants at your clinic.

3. I read with interest your article in *Women in the Workplace,* "The Double Standard in Sexuality in American Society." I have done some extensive research on this subject and have some theories that might be of interest to you.

4. Thank you for the opportunity to discuss my qualifications with you as they relate to the sales position you have available. As we decided, I will meet with you on Tuesday, April 5, 2005, at 10:00 A.M. I look forward to meeting with you in person to explore further the possibility of my becoming part of your sales team.

5. I am a recent Environmental Science graduate of the University of Colorado in Boulder, and I am interested in employment in the San Francisco area. Because my background experience and education are focused on the current problem of toxic waste and environmental protection, I am interested in any appropriate positions with Applied Environmental, Inc.

6. While employed at Resource Data Maintenance, Inc. as a Customer Service Engineer, I have enjoyed many opportunities to speak with some of your satisfied customers. Further investigation and research on your company has proven to me that I would like very much to become an employee of KOP Consulting Engineers, Inc.

7. I am most interested in determining if you have any openings for an Assistant General Manager or Manager Trainee at your hotel. I would like to relocate to the Dallas area, and from my research on the Raintree Inns, I know I would like to become an employee with a well-respected establishment such as yours.

8. Enclosed is my application for the position of Administrative Assistant that we discussed yesterday in our phone conversation. As I mentioned, I've just completed my Associate's degree in the Executive Secretarial program at American Career Schools here in New Rochelle, and I'm eager to apply my new skills to this position.

9. Glen Fries, Production and Engineering Systems Manager at Advanced Systems Engineering, Inc., suggested that I contact you concerning the openings you have for Electronic Technicians. He highly recommended your company as being a leader in digital/analog microprocessor-based circuitry, and this strongly appeals to me as I am very interested in this branch of technology.

10. In our brief conversation on the phone yesterday, you asked me to send you a resume with information about my abilities and achievements. I have enclosed

SAMPLE OPENING PARAGRAPHS Continued

a copy of my most recent resume as well as some letters of recommendation that I've received from my previous employers. I believe you will find that my skills match those of your current opening for a computer programmer.

11. Please accept the enclosed resume as application for the opening you have for an Automotive Technician. I've been involved with the automotive industry since the age of 12, when I spent my evenings and Saturdays helping my dad in his automotive repair shop. Now I have my Associate's degree in Automotive Technology from the Universal Technical Institute, and I can hardly wait to get started on my new career.

12. Your advertisement in today's *Herald* for a Computer Service Technician interests me very much. I will be graduating in June from Omaha Electronic Institute with an Associate's degree in Computer Servicing, and I am excited at the possibility of working for a firm such as yours because of the excellent reputation you have for innovative computer technology. Please accept the enclosed resume as application for the position of Computer Service Technician.

The closing paragraph.   The last paragraph of your letter, which will be either the third or fourth, is called the **closing**. In this paragraph, thank the reader for taking the time to review your qualifications; however, do not offer thanks for anything he or she hasn't done. Doing so implies that you assume the reader is going to do it, and that is insulting to the reader. *Always ask for an interview*; this is the reason you are writing, is it not? You may also suggest a date and a time when you are available and indicate that the interview be at the reader's convenience. If you say you are going to follow up with a call or other correspondence, make certain that you do so because this could encourage the reader to wait for your call instead of contacting you. If your address or phone number has changed since you printed the resume, give the new information. Never white out or write over anything on your resume. Reprint the resume or include the information in the closing paragraph of your letter.

PRINCIPLES OF COVER LETTER WRITING

- The purpose of your cover letter is to get the recipient to read your resume, to apply for a specific job (or to inquire about the possibility of employment), to arouse interest in you as a potential employee, and to request an interview.

- Each letter should be carefully adapted and personalized for each employer. Never reproduce a form letter and fill in the company name. Type or word-process each individual letter and sign each one by hand.

- Use a business-style format, either semi-block or block. Use the cover letter samples beginning on page 85 as a guide or consult any good business correspondence text for instruction on letter formatting.

- Use paper that matches your resume if at all possible.

- Include information about the skills and qualifications you have that could be of interest or benefit to the employer.

- Do not mention salary requirements or past salaries unless you have been asked to do so. If asked, it is wise to give a salary range and add that you are willing to negotiate. Including past salaries could affect your ability to get the salary you deserve, especially if they were lower than what you are now qualified for. (Note: *Before entering into any discussion on salaries, consult the section at the end of Chapter 4 on salary negotiation.*)

- Keep the letter to one page unless there is a valid reason for its being longer. Ideally it should contain no more than three to four paragraphs.

- Use concise, simple sentences and be especially careful to avoid sentence fragments. Avoid formal, flowery language; write in a natural, conversational tone.

- *Proofread and proofread again* for content, correct spelling, punctuation, and word usage. Ask yourself: Does the letter say what I want it to say? Is it clear and concise?

- Use the A-I-D-A checklist below to make sure your letter is complete and effective:
  - **Attention:** Did you attract the reader's attention in the first paragraph sufficiently to make him or her want to read further? You can do this by informing the reader of one of your accomplishments that is relevant to the job description or advertisement, or by mentioning something you have learned about the company that excites you.
  - **Interest:** Did you point out why you would be an excellent match for the organization? Another way to spark interest is to mention personal contacts, mutual acquaintances, etc.
  - **Desire:** Have you created a desire in your reader to call you for an interview by stating examples of how you could be of benefit to the company? Give results of your achievements that would match the company's needs. Be very specific about how these relate to the job. Now is the time to use the benefit statements you wrote in the first section.
  - **Action:** Did you ask for the interview? Did you suggest a time? Did you supply information about how to contact you?

How to Create All Your Cover Letters from One Letter

Once you've composed a basic cover letter template, you can modify it and use it again and again. Simply change the first paragraph to indicate the person's name to whom you are writing, the position that interests you, and information about the company. In the second and third paragraphs, focus on your skills and qualifications relevant to this specific position and company. In order to sell yourself to this particular company, list your qualifications, experience, or education (which may or may not be on your resume).

To see how a cover letter can be modified, study the two cover letters from John Jones (see Exhibits 2.19 and 2.20). You may also use the sample opening paragraphs in the previous box as a guide to how opening paragraphs change to adapt to the writer's intent. With these guides, you should have no difficulty in writing any cover letter that you'll need. Of course, don't hesitate to use your own creativity. (See Exhibits 2.21 through 2.30 for more sample letters.)

EXHIBIT 2.19   Sample cover letter.

11567 East 17th Street
Spokane, WA 01435
September 2, 2005

Mr. Kevin Schultz
ABC Data Processing
3498 South Ivy Way
Suite 1160
Spokane, WA 01437

Dear Mr. Schultz:

Jane Hill, Student Services Director at Spokane Technical Institute, recommended
ABC Data Processing as an excellent company to work for because of its reputation for total commitment to its employees' growth and advancement. My own
research of your company indicates that it is the kind of progressive company
I would like to work for.

My experience and education are summarized for you on the enclosed resume.
Not mentioned there is a computer operations and programming internship that
I participated in while attending classes at STI. The internship took place at the
Regional Transportation District, where I gained experience with Java, Pert, and
C++. I believe that my experience and education qualify me to work effectively
and productively in your department. I could contribute to the goals of ABC
Data Processing as I learn new concepts and ideas quickly, and this would save
you time and money in that I would require a shorter training period.

I would like to meet with you to discuss employment requirements and opportunities at ABC Data Processing. I look forward to hearing from you soon with
reference to a possible future with your company.

Sincerely,

John E. Jones

John E. Jones
(509) 555-4587
johnjones95@aol.com

Enclosure: Resume

11567 East 17th Street
Spokane, WA 01435
September 16, 2005

Ms. Elaine Calovet
Data Processing Manager
Seattle Medical Manufacturers
170 Denny Way
Seattle, WA 01539

Dear Ms. Calovet:

I enjoyed speaking with you on the phone yesterday and learning of the computer operations position that is available with Seattle Medical Manufacturers. I look forward to the opportunity to interview with you for this position.

If you will review the enclosed resume, you will see that I have experience in computer computations and data processing in addition to the education I've received at Spokane Technical Institute. The training there was in a work-simulated environment and consisted primarily of hands-on self-instruction. I believe that my education, coupled with an internship at the Regional Transportation District, qualifies me for this position. In the internship, I gained experience with Java, Pert, and C++.

I would very much appreciate an interview with you to discuss how my qualifications could serve as an asset to Seattle Medical Manufacturers. You may contact me at the number below or leave a message (I have voice messaging), and I will return your call as soon as I return. You may also contact me at my e-mail address: johnjones95@aol.com.

Thank you for taking the time to consider my application for the position of computer operator with your company.

Sincerely,

John E. Jones

John E. Jones
(509) 555-4587
johnjones95@aol.com

Enclosure: Resume, reference letters

LETTER STRUCTURE

Correct letter structure is important to any effective business correspondence. If you use an accepted format, your letter will be easier to read and understand. Every letter, formal or informal, contains a *heading*, a *salutation*, a *body*, and a *closing*.

HEADING

- In a business letter, this is your company's name and address. In a personal letter, or if you are not representing a company, this is your own address.
- The date.
- Name, title, and address of the person receiving the letter. Be sure to spell the name of the recipient correctly and use his or her correct title (if known).

SALUTATION

The salutation follows the inside address. A formal one is preferred for business letters unless you know the person very well.

BODY

The body of the letter contains your message and request for action. It is organized into three sections: introduction, main body, and conclusion.

- *Introduction:* The first sentence of the letter lets your reader know why you are writing, the purpose of the letter.
- *Main body:* The main body of the letter presents your message in organized, easily understood paragraphs. In a cover letter, it should contain no more than one or two paragraphs.
- *Conclusion:* In a cover letter, the conclusion should thank the reader for taking the time to consider your qualifications and end with a request for an interview. Always end your letter on a positive note.

CLOSING

All letters end with a complimentary close and your signature above your typed name. Accepted closings for business letters are:

Yours truly,	Sincerely,
Yours very truly,	Sincerely yours,

The closing used most often for cover letters is "Sincerely." After the complimentary closing, type your name and title (if you have one) four lines down from the close, and always sign your name above. It is also a good practice in cover letters to include your phone number and e-mail address after your typed name.

COVER LETTER FORMAT (Semi-Block Style, Standard Punctuation)

5101 Cherry Twig Road *RETURN*
Omaha, NE 68835 *ADDRESS*
October 25, 2005 *DATELINE*

4 lines

Mr. Randolf Manning
Omaha Central Power Supply *INSIDE ADDRESS*
P.O. Box 32789
Omaha, NE 68746
Line space

Dear Mr. Manning: *SALUTATION*
Line space

Please accept this letter and the enclosed resume as application for the position of Systems Analyst that you advertised in the *Omaha World Herald* on October 23, 2005. I am very interested in having an opportunity to apply my knowledge and background experience to program analysis, as well as put to use my fascination for the field of energy, to the continued success of Omaha Central Power Supply.

Line space

As you can see from my resume, I have a solid background in the field. My qualifications include training and experience as a programmer with skill application in program modification and design. I also have had some association with documentation and recommendations for program improvement methods. I believe that I fulfill the requirements of this position and will be an asset to your department.

Line space

I am a dedicated and loyal person as is demonstrated by my ten years of employment where I advanced to Chief Design Programmer at The Sterling Company in Lincoln. I believe in the old-fashioned work ethic and am committed to above-average job performance. I know I could save Omaha Central Power Supply time and money by implementing a program design I've developed that reduces energy costs by 25%.

Line space

Thank you for taking the time to consider my qualifications as they pertain to the goals of Omaha Central Power Supply. I look forward to meeting with you at your earliest convenience.

Line space

Sincerely, *COMPLIMENTARY CLOSE*

Cheryl Kowalski *WRITER'S NAME*
(308) 555-1462
ckowalski@gpcom.net

Line space
ENCLOSURE NOTATION

EXHIBIT 2.21   Sample letter.

7854 East Martin Luther King Blvd.
Aurora, Colorado 80010
October 15, 2005

Mr. Dennis Kelly
MAC Tools Corporation
1757 Hoyt Street
Lakewood, Colorado 80215

Dear Mr. Kelly:

I have recently earned my Associate's degree in Occupational Sciences of Automotive Technology
from the Westwood College of Technology (formerly Denver Institute of Technology) graduating
with a GPA of 4.0. This accelerated education, in addition to years of great interest in the field of
automotive technology, makes me eager to be placed in a position with your company.

The attached resume summarizes my experience and education for you. Westwood College offers,
to all graduates, the opportunity to receive lifetime training so I can keep current with new material and procedures. This benefit will be an asset to your company because I will have ongoing
retraining in my field at no cost to you.

As for my other qualifications, I have completed EDGE training that has taught me diagnostic
procedures for automotive repair. I am ASE certified and have a clean, no-ticket driving record. I
have most of the tools needed to begin my career and am in the process of purchasing more diagnostic equipment.

I believe you will consider me for a position with MAC Tools Corporation when you review the
enclosed resume and see that I match the qualifications that you ask of your automotive technicians. I look forward to meeting with you and becoming part of your team. You can contact me at
the number below between 5 and 10 p.m. weekdays and all day on the weekends. I have voice
messaging and pick up my messages regularly. Please do not contact my present employer as he is
not aware of my decision to leave, and I want to give two weeks' notice at the appropriate time.

Sincerely,

Harold Blake

Harold Blake
(303) 555-1221
blake56@yahoo.com

Enclosed: Resume

5094 Osceola Street
Westminster, Colorado 80030-3173
May 20, 2005

Michelle Graves, Legal Administrator
Smith & Graves, P.C.
10742 West 120th Avenue
Broomfield, Colorado 80020

RE: Network Administrator/Desktop Support Specialist

Dear Ms. Graves:

I am writing to respond to your advertisement for a Network Administrator and Desktop
Support Specialist which appeared in the Sunday *Denver Post*, May 15, 2005. I am
impressed with your firm's prestigious reputation and long-standing commitment to
client service.

The attached resume formally presents my qualifications. However, the personal attributes
that I am most proud of are my initiative and drive. I accomplish what is required, correctly
and on time. I know how to juggle a multitude of tasks—some critical, some routine—
while remaining courteous and professional. I have combined my long experience resolving
customer challenges with newly developed technical skills. My goal is to provide technical
support for customers and coworkers as they negotiate through complex and at times
mystifying computer network problems.

My unique combination of education, training, and experience allows me to offer your firm
great value as an employee. I look forward to meeting with you to discuss the specific
requirements for this position and my ability to meet them. Please contact me at your convenience at the number below to schedule an interview. Thank you for taking the time to
consider me as an applicant for this position.

Sincerely,

Mark T. Wheeling Jr.

Mark T. Wheeling, Jr.
(303) 555-9023
mtw@uswest.net

Attached: Resume, reference letters

EXHIBIT 2.23   **Sample letter.**

6998 Pearl Street
Dallas, Texas 75207
June 22, 2005

Randolph Minnick
South Polar Heating & Air Conditioning
4323 Maple Avenue
Dallas, Texas 75235

Dear Mr. Minnick:

I am most interested in obtaining an HVAC position with your company. With my training and interest in Heating, Air Conditioning and Ventilation Serving, I believe that your company would be an ideal place for me to begin. I believe that I can be a key person in the continued success of your reputable company. The enclosed resume provides the information detailing my background and abilities. I am confident that upon review of my qualifications, you will find that I am a strong candidate for your next available opening.

As my resume indicates, I have just completed a program at the American Trades Institute specializing in Heating, Ventilation, Air Conditioning, and Refrigeration. My abilities and potential for success can be greatly broadened by securing a challenging position with your company. What may not be adequately reflected in the resume are my computer skills, mechanical aptitude, and high level of energy and professional work ethic. Fast-paced environments and pressure are no stranger to me; I function well under both.

During the course of my studies, I was educated in HVAC maintenance and have knowledge and strong skills in refrigeration systems, air conditioners, gas/forced air furnaces, and electronic control systems. I also earned my Universal CFC certification in refrigeration. At this point in my career, I am seeking an opportunity that will allow me to fully utilize my education and skills, as well as gain new knowledge in the field.

I would consider it an honor to meet with you to discuss your requirements as related to my qualifications for the position of HVAC Technician. If at that time you believe we are a "match," I believe we could look forward to a long and mutually profitable relationship. I look forward to hearing from you, at your earliest convenience, with reference to a position with South Polar. You can contact me at the number below or at my e-mail address: rwallace@yahoo.com.

Sincerely,

Robert Wallace

Robert Wallace
(214) 555-4556
rwallace@yahoo.com

Enclosed: Resume and reference letters

1003 Massachusetts Avenue
Boston, Massachusetts 02115
August 23, 2005

Mr. Tom Flynn
Flynn's Graphics, Inc.
90 Marlborough Street
Boston, Massachusetts 02116

Dear Mr. Flynn:

At the forefront of every successful visual undertaking, whether it's a magazine cover, a business brochure, or an entire ad campaign, there should be a top-of-the-line graphic designer. As a graphic designer in the field, I am confident that I can provide you with ideas and images that can bring unquestionable recognition and extraordinary results.

I have seven years' experience (noted in my resume) in digital typesetting, electronic publishing, and computer graphic design. I am a proficient user of major computer page-layout, image creation/editing, illustration, and word processing software on both Macintosh and PC (DOS- and Windows-based) platforms. This experience includes knowledge and proficiency with PageMaker, QuarkXPress, Photoshop, and Illustrator. So as you can see, I am very familiar with all aspects of the graphic design process.

Self-motivation is one of my strong points. I worked full-time and attended college at the same time, earning my degree with a grade point average of 3.7. I have worked in several professional and management positions, and because of my skills in communications and dealing with people, I was considered a valuable team member.

At your earliest convenience, I would very much appreciate an interview with you to discuss how my qualifications could contribute to the continued success of Flynn's Graphics, Inc. I will bring my portfolio at that time to show you my designs.

Sincerely,

Steven Marks

Steven Marks
Residence: (617) 555-8090
Pager: (617) 555-4455
steven_marks@hotmail.com

EXHIBIT 2.25   Sample letter.

320 West 31st Street
New York, NY 10001
May 6, 2005

R. Rudy Lee, President
Traphagen Marketing & Advertising
257 Park Avenue South
New York, NY 10010

Dear Mr. Lee:

Our mutual friend, Karne Scott, suggested I write you about possible employment with your firm. Because of my training and interest in marketing and all types of advertising, in addition to your reputation for creative and innovative design, I am especially excited at the prospect of going to work for Traphagen Marketing & Advertising.

I will be graduating June 12 with a Master's degree in Advertising Design & Technical Illustration from New York State University. I made the Dean's list this year and was vice president of the University Advertising Club at New York State for the past two years. I promoted the club's membership program, which netted 50 new members, and I was responsible for the design, layout, and production of the advertising and marketing for an on-campus career fair.

As you can see from the enclosed resume, I worked in retail management at Conte Jewelers while I was attending the university. I began as a clerk and after six months was promoted to assistant manager. In this position, I had full responsibility for the advertising campaigns and the marketing strategies for new jewelry lines. This included complete layout and design, market surveys, and budget allocations. I believe that my education, coupled with this experience, would enable me to be a contributing member of your marketing and advertising team.

I'm excited about the prospect of discussing employment with Traphagen and look forward to meeting with you at your earliest convenience. You may contact me at the number below.

Sincerely,

Carolyn B. Greene

Carolyn B. Greene
(212) 555-5225
cbg118@aol.com
Enclosure: Resume, design samples

12103 Melody Drive, #404
Westminster, CO 80233
July 16, 2005

Emily Griffith Opportunity School
1250 Welton Street
Denver, CO 80221

Attention: Director of Education

I am most interested in exploring the possibility of obtaining a teaching position with Emily Griffith Opportunity School. Instructing English, Composition, Business Correspondence, or Career Skills would be ideal; however, I am open to any discipline that you believe I am qualified to teach.

As reflected in the enclosed resume, my experience and education, with a concentration in basic skills and career development instruction, provide a solid background in my field. I believe my qualifications, in addition to my intense love of teaching and a strong commitment to being an understanding, caring teacher, meet the requirements of an Emily Griffith instructor.

I have taken the liberty of including a few of the reference letters that I have received over the past ten years from my students, coworkers, and administrative staff. I believe you will agree that they reflect my commitment to being the kind of teacher who is dedicated to helping students recognize their educational and personal goals.

Thank you for considering my application for a teaching position at your school. I would appreciate an opportunity to discuss with you, in person, how I could become part of your teaching staff. You may contact me at the number below any time of day. If I am not there, please leave a message, and I will return your call promptly.

Sincerely,

Judy L. Dally

Judy L. Dally
(303) 555-0367
dally@idcomm.com

Enclosure: Resume, reference letters

EXHIBIT 2.27   Sample letter.

16205 Riverside Lane
Brighton, CO 80601
October 16, 2005

Mr. John Smith
Main-Tec, Inc.
2412 Rose Street
Suite 102
Honolulu, Hawaii 96819

Dear Mr. Smith:

I am a recent Electronic Technician graduate of the Westwood College of Technology in Denver, Colorado. I am interested in employment in the Hawaiian Islands. Because of my background experience and education, I would be very interested in any appropriate available positions within Main-Tec, Inc. My research of the islands indicates a rapidly growing electronics industry, and I would like to be a part of that development.

My experience and education are summarized for you in the enclosed resume. Following are a few of my skills that could be of use to your company. Knowledge of and proficiency with foreign languages allow me to relate to various cultural differences, which is an advantage in customer relations, a skill so necessary in field work. I have excellent mathematical and logical aptitude, which enables me to analyze situations and to determine efficient solutions. My programming experience on IBM and MacIntosh computers would be an asset in that I can readily troubleshoot and repair many kinds of systems. 1 am proficient in MS-DOS, UNIX/LINUX, and NT and am familiar with Java and Applescript. One final advantage to hiring me is that since I am a recent graduate, I am still accustomed to a learning environment and can be trained quickly, therefore saving you time and money.

Thank you for your time in examining my qualifications; I am looking forward to the opportunity of a possible future with Main-Tec, Inc. I will be in Honolulu the first week in November and will contact you then. Should you need to reach me before that date, I am available at the above address, or I will gladly accept a collect call at the number below.

Sincerely,

Richard Martinez

Richard Martinez
(303) 547-2183
rmartinez@attglobal.net

7816 Montview Drive
Orange, CA 92669
June 15, 2005

Stevenson's Office Machines
4500 Ocean Boulevard
Suite 2103
Long Beach, CA 98022

Attention: Data Processing Manager

The *Los Angeles Times* recently reported that Stevenson's Office Machines is building a new data processing center in the Compton area. I would like to apply for a position as a computer programmer and have enclosed a resume for your consideration.

I am a recent graduate of Systems Programming Development Institute with an Associate's degree in Computer Science. In addition to taking a broad range of courses in many business-related languages (noted in my resume), I was a tutor and consultant at the college for the students having difficulty with those languages. Most recently, I have been doing volunteer work in programming for the local high schools here in Orange County. I believe that you would find my skills valuable in assisting you in getting the center off and running.

I will be happy to meet with you at your earliest convenience and will provide any additional information you may need. You can contact me at (714) 555-6781 any time; I have an answering machine and check my messages regularly. In addition, you may e-mail me at ghrowlands@home.com.

Sincerely,

Gena H. Rowlands

Gena H. Rowlands
Enclosures: Resume, reference letters

EXHIBIT 2.29   Sample letter.

5336 West Tejone Street
Lakewood, CO 80333
October 28, 2005

Ms. Joan Fredericksen
Itel Corporation
1650 Stout Street, # 207
Denver, CO 80206

Dear Ms. Fredericksen:

I recently earned my Associate's degree in Electronics Technology from ITT Technical Institute in Denver, Colorado. This formal education, along with several years of great interest and devoted pursuit of computer systems, makes me eager to be placed in a position you may find suitable with your corporation.

I have enclosed a resume which summarizes my experience and education, yet some, I believe, require further explanation. For example, because I fluently speak three languages, I understand and respect cultural variety. This skill can be an asset with customers as well as fellow workers. I am also flexible, yet reliable.

As for my other qualifications, I especially like working with MS-DOS, which the advertisement in the *Rocky Mountain News* indicated that your corporation uses extensively. I am also experienced with digital/analog microprocessor-based circuitry. Furthermore, because your corporation manufactures telecommunications hardware, perhaps you should know that I am knowledgeable and interested in this branch of technology. In addition to these skills, I have an Amateur Radio license, and I actively participate in various forms of radio communications including Morse code, satellite, and packet radio.

Thank you for considering my qualifications. I look forward to the opportunity of talking with you in person about how I could become employed with Itel Corporation.

Sincerely,

Daniel Simone

Daniel Simone
(303) 555-9350
d1336@juno.com

Enclosure: Resume

16307 West Alaska Place
Lincoln, NE 68508-2478
May 18, 2005

Dale Skyhorn
Tri-City Design Corporation
Post Office Box 80245
Omaha, NE 68105

Dear Mr. Skyhorn:

The key to successful organizations is quality personnel. I would like to contribute to your success. Please accept the enclosed resume as application for the position of mechanical drafter with Tri-City Design.

As you can see from my professional background, I have extensive experience in the design, layout, and production of sheet metal fabrication. My current position demands leadership ability as well as interpersonal skills and comprehensive decision making. I am responsible for the production and design of all sheet metal fabricated parts. I also analyze and report on the progress and quality of each project and purchase all raw materials. Creativity and self-motivation are two of my strongest suits. Across the United States, I have established many successful relationships with vendors and suppliers.

Over the past eight years, I have gained invaluable experience at my present position with Norwest Systems, but I am now ready for new challenges that will expand my professional potential. I would very much like to speak with you about opportunities within Tri-City Design. I will be in contact with you within the next week; however, please feel free to contact me (discreetly) at work (402) 555-1587 or leave a message at my home, and I will return your call. Also, please consider contacting me via e-mail at mcordlin@yahoo.com; I check my messages daily.

Thank you for your consideration. I look forward to meeting with you.

Sincerely,

Micheal Cordlin

Micheal Cordlin
(402) 555-9034

Follow-Up Letters

Many job seekers breathe a sigh of relief after they've completed their resume and cover letter, thinking they are finally finished with the paperwork. Not so, if you want a final, professional touch to your job searching efforts. There are always follow-up letters to write. A note thanking the interviewer for his or her time, a letter to cultivate future job offers when you weren't granted an interview, a resurrection letter to remind an employer of your application, or a letter to refuse a job offer are all important parts of successful follow-up. Unfortunately, only about 10 percent of the people looking for jobs bother to send them.

Sending a thank-you letter actually could be the determining factor in your being selected over another applicant, all other things being equal, of course. Some interviewers consider this a vital part of the hiring process. It is a necessary step. To see why, imagine that an employer has interviewed all the applicants and is down to deciding between two candidates. The have equal qualifications, they both interviewed well, and both have a personality that the interviewer believes will fit with the organization. One applicant sends a short note thanking the interviewer, and the other applicant does not. If you were the interviewer, which applicant would you be more likely to choose?

A thank-you letter is short and concise, no more than two brief paragraphs. Should you type it or handwrite it? Experts disagree. Lettitia Balldrige, well-known expert on professional manners, advises typing it on nice stationery, following the same principles as you would for any correspondence. I agree that you should follow good correspondence protocol; however, I suggest handwriting your thank-you on simple note stationery. A handwritten note adds a personal touch. If you were in the place of the interviewer, when you pick up your mail, which envelope would you open first—the one that is standard business size, or the one that is greeting-card size? Note cards are inexpensive and can be purchased at department, stationery, or discount stores.

Always send a thank-you letter after *every interview*, and send one to each individual interviewer, not one for all of them. Also, it's a good selling point to send one to others in the company who have helped you. Whether you type it or handwrite it is certainly your option.

What does a thank-you letter say? First, it should convey that you appreciate the time the interviewer spent with you. Second, it should state that you are impressed with the company and why. Third, it should tell the reader that you really want the job (if you do), reiterating how your qualifications match those discussed in the interview. Something you can do to help clinch the interviewer's interest in you is to mention some problem the interviewer discussed during the interview and suggest a possible solution or strategy for resolving it. By the way, this is also an opportune time to add anything you forgot to say in the interview or to ask questions you neglected to ask.

When should you send it? Within five to seven days? No—sit down immediately after the interview and mail it that day. If you know they are making a decision that evening, you should e-mail one and follow up with a hard copy. You want it to arrive before the decision to hire is made and while the interviewer still remembers who you are. Faces and personalities tend to fade very quickly, especially when the interviewer is seeing a lot of applicants.

If you are declining a job offer, give the reason for declining and, as in the thank-you letter, thank the interviewer for the time and interest in you. Sometime in the future, that company may have an opening that you would be interested in.

SAMPLE THANK-YOU LETTERS

Dear Mr./Ms. _____:

Thank you for your interest in me as a possible applicant for the position of _____
with ___(company name)___.

I enjoyed meeting with you and am very interested in becoming an employee of your company. I was impressed with the state-of-the-art computer equipment and software programs you are using.

I wish you continued success and look forward to hearing from you.

Sincerely,

Dear Mr./Ms. _____:

I appreciate the opportunity I had to interview with you for the position of _____
on_____(date)_____. I was very interested to learn that you are using Quark and PhotoShop software, as those are my favorites. I believe that my experience with Quark and PhotoShop, in addition to my other administrative skills, would enable me to be an asset to _____(name of company)_____.

Thank you again for your time and your interest in me as a potential employee of your company. I would very much like to fill your opening for _____(name of position)_____.

Sincerely,

Dear Mr./Ms. _____:

Thank you for such an interesting and informative interview yesterday. I was extremely impressed with the emphasis you place on customer and employee satisfaction. My observation while there yesterday confirmed my research on _____(name of company)_____, that you do, in fact, genuinely care about your personnel.

I am excited about the possibility of becoming a member of your team. If you need any further information, you may contact me at (444) 333-4444 from 8:30 A.M. until 5:30 P.M. or in the evenings at (444) 222-1111. I look forward to hearing from you.

Yours truly,

If you've left the firm with a favorable image of you, it will be more likely to contact you about the new position.

Another time to write a follow-up letter is when you have submitted a resume to inquire about the possibility of openings or to apply for a known opening and have received a reply such as "We're sorry, but . . . we'll keep your resume on file"; in such cases, it is to your benefit to write a brief letter of thanks to the person for taking the time to review your qualifications. You do this for the reason mentioned above: you want to be considered for future openings.

The Application for Employment

More paperwork! During your job search, you will probably fill out many employment applications. The importance of this part of the paperwork is not to be minimized; employers also use this document as a screening device. If they see a half-completed, sloppily written application, they assume that the person who completed it is also sloppy and careless. Job seekers tend not to understand that if a job application is not filled out correctly and completely, it could cost them an interview, or worse, a job offer.

Employers design applications to give them specific information relative to their organizations, things you might not have included in your resume or cover letter. One absolute "no-no" is to write on the application "See resume." Do not put this anywhere on an application form; it is viewed as lazy and disrespectful. The saying is true: "Resumes tell the employers what *you* want them to know, and job applications tell them what *they* want to know."

Now it is reality time. You're facing a form that is asking for your life history, to account for every breath of your life since puberty, and you are not given very much space to do it. Heaven forbid that you now have to "reveal" yourself. I really believe this is the reason we all hate forms: the lack of space to write in and the darn things want us to "tell all." So you hurry through it, just wanting to get it over with and sometimes making fatal mistakes. You needn't suffer from "application phobia"—there is a painless and correct way to complete them. To help ensure that yours will be among the best that the employer sees, observe the following guidelines carefully.

- If possible, obtain an application form before going to the interview. If you can get one, fill it out in your own time, making sure that you have all your information correct. Then you can take it with you when you go to the interview. When you do have to fill one out in the employer's office before the interview, if you make an error, ask for another form. Erasures and whiteout are usually not viewed favorably. Whatever you do, do not turn an application in with scratched out words.

- Always take two or three pens with you to an interview. Try them out at home to make sure that they don't bleed or drop spots of ink. You should always use black ink pens, as blue does not reproduce well on most fax machines and some copy machines. Also, this is a legal document and should be filled out in black ink. Of course, any other colors, such as red, purple, pink, etc., are totally unacceptable.

- Have the necessary information with you. Never ask for a telephone directory to look up addresses and numbers; this is the ultimate sign of unpreparedness. You can use the resume worksheets in this book for this information.

- Read the entire application through before beginning, and then re-read each question before you begin writing to make certain you understand what the question is asking for. Filling out application forms resembles taking a test (actually, it is your first test with this employer). More mistakes are made from not reading carefully than from any other reason. One employer says that if he sees a sloppily filled out application form, that applicant has just failed the first test, and he will not hire that applicant no matter what the other qualifications are. This was an employer at a company where the employees had to complete service orders on a daily basis.

- If you need a dictionary to check terms and spelling, use one. Have one with you so you don't risk errors in grammar or spelling or in the use of technical terms. The term "technician" is misspelled more times than you might believe. Technical terms and jargon are especially tricky, so make certain you use and spell them correctly.

- Never leave anything blank. If you don't understand what a question is asking for, find out. If it doesn't apply to you, write "NA" (not applicable) in the space. If you leave it blank, the reader has no way of knowing whether you carelessly missed it or just didn't want to answer it.

- For open-ended questions, such as those that ask for an opinion, organize your thoughts carefully and write them on a separate piece of paper before transferring your response to the form.

- Always include a phone number where you can be contacted if you do not have voice mail or an answering machine. And give your e-mail address if you have one, since today so many people are communicating in that manner. Remember, a missed call might mean a missed interview or job offer.

- When you go to fill out an application form at the employer's place of business, take the following with you: Social Security card, a small dictionary, grade transcripts, any certificates or documents that you would need for verification of data, and all your history information, including a list of references.

- When you finish, go back over the form and double-check for errors or anything you might have missed.

Troublesome Areas

When I teach classes on the paperwork of job searching and we get to the session on employment applications, the questions I encounter most often are about legal and illegal questions. Another common concern is how to complete the "Reason for Leaving" line in the work experience section. Finally, applicants ask what they should put in the salary requirement blank. Let's tackle these questions first.

Illegal questions.   If I told you that you would never encounter any illegal questions, I would be lying. I have seen application forms that left me appalled at the obvious ignorance of the employer. If you are given an application with illegal questions on issues such as age, marital status, religion, or race, you may wish to write "NA" (not applicable) in the blank. You certainly do not have to answer them. (If they are on a separate page that states that the questions are for the company's Affirmative Action program, the information should not be used in the hiring process. Whether to answer them is your choice.) Believe it or not, some employers are not aware of the questions on their application forms, and many are ignorant of the legalities in the hiring process. If an employer is asking illegal questions on the form or in the interview, you probably should ask yourself, "Do I want to work for someone like this?" It's your call.

Reason for leaving.   If you are afraid to explain why you left a job because you were fired or asked to resign for other than favorable reasons, don't worry. You do not have to state the reason on the application. There are ways to answer without hurting your chances. First, you need to know that being fired is not usually a reason employers choose not to hire someone; it is how you handle the question in the interview that could disqualify you. Instead of writing that you were fired, you can write that you would like to discuss this in the interview. At that time, you have the opportunity to explain the circumstances surrounding the termination. For how to explain this during the interview, refer to the section titled "Questions You Could Be Asked and How to Answer" in Chapter 4.

Salary requirement.   Another area on employment applications that causes applicants to unknowingly eliminate themselves is the inquiry as to salary requirements. This is an important but also sensitive factor in the job search process that needs to be handled carefully. If you have done the necessary research, you know what is an appropriate range for you and also have some idea as to the salary this company is willing to pay. You can acquire this information about salary ranges from many sources, such as informational interviews (discussed in Chapter 3), magazines and newspapers that publish special sections throughout the year, directories in the library, college placement offices, the Internet, and people you know who are already working in the field. The best answer is to state a range (yearly, monthly, or hourly) and always add that it is negotiable. If you give a figure that is too low, an employer will most likely be delighted to give it to you. Employers have a commitment to make a profit, and they will hire you as economically as they can. On the other hand, if you set a figure or range too high, the employer might assume that you are out of reach. So, do your homework and know the range that is appropriate for you.

If you complete the application according to these suggestions, you will present yourself to the interviewer as a conscientious and thorough person who is serious about his or her job search. It will also give you an edge over other applicants who have not done their homework. To practice and prepare yourself for filling out employers' application forms, complete the sample form in Exhibit 2.31.

APPLICATION FOR EMPLOYMENT

PRE-EMPLOYMENT
QUESTIONNAIRE
AN EQUAL
OPPORTUNITY EMPLOYER

LAST

PERSONAL INFORMATION

NAME (LAST NAME FIRST)			SOCIAL SECURITY NO.	
PRESENT ADDRESS	APT. NO.	CITY	STATE	ZIP
PERMANENT ADDRESS	APT. NO.	CITY	STATE	ZIP

ARE YOU 18 YEARS OR OLDER?   ☐ YES   ☐ NO   PHONE

DESIRED EMPLOYMENT

FIRST

POSITION		DATE YOU CAN START	SALARY DESIRED
ARE YOU EMPLOYED NOW? ☐ YES ☐ NO	IF SO MAY WE INQUIRE OF YOUR PRESENT EMPLOYER? ☐ YES ☐ NO		
EVER APPLIED TO THIS COMPANY BEFORE? ☐ YES ☐ NO	WHERE?		WHEN?
EVER WORKED FOR THIS COMPANY BEFORE? ☐ YES ☐ NO	WHERE?		WHEN?
REASON FOR LEAVING			
NAME OF LAST SUPERVISOR AT THIS COMPANY			

WHO REFERRED YOU TO THIS COMPANY?

☐ EMPLOYMENT AGENCY   ☐ NEWSPAPER ADVERTISING   ☐ FRIEND

☐ STATE EMPLOYMENT OFFICE   ☐ COLLEGE PLACEMENT SERVICE   ☐ WALK IN   ☐ OTHER

MIDDLE

EDUCATION

SCHOOL LEVEL	NAME AND LOCATION OF SCHOOL	NO. OF YEARS ATTENDED	DID YOU GRADUATE?	SUBJECTS STUDIED
GRAMMAR SCHOOL				
HIGH SCHOOL				
COLLEGE				
TRADE, BUSINESS OR CORRESPONDENCE SCHOOL				

GENERAL

SUBJECTS OF SPECIAL STUDY OR RESEARCH WORK
SPECIAL TRAINING
SPECIAL SKILLS

EXHIBIT 2.31 Application for employment. Continued

FORMER EMPLOYERS

LIST BELOW LAST THREE EMPLOYERS, STARTING WITH THE MOST RECENT ONE FIRST.

NAME OF PRESENT OR LAST EMPLOYER				
ADDRESS	CITY	STATE		ZIP
STARTING DATE	LEAVING DATE	JOB TITLE		
WEEKLY STARTING SALARY	WEEKLY FINAL SALARY	MAY WE CONTACT YOUR SUPERVISOR? ☐ YES ☐ NO		
NAME OF SUPERVISOR	TITLE		PHONE	
DESCRIPTION OF WORK				
REASON FOR LEAVING				

NAME OF PREVIOUS EMPLOYER				
ADDRESS	CITY	STATE		ZIP
STARTING DATE	LEAVING DATE	JOB TITLE		
WEEKLY STARTING SALARY	WEEKLY FINAL SALARY	MAY WE CONTACT YOUR SUPERVISOR? ☐ YES ☐ NO		
NAME OF SUPERVISOR	TITLE		PHONE	
DESCRIPTION OF WORK				
REASON FOR LEAVING				

NAME OF PREVIOUS EMPLOYER				
ADDRESS	CITY	STATE		ZIP
STARTING DATE	LEAVING DATE	JOB TITLE		
WEEKLY STARTING SALARY	WEEKLY FINAL SALARY	MAY WE CONTACT YOUR SUPERVISOR? ☐ YES ☐ NO		
NAME OF SUPERVISOR	TITLE		PHONE	
DESCRIPTION OF WORK				
REASON FOR LEAVING				

Application for employment. Continued   EXHIBIT 2.31

REFERENCES
BELOW, GIVE THE NAMES OF THREE PERSONS YOU ARE NOT RELATED TO, WHOM YOU HAVE KNOWN AT LEAST ONE YEAR.

	NAME	ADDRESS	BUSINESS	YEARS ACQUAINTED
1				
2				
3				

SERVICE RECORD

BRANCH OF SERVICE	DISCHARGE DATE RANK

HAVE YOU BEEN CONVICTED OF A FELONY WITHIN THE LAST 5 YEARS?	☐ YES ☐ NO
IF YES, EXPLAIN. (WILL NOT NECESSARILY EXCLUDE YOU FROM CONSIDERATION)	

AUTHORIZATION

"I CERTIFY THAT THE FACTS CONTAINED IN THIS APPLICATION ARE TRUE AND COMPLETE TO THE BEST OF MY KNOWLEDGE AND UNDERSTAND THAT, IF EMPLOYED, FALSIFIED STATEMENTS ON THIS APPLICATION SHALL BE GROUNDS FOR DISMISSAL.

I AUTHORIZE INVESTIGATION OF ALL STATEMENTS CONTAINED HEREIN AND THE REFERENCES AND EMPLOYERS LISTED ABOVE TO GIVE YOU ANY AND ALL INFORMATION CONCERNING MY PREVIOUS EMPLOYMENT AND ANY PERTINENT INFORMATION THEY MAY HAVE, PERSONAL OR OTHERWISE AND RELEASE THE COMPANY FROM ALL LIABILITY FOR ANY DAMAGE THAT MAY RESULT FROM UTILIZATION OF SUCH INFORMATION.

I ALSO UNDERSTAND AND AGREE THAT NO REPRESENTATIVE OF THE COMPANY HAS ANY AUTHORITY TO ENTER INTO ANY AGREEMENT FOR EMPLOYMENT FOR ANY SPECIFIED PERIOD OF TIME, OR TO MAKE ANY AGREEMENT CONTRARY TO THE FOREGOING, UNLESS IT IS IN WRITING AND SIGNED BY AN AUTHORIZED COMPANY REPRESENTATIVE."

DATE   SIGNATURE

NOTES

1. Helen Lauer, "In Search of Resume Writing Excellence," [online]. Available at http://content.careers.msn.com/Getting Hired/Resumes (March 23, 2001).

2. Robert Lewis, "A Rising Tide: Suddenly, Older Workers Find They're in Demand." *AARP Bulletin* 40 (10) (November 1999): 22.

3. For some valid information on older workers in the workplace and a list of the best employers for workers over 50, refer to the *AARP Magazine* (2003 November/ December) 51–55.

4. Carol Kleiman, "Former Employees Fight Negative References," *The Denver Post*, August 16, 1992, Sec. J, 1.

5. Liz Pullman Weston, "How Bad Credit Can Cost you a Job." *MSN Money*, [online]. (February 7, 2004.)

6. "A Bull Market in Inflated Resumes," *U.S. News & World Report*, November 13, 2000, 78.

7. Mary B. Nemnich and Fred E. Jandt, *Cyberspace Job Search Kit 2001–2002 Edition, The Complete Guide to Online Job Seeking and Career Information* (Indianapolis, IN: JIST Publishing, 2001), 94–109. Reprinted by permission.

8. Ibid.

9. Ibid.

Organizing, Searching, and Planning

Now that you're all "inventoried" and your paperwork is done, you are ready to begin your search for information, leads, and bona fide job openings. The first step is to organize your search. You need to learn the specific requirements for the job(s) you are targeting, discover where the jobs are, and decide how you can best utilize your time while you are searching.

3

In this chapter, we will look at one of the best known ways to get information on companies, job titles, and job definitions and describe sources for leads to jobs, including those in the mysterious "hidden job market." You will also learn ways to organize and manage your time during the job search to maximize your efforts for the greatest success and the least possible stress.

Organizing

Where Do You Begin?

To begin organizing your job search, you need a list of companies in your targeted industry and some information on occupational titles and definitions. Without this information, you will most likely waste your time going off in all directions, totally unorganized, unprepared, and unproductive. So, your first assignment in organizing the search is to prepare a list of the companies that you would like to work for and to get information on job titles and their definitions. This kind of information can be found in the library and on the Internet. Your local library is a good place to start. Books on organizations are classified by industry, size, and location, so you can go directly to the ones that will give you the information you need. Look for directories, trade publications, and even the Yellow Pages. Local newspapers and magazines are also very good sources of information on companies in your area. Below is a list of some of the many sources available to you at the library.

- Fitch Corporations manuals
- *Standard & Poor's Register of Corporations*
- *Peterson's Guide*
- *The Wall Street Journal*
- *Job Seeker's Guide to Private & Public Companies*
- *Thomas Register*
- Dun & Bradstreet's *Million Dollar Directory*
- College Placement Annuals
- *The Best Hospitals in America*
- *Travel & Hospitality Career Directory*
- *Therapists and Allied Health Professionals Directory*
- *Applied Science & Technology Index*
- *Business Week*
- *U.S. News & World Report*
- *World Almanac*
- *Business Periodicals Index*
- *Directory of Corporate Affiliations*
- *Directory of American Research & Technology*
- *U.S. Government Manual*
- National Trade & Professional Associations of U.S.
- American Federation of Information Processing Societies
- Data Processing Management Association

The library also has two publications that cover career information and jobs: the *Occupational Outlook Handbook (OOH)* and the *Dictionary of Occupational Titles (DOT)*. The *Occupational Outlook Handbook* describes what workers do on the job, working conditions, the training and education needed, earnings, and the expected job prospects in a wide range of occupations. The *DOT* contains definitions for nearly 13,000 job "codes" and encompasses approximately 20,000 job titles and nearly 13,000 detailed definitions. Ask the librarian for assistance in locating information about the occupation that interests you.

The Internet offers a wealth of information about companies. To learn about companies, visit the sites of magazines and newspapers, or search the career sites listed on page 127. For information about jobs, go to the *DOT* online at www.wave.net/upg/immigration/dot_index.html or the *OOH* at www.bls.gov/oco. On the *OOH* site, to find information by occupation, enter the name of your specific occupation in the box labeled "Search by occupation." If you would like to see a listing of all occupations, click the A–Z button.

As you find information at the library and on the Internet, build a comprehensive list of names of companies and be sure to record exactly where you got the name of the company. If you find later that you want to go back and get more information, there is nothing more frustrating than to have to try to remember which directory, publication, etc. listed that company. Once you have compiled a list of the companies you are interested in (depending on your field, you should have at least 20–50 names), you are now ready for the next step in organizing your job search, the *informational interview*.

The Informational Interview

It has been said that if you want to find out how to get where you want to go, talk to someone who's already there. That is exactly what informational interviews are for. The one sure way to find out if your skills and abilities match your targeted job is by talking to those working in your field. You can find out all about the characteristics and requirements of the position, plus many tips for success and insight into the future of your field. An informational interview can eliminate "surprises" in the job interview and give you some intelligent questions and answers for your interviewer. Moreover, informational interviews can help you develop employment leads and gain experience with interviewing. It is not unusual for informational interviews to lead to job offers.

Strategies for Conducting an Informational Interview

Choose the top five companies from your list.   Not all of the companies you call will have someone available to meet with you, so choose the top five from your list and work down from there.

Plan your call.   Before you pick up the phone, you must plan your call. You don't want to waste the person's time or risk sounding like you're unprepared. Write out what you're going to say and then practice it. Your conversation should not sound "canned," but you do want to sound professional.

Get to the person in charge of the department for the type of job you are targeting. The person who answers the phone is usually a receptionist or a secretary who has been trained to screen calls; therefore, you must be prepared to handle the person's attempt to screen you out. Be firm but polite, and state that this is *not* an employment call, but an information call. Stress that you are not looking for work at this time; you simply would like to learn more about the field and would appreciate speaking with someone who has that information. If the employee is reluctant to transfer your call and puts you off by saying that the person you want to speak to is "out," "in a meeting," or "on the phone," *get a name* and call back and ask for that person directly. If the employee asks you to leave your name and number, *don't.* The chance that you will receive a return call is next to none. Just say that you are going to be away from your phone and that you'd like to try again, and ask what would be a good time to call.

Identify yourself and state the purpose of your call.   When you have been connected to the person you wish to talk to, don't waste that person's time. Be prepared and immediately explain who you are and why you are calling. Be sure to emphasize that you need his or her expertise; this is one of the highest compliments you can pay anyone and should help you to gain an interview. It's true; you *do* need that individual's expertise. Ask for a few (15–20) minutes of time when it is convenient to meet with you. Some busy people may try to conduct this interview over the phone; therefore, you must stress that you are very interested in observing just how the job is performed and would learn much more by visiting in person. Once you have confirmed a date and a time, ask if there is anything you need to know about the location, restrictions on parking, or entry into the company, etc. Some computer companies and government organizations have security measures to protect their operations. *Write down all of this information; do not trust it to memory.* (See the techniques and tips for using the telephone for job and interview calls at the end of this section.)

Prepare your questions.   Part of the preparation for an informational interview is to decide on the kinds of questions you are going to ask in the interview. What is it that you would like to know? What kinds of things are pertinent and appropriate to ask? The objective of your interview is to find out all you can about the requirements and characteristics of the job you are looking for and your industry. To help you stay on target and not waste your time and that of the interviewee, either choose questions from the list below or make up your own.

SAMPLE QUESTIONS

1. What does the company do?
2. How old is the company; how long has it been in business?
3. Where are its plants, stores, locations?
4. What are its products or services?
5. Who are its competitors?
6. In each major division, what types of positions are offered?
7. What are the requirements for entry level and experienced positions (education, skills, abilities, etc.)?
8. What are the main duties and responsibilities of the job?
9. Where is the job performed (indoors, outdoors, travel)?
10. What personal qualities does the company look for?
11. Is any certification or licensing required to be eligible for hire?

12. What, if any, are the tools, equipment, software, computer languages, experience, etc. needed in order to perform the job?

13. What are the opportunities for advanced training, on-the-job training, or academic coursework? Is this paid for by the firm?

14. What is the salary range? What could one expect to make five years from now?

15. What benefits are provided by the company?

16. What does the interviewee see as the future of this occupation? Will there be an increase or a decrease in demand for it?

17. What changes could arise in this position or field over the next few years? How could you prepare for these changes?

18. How much involvement do employees have in decision making and policy making?

19. What other companies might employ individuals wishing to enter your field?

20. Could the interviewee suggest any other people you could talk to for more information about opportunities in your field?

Conduct the interview professionally.   Bring your questions with you to the interview and use them as guidelines to keep you from straying from your objective, which is to get information. Treat this interview as seriously as you would an actual job interview: dress professionally, be on time, listen carefully, and make good eye contact during the interview. *If you have cleared it with the person you are interviewing*, you might want to bring a tape recorder as it will allow you to be more relaxed and not have to concentrate on taking notes during the interview. Keep to the allotted time unless the person you're interviewing willingly offers more. When the interview is over, always thank the person for spending time with you and don't forget to ask for referrals.

Follow up.   There is only one way to follow up an information interview: with a thank-you note. Writing the thank-you is a professional courtesy. All you need to say is that you really appreciate the time the person took from a busy day to spend with you and how much it has helped you in your research. Send the thank-you as soon as possible after the interview. If other people helped you to arrange the interview, write to them as well.

Caution: Don't take your resume to informational interviews. I hear lots of objections from people about this, such as "But what if they offer me a job or ask for my resume, shouldn't I take it with me?" Well, what did you tell the interviewee that you were there for? Was it for getting a job or for getting information? Do you want the interviewee to think that you had ulterior motives, that you're not honest? Besides, not having your resume with you gives you the opportunity to offer to bring it by later and maybe get a job interview at the same time.

Making Calls for Information and Job Openings

The telephone is one of the best tools available to you when job searching. Whether you use it to arrange for informational interviews or to locate job openings, it is the swiftest way to contact prospective employers. However, to avoid wasting the time of the person you are calling, or worse, losing a possible job opening, you must be prepared. You need to be clear about your objective (the reason you are calling) and have a well thought-out plan that includes a prepared phone "script."

Your Objective

If you are calling for an informational interview, your objective is to speak with the person who is qualified to give you the information you're seeking and to grant you an interview. If you are calling about job openings, your objective is to get to the person who knows firsthand about those openings. If you are calling from an advertised opening or referral, you will probably have been directed to ask for a certain person; when you reach that person, begin by asking for an interview.

Planning Your Call

A receptionist or secretary will probably answer your call; therefore, your first strategy should be to obtain the name of the person with whom you wish to speak (unless you already know it). Keep in mind that secretaries and receptionists have often been trained to "protect" their superiors from unnecessary calls and might not readily give out their names. What you say at this time can be crucial. It is always best to ask for the person in charge of the department that you are interested in, *not* the person in charge of hiring. You may be asked if this is an employment call. If it is, say so. If the reply is "I'm sorry, but we're not hiring at this time," or "We have no openings at this time," simply say, "But if you were hiring, to whom would I speak?" Once you have a name, thank the employee, hang up, and call back later asking for that person.

If the receptionist or secretary refers you to someone in the personnel department, go ahead and speak with that person. However, avoid personnel people if at all possible, as they are usually the last ones to know about openings and many times will screen you out based on preset guidelines. Instead, you want the opportunity to sell yourself to the person who is qualified to judge whether or not you could be of use to the company.

If you are successful in getting the name of the person who is in charge of the area you're interested in, but are told that that person is out or in a meeting, don't leave your name and number. Just say that you are going to be in and out and that you will call back.

Whatever the result is in your dealings with receptionists or secretaries, always remember this: Treat them with respect and courtesy. Not only is this the right thing to do in dealing with anyone, but you also want them to be "on your side." They can be very helpful should there be an opening. They can help you arrange an interview, and they often have a say in who gets hired.

Your Telephone Script

Once you've been connected to the person you wish to speak with, your call should be brief and to the point. Whatever the reason you are calling, whether for a job opening or information, begin by telling the person who you are and the purpose of your call.

For information: "Good (morning, afternoon), my name is John Smith, and I am interested in learning about the field of (computer programming, drafting, engineering, hospitality, medical, etc.) and about career opportunities in this field."

For job leads: "Good (morning, afternoon), my name is Mary Jones, and I'm interested in any openings you have in _____. I'm a recent graduate of (name of college) with a/an (Associate's, Bachelor's, Master's) degree in _____."

If you are calling to inquire about job openings, after your introduction, be prepared to offer some strong selling points for meeting with you. Mention special skills, experience, and abilities. Have your resume handy and use it to summarize your strongest qualifications for the position. Be brief but assertive, and describe why your abilities would be of value to the company.

The Close

Get the interview!   This is the objective of your call; don't lose sight of it. If this is a job call, now is the time to remember that you are not asking for a "handout," you are offering something of value, an opportunity for the employer to hire a dedicated, hardworking, and valuable employee—you! A closing statement to help you get an interview might be: "I would really appreciate the opportunity to meet with you to discuss my qualifications as they relate to the opening in _____. I have tomorrow morning or anytime on Tuesday free; which is most convenient for you?"

Additional Tips for Successful Cold Calls

- Be enthusiastic, smile, and project a positive attitude. Even though the other person can't see you, your attitude and the way you feel projects over the phone.

- Make your calls in a quiet place without distractions from children, pets, roommates, etc.

- Have all your paperwork in front of you: script, resume, daily planner, whatever other information you need.

- Choose the best time to call. Anytime after 9:00 A.M., even during lunch hours, is a good time to call. In some small- to medium-sized companies, managers and even owners will cover the phones while the receptionist is out to lunch. After 3:00 P.M. can also be an opportune time to call because it's usually a less busy time of day. Friday afternoons may also be good because people are looking forward to the weekend and are in a good mood. Avoid calling on Monday morning or before 9:00 A.M. on any day. Most business people like that time to be uninterrupted by phone calls.

- Be prepared for rejection. Keep in mind that a "no" is not about you personally. Making job calls and looking for openings is a numbers game. The law of averages says that after a certain number of no's, it is inevitable that a yes will follow. Just keep calling; be persistent!

- Always get all the information you need for follow-up, interviews, and so on, and *write it down*!

- If you have voice mail or an answering machine, always record a simple, but professional, message. A caller could be offended by an unprofessional message.

TELEPHONE LOG

Date _____   Telephone Number _____

Name of Company _____

Address of Company _____

Name of Contact Person _____   E-mail _____

Information Interview _____   Position(s) Open _____

No Openings _____   Future Contact Date _____

Comments _____

_____

_____

Date _____   Telephone Number _____

Name of Company _____

Address of Company _____

Name of Contact Person _____   E-mail _____

Information Interview _____   Position(s) Open _____

No Openings _____   Future Contact Date _____

Comments _____

_____

_____

Date _____   Telephone Number _____

Name of Company _____

Address of Company _____

Name of Contact Person _____   E-mail _____

Information Interview _____   Position(s) Open _____

No Openings _____   Future Contact Date _____

Comments _____

_____

_____

INFORMATIONAL INTERVIEW RECORD

Date of Interview

Name of Company

Address

Name and title of person being interviewed

Phone Number   E-mail

Time spent interviewing

What information did you gain from the interview?

Was the interview useful to you?   Did you enjoy it?

Comments

INFORMATIONAL INTERVIEW RECORD

Date of Interview

Name of Company

Address

Name and title of person being interviewed

Phone Number   E-mail

Time spent interviewing

What information did you gain from the interview?

Was the interview useful to you?   Did you enjoy it?

Comments

LIBRARY SEARCH REPORTS

Source Information (title of publication, Website URL, etc.)

Name of Company

Address

Phone Number(s)

Contact Person

Summary of important and useful information

Source Information (title of publication, Website URL, etc.)

Name of Company

Address

Phone Number(s)

Contact Person

Summary of important and useful information

LIBRARY SEARCH REPORTS

Source Information (title of publication, Website URL, etc.)

Name of Company

Address

Phone Number(s)

Contact Person

Summary of important and useful information

Source Information (title of publication, Website URL, etc.)

Name of Company

Address

Phone Number(s)

Contact Person

Summary of important and useful information

Searching

Where Are the Jobs?

There are many ways to find job openings. Approaches to finding job leads can vary with some industries, but for 98 percent of the positions available, you can employ any or all of the methods listed below. When you are looking for work, you should utilize all available resources for a successful job search. The more you use, the sooner you'll find the job you want. Most job searchers mass-market themselves by indiscriminately mailing hundreds of resumes, believing that this will get them interviews and, ultimately, a job. Not true! This is the most *inactive* way to job search; it could take you months or even a year to find a job this way. The only effective way is to focus your search *actively* using the following strategies.

Newspapers and Trade Publications

The classified section of the newspaper is, as you probably already know, a good place to begin your search. However, you need to know how to get the most mileage from this source. There is nothing wrong with using the classifieds, but you should know that only a very small percentage of the available jobs at any given time are ever advertised, and the competition for advertised jobs is extremely high. The average ad, depending on the field and the job market, of course, will net anywhere from 75 to 300 resumes. Consequently, your chances of getting an interview, much less getting a job offer, from a classified ad could be very slim. If you are going to use the classifieds, use the techniques below to maximize your efforts.

Check prior newspaper ads.   When you begin your job search, go to the library or to someone you know who saves newspapers and collect all of the Sunday and Wednesday issues for the past 10 to 12 weeks. Why? Well, think about it . . . what is the probationary period for most jobs? That's right, 60 to 90 days. During this period, the employer is considering whether or not to keep the person they've hired. If the employer is not going to retain the employee, the chances are that he is dreading the prospect of advertising, interviewing, and selecting another employee. Also, many times companies are unable to find someone to fill the job and continue to look long after the ad runs. For either reason, if you are qualified, the company will be delighted to hear from you.

Expand your search.   When you are deciding which ads to respond to, consider ads for positions that are a little above or below what you are actually seeking. Employers are often willing to talk to you about upgrading or downgrading a job if they see that you could be a contributor to their company. Look for ads for related positions. Notice those businesses advertising for sales or accounting personnel. If they are advertising for these positions, this could indicate that they may be planning to increase their business by adding more services or products. They might need people with your skills. Always check out the ads for part-time and temp positions because many are tryouts for full-time positions. And many times blind ads are placed for legitimate jobs, so go ahead and check them out, but not if you think that your employer might have placed it.

Read the business section of the paper.   This is where you will find out about new companies coming to your area, branch offices opening up, expansions in already existing firms, and the names of people being promoted to positions of management. If you're really serious about making some good contacts, send a letter of congratulations on the promotion and include a resume (a nice gesture that just might get you an interview).

Read the trade journals for your industry.   You will find articles and advertisements that will give you information on companies to contact. Many of these journals also have classified ad sections that list job opportunities. Even if the ads are not for the kind of position you are looking for, again, they could indicate growth and that openings may be coming soon in other areas. Some trade journals list meetings and conventions that could be useful in your job search. If you're looking for positions with specific firms, you might be able to attend these functions and make contacts with key personnel.

Associations

The *Encyclopedia of Associations* gives the names and addresses of trade associations that are affiliated with all industries. These associations are always looking for new members and are usually happy to speak with job hunters like you. Many times they will invite you to one of their monthly or quarterly meetings, where they sometimes have workshops or dinners. It is a wonderful and fun way to obtain many contacts with local companies in your industry. And if you do become a member, it is a definite plus to be able to add it to your resume.

State and City Job Service Centers

These are employment agencies operated by the government and are open to the general public. They have free daily listings of jobs within your state and city. The listings are usually for lower-level, minimum-wage jobs, but sometimes these entry-level openings are with companies that offer advancement.

Career Fairs

Attending career fairs can allow you to talk with many employers in one day. Fairs are usually held in large hotels or convention centers and feature many of the larger companies in your area, along with others from all over the country. You should dress as if you are going to an interview and take several copies of your resume with you. The companies usually do not hire at career fairs, but they do take resumes and applications. The majority of them will be looking for persons with at least a Bachelor's degree; however, don't let this intimidate you if you don't have one. Speak with them anyway and sell what you do have! Not all organizations are locked in to these requirements; most will take an honest look at anyone who is positive and enthusiastic. Be prepared for wall-to-wall people, and get a good night's sleep before you go. In times of high unemployment and particularly in the spring when hundreds of college graduates are looking for jobs, these fairs can be swamped with job applicants.

Chambers of Commerce

Most companies register with the local Chamber of Commerce, and new businesses use this membership for advertising and promoting themselves in their communities. Be sure to ask if there is a charge for the Chamber's handout materials; some charge a fee. If you are relocating to another state or city, the Chamber of Commerce is one of the first places you should visit to receive a wealth of information about all of the activities and companies in their cities.

Career Resources and College Placement Centers

If you are a graduate of any college, the career resource or placement center is the first place you should go. Nearly all technical, business, and community colleges provide placement assistance for their graduates. Universities are now realizing that they must offer more services for their graduates and are expanding their career resource centers to include their alumni. Recruiters from companies all over the United States visit colleges on a regular basis to interview potential employees.

Remember that your placement or employment assistance office will provide you with job leads; however, it is still your responsibility to duplicate those efforts and conduct your own intensive search. If you want a job soon after, or even before, you graduate, the possibility of this is greater if *both* of you are seeking.

College placement centers are excellent sources for information on employers even if you are not a graduate, as they have daily contact with employers and know what kinds of applicants companies look for. They also know the current salary ranges offered by a lot of the companies.

Bulletin Boards

Many public places have bulletin boards where companies post job listings. Check the boards at state and city government offices, libraries, courthouses, supermarkets, and recreational centers. These can be viable sources for job leads.

Temporary Service Agencies

Temporary agencies are a reliable source for job openings. Temporary agencies match up employees with employers who need short-term help in just about every field. Companies appreciate the freedom to add an employee for a short time without the commitment of permanency or the cost of benefits. Temp agencies contract you out to these companies, and they pay your salary, which is usually lower than the going rate. This can be a good way to get your foot in the door of well-established firms who might not hire you directly. In addition, statistics show that the length of time that temporary employees stay with an agency varies from 3 to 5 weeks because many times they are hired by the client firm. If you are changing careers and have little or no experience in the field you are entering, temporary positions are an excellent way to get that experience.

Job Placement Firms

Be very cautious about using job placement firms. A scam alert from the *AARP Bulletin* warns job seekers about placement firms that ask for money up front and guarantee you a job in your field, but never deliver. The article, "Bum Job Leads," June 2002, states that "Sheila Adkins of the Council of Better Business Bureaus, which logged more than 1,000 complaints last year involving job placement services, says consumers should ask how long a business has been in existence—and what the company's success rate has been for placing clients in jobs."[1] Believe me, *no one* can guarantee you a job. For more information on how to protect yourself from unscrupulous job placement firms, visit the AARP website: www.aarp.org/bulletin/scamalert.

Direct Contact—Visits or Calls to Potential Employers

You've probably heard of the "hidden job market" and wondered where it was and how to find it. Well, there's no mysterious secret; it exists all the time, and the way you find it is simply to contact companies directly. Openings are created every day in all organizations by terminations, retirements, and deaths, as well as by relocations, resignations, and promotions. When you call or visit employers directly, you will discover this "hidden" market. Telephoning and visiting the company are two of the most effective ways to find job openings, and more jobs are acquired in this way than through more traditional methods. Because you make the contact before employers have advertised or announced the opening, you have the opportunity to present your qualifications ahead of everyone else. The advantage of using the telephone is that you can reach more companies in a shorter time. If you go in person, however, you may be offered an interview on the spot.

Using the United States Postal Service

Mailing resumes and cover letters may be something that just about all job seekers do, but it is the least productive. Your return on mailing resumes, if you are lucky, is probably about 1 percent. It is so easy for employers to send you a rejection letter in the mail or, worse, to ignore your resume completely. Since so many people approach job searching in this way, the competition is staggering. If you are going to mail resumes, be selective and follow the guidelines given in Chapter 2 (with respect to who gets the resume). Remember that in today's market, your documents are very likely to be scanned, so use a 10- by 13-inch envelope. You want your letter and resume to arrive flat and unfolded, scanner ready. If you haven't received a response from the company in a week (for small companies) or three weeks (for larger companies), send a second resume and call if you have the number.

Networking

You've probably heard the saying, "It's not what you know, but who you know." Well, when it comes to job searching, this could be true. Most of the best jobs are never advertised. Organizations themselves do their own networking when they need new employees. They consult with their current employees, vendors, customers, and so on. Many of the firms I have worked with over the years have told me that 30 to 40 percent of their openings are filled by a referral from one of the above sources. One of the reasons that job seekers miss valuable connections to job openings is that they fail to network. *Networking* is one of the most effective and productive ways of getting leads and job offers. It is also a source for the "hidden" job market. **Networking** is telling everyone you know that you are looking for a job and what kind of positions you seek.

Making an assumption that your family and friends know what kind of job you are seeking could be a grave error; they probably don't. Be sure that you tell them what you're looking for in a job. When I ask the people in my job search workshops and classes how many of their families could describe the kind of job they are looking for, very rarely do any hands go up.

Talk with everyone you meet about your job goal, even at social gatherings. At any gathering, people will be talking in groups. Casually join a group and take a moment to tune in to the conversation. Don't monopolize the conversation; listen. You can learn a lot by listening. Ask people where they work and if they know of any openings. You are probably doing this right now without even being aware of it. Think about it: How many people have you had association with in the past month? Did you talk about your job search? I'll bet you did. Now is not the time to be shy, proud, or zealous about your privacy; you have to open your mouth and ask. (If you are very shy and just can't bring yourself to speak up, try getting some inexpensive "Situation Wanted" cards printed to give to people. You can buy them like business cards or make your own, very inexpensively, with one of the many low-cost software packages on the market.) There are also networking groups you can join such as the Five O'Clock Club (800-538-6645) with a fee of $40 per month, or the 40-Plus Club (202-387-1582) with an initiation fee of $600 and $30 per month. To begin your networking process, complete the worksheet "Networking Prospects" with as many names as you can.

NETWORKING PROSPECTS

List the names of all the people, businesses, groups, etc. that could be sources for leads or referrals.

Family
_____
_____
_____

Friends
_____
_____

Neighbors
_____
_____

Service suppliers (grocers, service stations, etc.)
_____
_____
_____

Former employers, coworkers
_____
_____
_____

Schools, colleges, churches
_____
_____
_____

Clubs, associations, memberships
_____
_____
_____

People and companies from the business cards you collected
_____
_____
_____

Searching for Jobs on the Internet

The Internet is a valuable source for job searching. It offers enough job bank sites to fill a book. While it hasn't totally replaced conventional methods of job searching, the Internet has become a vital tool for searching hundreds of job databases, job listings, and company websites around the globe. If you plan to post your resume, you must prepare one that can be read by software or computer systems. *Caution:* Before posting your resume on the Internet, if you are currently employed, be sure the site guarantees confidentiality, and *don't mail it from your employer's address.* Companies sometimes search the Net on their own names. (See Chapter 2 for instructions for preparing an electronic resume.)

Corporate Internet Sites

Many companies and public organizations have established their own websites and include vacancy announcements online. They also now put their Web addresses in their newspaper ads. The vacancies listed on a company's site will contain more information than the ones published in newspaper ads, often giving an e-mail address, a fax number, and a postal address. If you don't have a definite company that you want to work for but want to investigate some corporate sites, go to Yahoo! (www.yahoo.com), then click on Business and Economy. Click on Companies and select the type of company. You will then be able to go directly to the company's home page. For classified ads from major U.S. newspapers, go to www.careerpath.com.

Internet Job Banks

The Internet offers hundreds of job banks with information about job openings, companies, and job search services. Job banks often change their names and URLs, and some will close as new ones appear. The following URLs were current as of this writing.

America's Job Bank: www.ajb.dni.us

Canada's Job Bank: www.mbpcanada.com/canadajobbank

CareerPath: www.careerpath.com

CareerBuilder (searches by location): www.careerbuilder.com

Hotjobs.com: www.hotjobs.com

Monster.com: www.monster.com

Joboptions: www.joboptions.com

Other notable job banks include the following:

www.careerfile.com

www.jobs.com

www.careermart.com

www2.jobtrak.com

www.headhunter.net

www.taonline.com (transition for moving from military to civilian life)

www.JobNET.com

JobCircle.com

SEARCHING THE INTERNET

To test your competence in searching the Internet, select a job bank or a corporate site and go online to find openings for the job you desire. If you have difficulty finding a site or would prefer a fast search, try using a search engine. Search engines scan the Web for keywords you specify. A few popular search engines are at www.altavista.com, www.hotbot.com, and www.metacrawler.com. For best results, use quotation marks for phrases "you want to appear exactly as typed," be specific, and enter more than one keyword in order to narrow your search.

Focus your online search as narrowly as possible, whether it is for a particular industry or geographical location. Pick the right sites, those directly related to the field you have chosen. If you don't know where to begin, refer to the suggestions in the box above.

Planning   "Fail to Plan, Plan to Fail"

When you begin your job search, careful planning and good time management are of the utmost importance. Procrastinating and delaying are usually the result of poor organization, and a lack of organization is a direct result of a failure to plan. So as you can see, one leads to the other, which leads you to *nowhere*. Since almost everyone is prone to procrastination, it is necessary for you to have a workable plan in order not to fall victim to this trap when you are job searching. In a job search, procrastination means missing appointments, interviews, and ultimately, a job.

Your job search plan should include some realistic objectives for each day of your search, a deadline for each weekly goal, and checkpoints to monitor your activity and your progress. Setting goals and listing some definite actions to acquire those goals will keep you motivated and help you to deal with rejection in a positive way. Go back to your goals worksheet and review the steps you listed there. You will be better prepared for your interviews and feel a lot less anxiety and frustration.

You should view your job search as a full-time job because that's exactly what it is. Of course, you do need to schedule some time for relaxation, but don't get off-track by taking time out to clean the closets, paint the downstairs bedroom, or anything else that can wait until after you land that job. It only makes it more difficult to get started again if you lose your momentum. Keep with your plan, and remember that persistence always pays off!

The particulars of a well-organized job search are:

- Make your job search a 40-hour week.
- Once you begin your search, keep going until you have your job.
- Always plan your week in advance.
- Always begin your day early.

- Make calls and visits to employers every day.
- Follow up on leads, requests for resumes, etc. immediately.
- If you are currently employed, make calls or visits on your lunch hour. You can also take some personal leave days to interview. Employers may be willing to meet with you after hours, even on Saturday if they are interested in you.

The Daily Performance Planner and the Performance Record sheets on the following pages will help you to get started and to keep going. Begin by setting up your daily performance plan for each day of the week. At the end of the week, summarize your progress and fill in your plan for the next week. Analyze what you are doing and the results you are getting as you go along so that you can realistically assess your progress. If you are not getting interviews, or if you are interviewing but not getting offers, you need to examine what you're doing or not doing. Spend some time to figure out a new game plan and find solutions to these problems. Maybe you need to take a serious look at your resume or call the employers who have interviewed you and ask for frank, constructive feedback. Have you been procrastinating? Are you selling yourself? An honest evaluation of your activity is always helpful to get you back on track. Search for other job seekers, possibly classmates you graduated with. Also, check with the Career Development office of your college to see if it has meetings for graduates who are still looking for work. There is a lot to be said for getting together with others who are in the same situation that you are for sharing information, leads, and tips on what works or doesn't work.

DAILY PERFORMANCE PLANNER

Date: _____

Job Search Activities:

NAME/ADDRESS OF CONTACT	VISIT, CALL, MAILING	RESULT
1.		
2.		
3.		
4.		
5.		
6.		
7.		
8.		
9.		
10.		

PERFORMANCE RECORD AND SUMMARY

Week of

Total contacts made

Number of interviews

Job leads acquired

Follow-up needed

NOTES

1. Bum Job Leads. *AARP Bulletin* (June, 2004): 22.

Interviewing Made *Almost* Easy

Of all the phases of job searching, from writing your resume to the time you say "yes" to a job offer, the one most traumatizing to job seekers is the interview. No wonder: The interview is the most critical part of the job search. *The interview is where you are hired or not hired.* It's the zero hour, and you must be prepared to be scrutinized. During the interview, you are the "bug under the glass," to put it bluntly.

What can you do to minimize the fears, the anxiety, the sweaty palms? How can you get through the interviewing process with your self-confidence intact and get the job you want? That's what this chapter is about: helping you take the fear out of interviewing and showing you that you *can* have the job you desire. No matter what your age is or what field you're in, there are certain strategies and techniques you can use that will help you handle this phase of the job search with more confidence and less stress. Knowing how companies conduct interviews, what their expectations are of you as a prospective employee, what subjective assumptions are made in 75 to 80 percent of all interviews, and how to evaluate your performance are just a few of the things that can make interviewing *almost* easy.

How *Not* to Interview

 ome of the most common mistakes that will keep you from being hired are:

- Not conducting the necessary research on the company and the industry.
- Not practicing (role-playing) for interviews.
- Not knowing the job requirements.
- Improper dress or sloppy appearance.
- Giving inappropriate or untruthful answers to interview questions.
- Not having questions to ask the interviewer other than "What are the salary and benefits?"
- Poor communication skills and body language that "give you away."
- Criticizing former employers or supervisors.
- Not selling yourself, being too passive, lacking enthusiasm.
- Not knowing salary ranges and your worth.
- Lack of career direction and goals.
- Not knowing how to close the interview.
- Overemphasizing money.
- Being late to the interview.
- Sharing a marked dislike for school work.
- Failing to follow up after the interview.

Would you like to hear about just a few of the outrageous reasons that applicants didn't get hired? Vice presidents and personnel directors from 100 of the largest corporations were asked to describe their most unusual experience interviewing prospective employees. Here are a few of the incidents they reported:[1]

- A job applicant challenged the interviewer to an arm wrestle.
- The candidate fell and broke an arm during the interview.
- The candidate announced that she hadn't had lunch and proceeded to eat a hamburger and fries in the interviewer's office.

- One candidate brought a large dog to the interview.
- The applicant interrupted the interview to phone her therapist for advice on how to answer specific interview questions.

In this chapter you will learn how to avoid the common pitfalls. You will learn how employers conduct interviews and what they are really looking for, what is the necessary preparation, how to find out about salary ranges, and how to sell yourself. In addition, this chapter will give you some advice about what to do between interviews, how to deal with rejection, how to negotiate for the best salary, and how to evaluate a job offer.

Interviewing is not as difficult as most people think. Yes, it does make you feel very vulnerable. After all, the interviewer could say, "Sorry, you don't measure up; you're not what we're looking for." And that hurts! It is not an attack on your self-worth, and you can save yourself a lot of agony if you prepare for your interviews properly and know how to present yourself to a prospective employer confidently and professionally. You will have a much greater chance of getting the job of your choice, and to deal with rejections effectively.

I can promise you this: If you do your "homework," follow the suggestions in this chapter, and remember to believe in yourself, interviewing will be less fearful than it has ever been. Who knows . . . you might even consider it an exciting challenge.

Successful Interview Preparation

Preparation, the first step to successful interviewing, is the most neglected. People searching for work usually do not have the vaguest idea how to prepare for an interview correctly. And not being prepared creates about 75 percent of your fear. You simply cannot expect to make a favorable impression on the employer who is interviewing you if you do not prepare yourself beforehand. First, you must know something about the company to which you are applying. If you go into the interview with no idea what this company does, you are asking for rejection. It is an insult to them that you didn't care enough to find out what they're all about, and the last thing you want to do is to ask them about their company in the interview.

What Does the Company Do?

It's actually quite easy to research companies. Now is the time to put your library and Internet techniques to use. Using the guidelines in Chapter 3, learn as much as you can about the company to which you are applying. Interviewers try to determine not only your interest in obtaining the job, but also why you wish to work for them as opposed to other companies. Two questions they may ask are "What do you know about our company?" and "What contribution can you make to our organization?" In order to answer these questions knowledgeably, you must have done your research. The more information you have on the company, the better qualified you will be to answer their questions about your ability to contribute to their growth and prosperity—which is, by the way, the most important thing to them. Below are lists of library and Internet sources to assist you in your search for information on companies, the latter taken from the *Cyberspace Job Search Kit*.

Library Research Sources

- *New York Times Index.* Twice monthly index of newspaper articles in the *New York Times*, according to subject matter, dates, etc.

- *Applied Science & Technology Index.* Index of articles from magazines devoted to aeronautics, automation, chemistry, construction, metallurgy, transportation, and other related subjects.

- *Facts on File.* Weekly 8- to 10-page news digest that gives unbiased coverage of significant news events of each day, indexed for easy location.

- *Information Please Almanac.* In addition to statistical information, it features brief articles summarizing developments in various fields during the previous year.

- *World Almanac.* One-volume, yearly publication that presents statistics on business, education, industries, governments, population, sports, foreign countries, etc.

- *Business Periodicals Index.* Indexes more than 100 magazines in accounting, advertising, banking, business, insurance, labor, and other related fields.

Libraries also provide access to CD-ROMs such as InfoTrac and ProQuest, which are collections of magazine articles, and microfiche copies of newspapers and journal articles.

Internet Sites for Employer Information[2]

- *EDGAR.* The Electronic Data Gathering, Analysis, and Retrieval system. Contains the publicly available filings submitted to the Securities and Exchange Commission (SEC). At this site, you can find a public company's annual report, or 10-K, which describes the company's overall direction and includes financial data, information on research projects in development, and other plans. www.sec.gov/edgar.shtml

- *Hoover's Online.* Contains "company capsules" on every U.S. company traded on a major stock exchange, as well as some 2,000 private companies, that offer information on recent reports, brief financial data, and links to each company's website. www.hoovers.com

- *Forbes 500 Largest Private Companies.* Includes a brief company description, number of employees, sales rank, and a link to the company's website. www.forbes.com/private500

- *Companies Online.* A joint project of Lycos and Dun & Bradstreet that includes private companies. www.companiesonline.com

- *Fortune. Fortune* magazine's 100 Best Companies to Work for in America. www.fortune.com/fortune/bestcompanies/index.html

- *Fortune.* The magazine's ranking of the most admired companies. www.fortune.com/fortune/mostadmired/index.html

- *Women's Wire. Women's Wire's* list of the best companies in the United States for women, based on salary, benefits, and opportunities for advancement. www.womenswire.com (bottom of page, key in city, state, ZIP for localized search)

- *Working Woman.* Contains the magazine's list of the top 500 women-owned companies. www.workingwomanmag.com

- *The Hispanic Business 500 Directory.* www.hispanicbusiness.com/research/companies/default.asp

Where Is the Company Located?

Another vital step in preparing for a successful interview is to make certain that you know exactly where the company is located and how to get there. Don't make the grave error of thinking you know approximately where it is and then end up walking in late for the interview because you didn't know for sure. When you schedule the interview, ask for directions. If you forget to ask, call and find out. Ask about parking: Is there a special lot or space for visitors? Is it controlled by security? Find out if there is more than one building, and if so, which one are you to go to. Next, if at all possible, take a trial run to the business so that you are prepared for any detours, street repairs, etc. By doing this, you will also know how long it takes to get there. Take into account the hour of the day when you will be interviewing. Is it during the rush hour? If so, be sure to allow sufficient extra time, depending on the distance.

What *Is* Professional Dress?

This question usually brings up a lot of discussion and a lot of different ideas about what is or is not professional dress. Unfortunately, there is no one simple way to describe, for everyone, what it is. A few years ago, the concept of what is professional dress in the workplace underwent a dramatic change. In many companies, suits and ties were replaced with the "Dockers look" and "casual Friday" became a common trend. According to Kim Johnson Gross, coauthor of *Work Clothes: Casual Dress for Serious Work*, this change reflected what people were wearing outside the workplace to what they wear to church and the theater.[3] It appears that the concept of professional dress changes with the values of society as it has now in the twenty-first century. I am now hearing from some employers that the casual Friday dress code is being abandoned because their employees were abusing the privilege and coming to work in sloppy apparel; however, one thing remains constant: We definitely have a good idea of what is not professional. Also, what is appropriate for one industry or person may not be for another. Standards differ from profession to profession and industry to industry. For example, an automotive technician probably would not wear a pin-striped suit complete with vest and tie to apply for a job; likewise, a senior networking administrator or human resources manager would most certainly not show up for an interview in blue jeans. What is needed here are some general guidelines to use in determining what you should wear so that you are seen as a professional in your field and so that you make a good first impression.

First impressions stay with an interviewer, and like it or not, the clothes you wear create an image and play a major part in how you are perceived. Nemnich and Jandt say "The amount of care you take in dressing appropriately for your job interview equates in an employer's mind with how much respect you have for the proffered job."[4] Consequently, if you wish to be treated as a professional, you must create a professional image, and that is determined, in a large part, by how you dress.

Color

One of the important aspects of your dress is the color you choose. Some colors convey a message of power or energy, some are interpreted negatively, and some convey a positive impression. The most desirable for an interview would, quite obviously, be colors that emphasize the positive.

Many people assume dark colors are always safe, but this is not always true. Black is a power color, and wearing a completely black outfit could intimidate your interviewer. Think about it: Who is always dressed in black? Judges, ministers, and, of course, people in mourning wear black. If black is your very best color, and it is the only thing you have to wear, then add a brightly colored accessory to offset that authoritative tone. Blues are always safe colors, especially navy blue. Blues convey serenity and a sense of balance. Greys and burgundy are also considered to be good choices as they represent dignity. Brown is a very somber color and can project a mood of despondency, so again, if it is the only thing you have, give it a spot of cheer by adding another color. Pastels such as yellow, pink, and light blue do nicely as a contrast color, but not as a total look.

Other colors that could convey the wrong message are green and yellow—studies show that green and yellow are the least-liked colors of executives. In general, wear a color that looks good on you and one that isn't going to shock the person with whom you're interviewing.

Style

The second aspect of being professionally dressed is the style of clothes you wear. *Conservative* is the key. For women, it is especially important to convey the image of someone who is serious about her career. Avoid frilly blouses, see-through materials, or "little girl" clothes. If you want to be taken seriously, you must dress seriously. Authors Greenleaf and Schaefer say, "While looking good is important, leave your sex appeal at home. The key is to be attractive through class and attention to detail, not through revealing clothing."[5] A simple suit or skirt and jacket is always a good choice. Women should wear closed shoes with medium-height heels and flesh-colored nylons. Men should avoid casual sportswear, faddish apparel, and sneakers. Your socks should be the same color, or a close match, to your suit or pants and jacket.

Jewelry should be worn sparingly and should be either gold, silver, or good-quality costume jewelry. Anything that dangles and is heavy makes you look as if you're going out for the evening. We see many men today wearing a single gold or diamond earring in one ear. Even though this is more common and much more accepted than it was a decade ago, conservative companies still frown on this practice and do not view it as professional. Wearing an earring is certainly your decision, but you should be aware of the consequences. Obviously, multiple body piercings can be viewed as unacceptable when employees are required to greet and work with the public. Makeup and perfume can be inadvertently overdone, so moderation is essential. Remember that you are going to an interview, not on a date. Anything that could be labeled as "far out" can distract your interviewer and give him or her the opportunity to make assumptions that could hurt your chances of being offered the job.

An equally important factor in achieving a professional appearance is to choose apparel appropriate to the current season. Don't wear linens and lightweight fabrics in the winter or heavy woolens in the spring or summer. Cotton for shirts and blouses is a good selection year-round and always looks professional. White shoes, in most parts of the country, are not considered to be in good taste from September through April. The part of the country you live in has a definite bearing on what is appropriate. If you are new to the area and not sure what to wear, talk to a sales clerk in a well-known clothing store; he or she can usually give you some sound advice.

Don't observe what the employees of the company for which you are interviewing are wearing and use that as a guideline. It could be very misleading. They already have their jobs, so they are sometimes not concerned with what they wear on a day-to-day basis. Besides, everyone has "bad hair days" when they do not look their best. If it is a Friday, the employees might be wearing casual apparel if that is a custom at the company. Interviewers want to know that *you* know how to dress professionally. After you get the job, you can wear what the others are wearing. Even then, if you are interested in being promoted, you might want to dress "up," that is, dress as if you already have that position. How you present yourself is one of the criteria on which many promotions are awarded. For additional tips for men and women, see the interview attire and grooming suggestions in the Appendix.

Whether you're an automotive technician, a chief financial officer, or a graduate with a degree in Business Administration, the same rules apply: The employer is judging you as to how you would fit in as a potential representative of the company image.

INTERVIEW DAY CHECKLIST

Use the checklist below on the day of your interview.

○ 1. I have prepared a list of appropriate questions to ask the interviewer.

○ 2. I have my list of references ready should it be requested.

○ 3. I have reviewed my benefit statements and am prepared to sell myself to get the job.

○ 4. I have done the necessary research on the company with which I'm interviewing.

○ 5. My hair is cut, washed, combed, and styled in a professional manner.

○ 6. I have bathed and used deodorant.

○ 7. My makeup, jewelry, and perfume or after-shave lotion are not excessive.

○ 8. My fingernails are trimmed, clean, and if polished, have been freshly done.

○ 9. My teeth are clean, and I have used a mouthwash for fresh breath.

○ 10. My shoes are clean, neat, and unscuffed.

○ 11. My clothes are clean, pressed, and styled appropriately for the job for which I'm interviewing. I feel comfortable in them.

○ 12. I promise myself that I will not fuss with or rearrange my clothing, hair, etc. once I arrive.

○ 13. I promise that I will be myself whatever the circumstances of the interview.

○ 14. I will take extra copies of resumes, transcripts, and portfolios with me in case they ask for these.

○ 15. I have all the necessary tools to correctly and neatly complete the application form should I be asked to fill one out.

How Interviews Are Conducted

One of the factors that makes interviews stressful is that you really can't be sure of what to expect. What questions will be asked? How are you going to be treated? Are you going to get the opportunity to sell yourself? What can you do about a question you don't understand or feel you can't answer? Are you going to be tested? And on and on and on. It is always the unknown that is so scary. This is why doctors and hospitals usually "walk a patient through" a surgery before the actual operation takes place. They have discovered that if the patient knows what to expect, a lot of fear can be eliminated. Being interviewed is a little like being operated on, wouldn't you agree? So if knowing what to expect can minimize the fear of surgery, then it should work as well for interviewing. What then, can you generally expect to happen in an interview?

Before the Interview

In most instances, you will be asked to complete an application form before interviewing. This is a very good reason to be early for the interview. If your interview time is set for 10:00, be there at least by 9:45. Also, your interviewer will love you for this, especially if he or she has finished with the one before you a little early. Interviewers are always eager to get on with the next one, and there you are, all ready to go! Being early also gives you time to check your notes and your appearance one last time before you meet your interviewer. It allows you to enter the interview relaxed and ready.

Many employers prefer to test an applicant before the interview, particularly in technical fields. Positions in electronics, mechanics, computer programming and networking, drafting, graphics, and word processing require levels of dexterity and accuracy that can be measured by performance tests or paper-and-pencil tests. Some employers evaluate prospective applicants through psychological testing (such as general intellectual ability and personality tests).

According to Caroline Hsu in *The Testing of America*, "Personality tests are increasingly a part of American life . . . and they are big business. The tests are being used in hiring, promotions, and professional development by a third of U.S. businesses. . . . In the last three months, the online testing website *Tickle* administered 10 million personality tests."[6] The objective of psychological assessment is to obtain as pure an estimate as possible of characteristics such as intelligence, leadership potential, creativity, and so on. However, the downside of these tests is that they are highly controversial and widely criticized, are not regulated by state and federal agencies, and are very costly to the employer. However, as quoted by Ms. Hsu, John Putzier, a performance consultant and author of the new book *Weirdos in the Workplace*, "argues that personality testing can be enormously valuable, precisely because often what is revealed as a weakness may actually be a strength."[7]

Whatever the type of testing the employer uses, you should make every attempt to find out if you are going to be tested before the interview; the best way is simply to ask. You don't need any surprises the day of your interview; your anxiety level will be high enough.

Types of Interviews

There are as many kinds of interviews as there are companies and interviewers because everyone does things a little differently. How an employer decides to administer the interview could vary from a personal face-to-face interview to videotaping an applicant to possibly a lunch or phone interview. Still, interviews can generally be categorized in four basic types: the *group* or *committee/panel* interview, the *unstructured* (discussion) interview, the *structured* (direct) interview, and the *stress interview*.

The kind of interview you will have is sometimes determined by the size of the company. The larger the company, the more structured and extensive your interview is likely to be. Larger companies have personnel staff who are usually skillful and experienced at conducting interviews, whereas smaller companies usually lack personnel staff, and managers and supervisors conduct all interviews. When you interview with a manager or supervisor, you might find that you know more about interviewing than the person sitting behind the desk. Whatever you encounter, it is best that you leave the control of the interview in the hands of the interviewer. If you are too aggressive or come across as a "know it all," you could be seen as a usurper, a person who likes to infringe on others' authority.

Group or committee interview.   In a *group interview*, several people ask questions of the applicant; the interviewers could include those who will be your peers if you are hired. Sometimes, applicants are interviewed more than one at a time and are asked to react to one another rather than to the interviewer(s) so they can determine how well you function in a group or team setting. You should make eye contact with, and speak to, each individual.

In a *committee/panel interview*, generally used for hiring for high-level positions, one candidate is interviewed by several interviewers. Group or committee/panel interviews can be somewhat intimidating, but they needn't be. Do expect that you will have less time to think about your answers, but take your time answering and try to establish a degree of rapport with everyone in the group. Do not feel pressured to be totally spontaneous. Keep your answers short and direct. You might want to ask yourself why you are being interviewed in this way. Does it mean you are going to have more than one boss?

Unstructured interview.   The *unstructured interview* is rather informal. The person interviewing you will expect you to do most of the talking by asking broad questions and may respond only with "Yes?" or "Is that so?" This type of interview usually yields more information about the applicant's opinions and reactions. In this kind of interview, job seekers often talk themselves right out of a job offer. Remember to stay focused on facts about your ability to fill the position, your qualifications, and what you can do for the company. Don't let nervousness sidetrack you into talking about irrelevant topics or personal trivia.

Structured interview.   The *structured interview* is the most commonly used and involves a predetermined pattern of questions that will be asked. It is considered to be the most valid for employee selection, as the questions are usually drawn directly from the job description. The drawback to this type of interview is that it does not allow you to exhibit your personality, communication skills, or other attributes.

Stress interview.   The fourth kind of interview is the *stress interview*. It is designed intentionally to put you under stress so that your behavior and your responses and reactions can be observed. It is not often used, and when it is, the reason is usually because the position for which you are applying is a high-stress one. The reason could be merely that you are being interviewed by someone who enjoys watching others in the "hot seat." If you find yourself in a stress interview, you must stay calm, cool, and collected. The interviewer may deliberately and frequently interrupt you, remain silent for long periods of time, or ask stressful and intimidating questions. Try not to take anything personally. Just answer as well as you can and keep in mind that you are being tested to see if you can handle stress.

If you are applying for a job in another city and cannot meet with the interviewer in person, you could be asked to do a videotaped interview via a third party such as a career service agency. To prepare for facing a video camera, you might want to practice beforehand. Your nonverbal communication (discussed later) is especially critical in this type of interview because the camera picks up and clearly records your body language more than an interviewer might in a face-to-face interview. You should speak slowly and clearly and show enthusiasm, but don't overdo it. An employer might also require a phone interview either because an in-person interview is not possible or because the person interviewing you wants to see how you respond to questions over the phone. It is very important to prepare for this interview just as you would for a one-on-one. In addition to regular interview preparation, review the telephone tips in Chapter 3.

Lunch interviews are usually more casual than interviews done in the office, but don't forget it is still an interview. Follow the person doing the interview in whatever manner he or she sets. Whether it is casual or professional, don't order messy foods or alcohol. Also, even where it is still allowed, it is wise not to smoke.

For all types of interviews, always do your homework beforehand, show self-confidence, and trust yourself to manage anything that comes up tactfully and professionally. Then, no matter how *they* rate you, *you* will know that you did your very best.

How Employers Evaluate You

The one thing you can be sure of in any interview is that you will be evaluated. During the interview, an unconscious evaluation is taking place, and after the interview, a formal evaluation is done.

There are no standardized evaluation or rating forms that all employers use. Each company evaluates its applicants differently, according to the needs of the company or the division for which you would be working. The following list will give you an idea of some of the things that employers say they observe when interviewing a prospective employee.

- Attitude
- Personal appearance
- Ability to communicate, orally and in writing
- Skills, ability to perform the job
- Self-confidence, poise

- Enthusiasm for the job and the company
- Criticism of past employers, coworkers
- Goals, self-motivation
- Willingness to do whatever is asked (overtime, additional training)
- School grades/attendance
- Educational requirements of the job
- Pre-employment testing
- Leadership potential

Overall, your level of self-confidence will be measured by the way in which you present yourself to the interviewer. How you dress and speak, your mannerisms, and the validity and content of your answers to questions will all influence the employer's evaluation. A study done at UCLA a few years ago revealed that the impact of a performance was based 7 percent on the words used, 38 percent on voice quality, and 55 percent on nonverbal communication. So—do your research, prepare your answers to possible questions, and maintain a positive attitude; this will carry you through most interviews with a good rating.

What Employers Are *Really* Looking For

 side from the technical, administrative, or management skills that are called for in the job description, what kinds of personal and interpersonal skills do employers look for? Frequently, applicants who have the best skills, education, and abilities are not hired. Quite often, the applicant who gets the job is the one who doesn't have quite all of the required experience or education. Wondering why this is the case, I began to question employers about their reasons for choosing one applicant over another. What would be the strongest selling points for their choice?

I discovered that there is much more to winning the approval of the interviewer and getting the job than skills and education. Being chosen over other applicants has everything to do with your interpersonal skills, your personality, and how you conduct yourself in the interview. Employers are looking for the applicant who "fits" with the company and its culture. Many interviewers told me that they hired the person with whom they felt the most comfortable, the one that they believed would be a good "match" for their employees. Of course, this person also had to have most of the qualifications for the job to even get the interview, but the candidate was hired because he or she was *liked*.

By the time you're in the interview, the employer usually knows about your employment background, education, and skill level. Now the interviewer will try to determine if you are compatible with the company. This is one time when the old saying "Opposites attract" does not apply: employers are looking for someone who is *like* them. The decision to hire or not hire becomes very subjective, so the more you understand about what takes place in the interviewer's mind, what she is looking for or feeling about you, the better chance you have of getting the job. An excellent way to do this is to practice "reading" people so that you can respond accordingly. What kinds of cues is the interviewer giving you? What kinds of body language is he or she exhibiting?

Interpersonal Skills

The employer is interested in the occupational skills you have (such as typing 65 words per minute, programming, networking, repairing computers, designing a building, or doing a blood analysis) but he wants to know other things about you as well. Can you take criticism and direction? Can you follow instructions? Are you a good team player? Are you flexible and adaptable? Can you communicate clearly? Can you handle change and conflict? Are you reliable, dependable, and responsible? Do you have initiative? Can you "hit the ground running?" Can you take on additional responsibilities? Can you demonstrate uncompromising integrity, professional ethics, and morals? Over the past few years, we have observed the flagrant abuse of authority and the complete lack of integrity by many of our nation's top senior-level executives, so employers are screening applicants for these most important traits. Most important, over and above performing the duties of the position, are you going to get along well with your coworkers and your supervisors? Are you able to work with others who have different values, work habits, and cultures than you? Research shows that approximately 78 percent of all terminations take place not because the employee didn't perform the job well but because he or she had difficulty with coworker/supervisor relationships.

Personality

The employer's subjective evaluation also includes a determination on the kind of personality you have. In order to learn how to respond to the needs of the interviewer, you need to learn more about yourself. Gaining an in-depth understanding of your personality style has enormous value in your career, and learning how to use this knowledge will make you more successful in your job search. How perceptive or creative are you? Do you have warmth and diplomacy? Are you self-confident? Depending on the culture (personality) of the company, how closely does your personality match that of the company's current and most valued employees? If the company is filled with outgoing and gregarious people, you might not be a good choice if you are generally quiet and reserved—and vice versa. The other side of this coin is that *you* probably would not be happy working there. Before you begin interviewing, go back and review the exercises you completed in Chapter 1 on your interests, wants, and needs, and re-read the information I presented on employer testing, page 140. What kind of personality do you have?

You may disagree with judgments of this kind, thinking that it shouldn't matter what your personality is as long as you can do the job. But it does matter. In today's world of committees, teams, quality circles, and participative management, you must blend in and be cohesive with your coworkers and management. If you don't, you will not only be very uncomfortable and dissatisfied, you will not be a productive worker—and neither will the people who must work with you. Also, it is highly probable that you will not stay long at the job. Enlightened management knows this, and so to avoid constant and expensive turnover of employees, they do everything they can to hire the "right" employee.

Are You a "Match"?

How does the company determine if you are a "match"? Do employers have a crystal ball? No, they just practice a little detective work. From your answers to the questions they ask, they can learn a lot about your personality and character.

Questions such as the following can uncover things that your resume and cover letter don't tell them:

- Tell me about yourself.
- What kinds of things do you do for relaxation?
- What are the qualities that you consider necessary in a good supervisor?
- If you've ever had a disagreement with a former coworker or supervisor, how did you deal with it?

In addition, if your answers are in any way negative or derogatory, this might indicate that you have difficulty in relating to others or that you may not function well as a team member. Likewise, if you are not prepared with well-thought-out answers, the interviewer could draw a negative conclusion about your reliability: Maybe you can't be relied on to be prepared in the workplace either.

Conduct in the Interview

General Guidelines

Some basic rules of behavior and appropriate conduct should be observed during an interview. Remember, everything you do and say is observed by the interviewer and is important. These guidelines may seem trivial, but whether you follow them or not can determine the success—or failure—of the interview.

- Do not take notes during the interview unless the interviewer asks you to do so or you ask permission to do so. (*Do* make notes immediately afterward while it is still fresh in your mind.) It is sometimes intimidating for the interviewer to see you taking down what she is saying. If the company does not hire you, they could fear being accused of discrimination based on some innocuous statement made in the interview.
- Remember your interviewer's name and use it when speaking to her during the interview. Refer to the person as Mr. or Ms. unless invited to use their first name.
- When introductions are made, do offer to shake hands, whether the interviewer is male or female, and make it a firm handshake. Be careful of "bone crushers"! If your hands are prone to perspire, either use a moisture-absorbing powder or run them under cold water for a few minutes just before you go in to the interview. There is nothing more "dampening" to the interview than a wet, limp handshake.
- Do not smoke, chew gum, or drink anything in the interview. Even if a beverage or cigarette is offered, you are probably better off turning it down. Today, smoking is prohibited in most offices, chewing gum is very unprofessional, and trying to balance a drink while being interviewed is risky. The last thing you need is to spill something on yourself, or worse, the carpet.
- Wait for the interviewer to offer you a chair before you sit down.
- Present yourself as an honest person. Do not try to hide anything, and above all, *never, never lie!* It will only come back to haunt you later. A lie

that you "get away with" during an interview could come up after you're hired and cause you to be dismissed.

- Sell yourself! Your job as an interviewee is to sell your assets to the interviewer. If you wait expectantly for questions and dutifully answer them, you have done absolutely nothing to distinguish yourself from the other applicants.

- Bring the necessary paperwork that may be required: an extra resume, college credentials or transcripts, work portfolios, and a reference sheet. Do not, however, load yourself down with unnecessary props.

- Show enthusiasm and sincerity.

- Close the interview using the suggestions given in the section "How to Close the Interview."

Body Language

A very important part of your conduct in the interview is your body language. Sometimes it's not what you say in an interview but what you do that reveals many things to the interviewer. Volumes have been written about **body language**: the nonverbal messages that your facial expressions, physical stance, and gestures convey to a listener. Evidence shows that body language plays a vital part in communication. Experts estimate that as much as 65 percent of communication is nonverbal. Some common types of body language, such as the position of the body, hand gestures, and facial expressions, can enhance or even contradict what you actually say.

Facial expressions.   Eye contact is extremely important during the interview. Continually averting your eyes could be interpreted as a sign of guilt, lack of self-confidence, or even dishonesty. You don't want to stare either, so just glance away from time to time. Your mouth also is a major silent communicator. Smiling too much conveys an unnatural message, and pursed lips can be a signal of disapproval or a sour personality. You can gauge what is too much or too little by watching your interviewer and responding accordingly. Avoid touching any part of your face or hair during the interview: It can indicate nervousness or insecurity.

Body gestures.   Crossed arms can mean defensiveness, dissatisfaction, or simply that you've found a comfortable place for your hands. Since the meaning is ambiguous, it is best to keep your hands in your lap. The head tilted far up indicates superiority; if it's tilted down most of the time, you are giving a message of submission. A ramrod straight posture can signal inflexibility, and the other extreme, slouching in the chair, could be viewed as an indication of laziness or disinterest. The physical distance that you put between yourself and the interviewer is very important. Everyone has his or her "space," and you should not invade it. Don't lean on the desk or get too close when you are speaking with the interviewer. You will know if you've crossed that boundary by watching the person's eyes and stance. If you are too close to someone, she will usually move backward in an attempt to gain her space again.

Hand gestures.   Try to keep from gesturing too much with your hands, as it can be distracting or irritating to the interviewer. Avoid clenched hands—the "white knuckle" look—as it can reveal anxiety or fear. If at all possible, keep your hands in your lap and certainly not in your pockets. Keep them away from your face, hair, and clothing. Straightening your clothing or hair can be viewed as sign that you are unsure of yourself.

Questions You Could Be Asked and How to Answer

There is no guaranteed way to determine exactly what questions are going to be used. All companies have specific needs and will ask questions related to those needs. Some questions, however, are very likely to be asked and are worth taking the time to prepare for. Some questions can be very difficult to answer extemporaneously. If you are not prepared with appropriate answers, you could be eliminated.

There is a story about a young man who applied for a job that involved operating a small train station along a remote section of the track. The personnel officer of the train company interviewed him carefully to find out his qualifications. Then the officer said, "Well, it looks like you have the basic qualifications for the job, but we need somebody who can think on his feet and solve problems if they come up. Can you do that?" The young man replied, "Well, I think so." The personnel officer then said, "Okay, I'll give you a hypothetical problem concerning train operations, and you tell me how you'd solve it. Suppose you find out one day that there's a southbound train headed down the only track that runs by your station. You also find out that there's a northbound train coming up the same track. The engineers of the two trains don't know about each other. What would you do?"

The applicant replied, "I'd get on the telephone and call the stations down the track to notify them of the problem." Said the interviewer, "What would you do if you found out the telephone didn't work?" "Well," said the young man, "I'd use the telegraph." "Suppose the telegraph didn't work either?" "In that case," said the young man, "I'd run outside and throw the switch so that one of the trains would be shunted off onto the spur." The personnel officer said, "And what would you do if the switch was jammed?"

"Well, in that case I'd run home and fetch my brother." This left the interviewer somewhat puzzled, so he asked, "Why would you go home and get your brother?" To this, the young man replied, "Because he ain't never seen a train wreck before."

All joking aside, you do need to be prepared before tackling the interview process. The following 26 questions are likely to arise in interviews. Rehearse the questions and become very familiar with your qualifications so that you can show the employer how you can benefit the company.

1. *Tell me about yourself.* What does the interviewer want to know? That you took lessons in knitting or home improvement? Hardly. He is not looking for personal information. Don't begin by saying that you are single or married, that you have X number of children, or that you are looking for a job with security. Take this opportunity to present your key qualities and your interest in and understanding of the company; focus on the needs of the company and its people, not what *you* want in a job. Don't be tempted to rattle off your employment history. This is the opportune time to sell yourself, to give some of the benefit statements you wrote in Chapter 1.

2. *What do you see yourself doing three (or five) years from now?* This question helps the interviewer determine if you plan ahead or just live from day to day. She wants to know if you have goals. If you have never before set goals and written them out, now is the time to do so. Preferably, your answer should relate to a possible career with their company. This is also the perfect opportunity to ask what the career path for this position is. If you've done your research, you should have a pretty good idea of where you want to go with your career. Do not say you want to be in management without stating exactly what kind of management. So many people say this, thinking that it shows planning for the future; believe me, it does not. It just puts you in a category with those who have not done their homework.

3. *Which is more important to you, the money or the type of job you do?* With this question the interviewer attempts to find out whether you are "paycheck oriented." Be honest; explain that you, like everyone else, have to be concerned with the salary you receive because you have to support yourself (and your family, if that is the case), but that you also want a job that you enjoy doing. Some applicants make the mistake of answering this question by saying that money is not important to them. Usually, this will only lead the employer to believe that you will take a low salary.

4. *How would you describe yourself?* This is a tricky question, so be careful how you answer it. The interviewer is asking you to describe yourself in terms other than "I'm 28 years old; I have a degree in Business Administration," etc. She is looking for information about your personality, your character, and what kind of worker you are. This is a good place to mention your functional skills, flexibility, communication, and responsibility.

5. *What is your greatest weakness (or strength)?* Most job seekers are completely stumped by this question as they have never taken the time to consider what their weaknesses or strengths are. Also, some people find it very difficult to talk about themselves. As with all questions, avoid giving answers of a personal nature. An appropriate answer would be to mention one of your work-related weaknesses or strengths. Are you a workaholic, or too detail-oriented? Does your strength lie in the fact that you get along well with coworkers, or that you have excellent communication skills? These are the kinds of things interviewers look for. If you describe a weakness, mention as well that you are aware of the weakness and are working on correcting it.

6. *What motivates you to put forth your greatest effort?* Employers know that in order to obtain the most productivity from their employees, they must offer motivation. When the employer knows what motivates you, she can provide you with greater job satisfaction, and in turn will have a more productive worker. Are you motivated by money, rewards, recognition, responsibility, self-satisfaction? Think about this before you interview and prepare an answer in case you are asked. (For help, review the section on values in Chapter 1.)

7. *Why should I hire you?* If you are unable to sell yourself because you don't know the answer to this question, you could lose the job offer. Your research should have given you some information about the company and what they are looking for in an employee. Remember that all companies are looking for people who can help them make a profit. Show the employer that you have qualities that can help to save time and make money, and you have just provided a reason

to hire you. Use your benefit statements and be specific. Can you increase productivity, cut expenses, and build good customer relations?

8. *Why are you leaving your present job? Why did you leave your last job?* Stress reasons that put you in the best light, such as that you need more room for growth and advancement. Above all, *do not criticize your present or past supervisor or employer.*

9. *How do you feel about relocating?* Unless you absolutely do not want to relocate, or can't because of personal reasons, you can say that you are open to discussing relocating at the appropriate time. Things change, and it's always a possibility that, at a later date, you might want to relocate.

10. *What salary do you expect?* In the first interview, try to avoid this subject and do not ask about salary yourself. James E. Challenger, president of Challenger, Gray & Christmas, Inc., an outplacement firm, advises applicants not to bring up the subject of money in the first interview because it sends a message that you are more interested in yourself than in the job. However, if it is asked, you need to be prepared with an answer without locking yourself into a set figure. Answer that you believe the salary should be commensurate with your ability to perform the job and to contribute to the firm's goals, and that you would like to wait to discuss salary when you have the details of what the job entails. If you are pressed for an answer, never give a single figure; always give a salary range and add that you are willing to negotiate.

11. *Do you smoke, drink, or use drugs?* If at all possible, avoid any emotional reaction to this question. Whether you do, have, or never have, it almost always gets an emotional reaction. To some interviewers, this could signal guilt. An employer can legally ask questions of this nature and require pre-employment drug and alcohol testing as long as the reason is to determine whether an applicant can regularly and successfully perform the job for which the employer is hiring. If this question is asked, do not try to avoid answering. Just be prepared to give an honest answer.

12. *What do you do to reward yourself after a difficult and stressful day or week?* Employers are interested in whether you are able to relax and to lead a balanced life. Since they cannot ask this directly because it is of a personal nature, they get the information by asking the above question. They also want to know if you are pursuing additional education or training, or are an active, industrious person. Let's face it, you might be considered a not-too-motivated person if you sit in front of the television set from Friday through Sunday.

13. *I see you're not married. Do you live with a man (or woman)? Do you plan to have children? Do you have adequate child care?* It is illegal for an interviewer to ask any of these questions. As with all illegal questions, you should ask politely if this has a bearing in any way on your ability to perform the job. Or you could reply that you are willing to answer any questions about your skills and qualifications to perform the job and ask if this is required information for the job. You also might ask yourself at this time whether you would want to work for a firm that is so insensitive and ignorant as to permit questions of this nature. As to reporting them, go ahead if you want to, but remember the burden of proof is on you. It will be your word against the interviewer's, and the EEOC requires proof to prosecute.

14. *Have you ever been fired or asked to resign?* This is a legitimate question, but a very sensitive one, and how you answer could mean the difference between getting and not getting a job offer. If you have been fired, the most appropriate answer is, "Yes, I have, and as I look back on it, I realize that I could have done things differently. I learned a lot about myself from that experience." Then stop, and don't say any more unless you are asked for details. I've found that 95 percent of the time, you won't be. You probably have given the needed information, that *you take responsibility for your role in that termination*. One thing you must never do is bad-mouth a former employer or supervisor. You will not be hired if you do. No one wants to deal with an employee who is insubordinate, blames others for what happens, and does not accept responsibility for his or her actions.

15. *Why do you want to work for us?* "I don't know" or "I need a job" are not exactly the best answers. Your goal should be to convince the interviewer that this company is the one you really want to work for. You can do this by saying that you are sold on the company's product or service, or that from your research, you found that the company is employee oriented and offers opportunities for growth and advancement. Of course, you must do your research so that you have a factual answer, not a glib statement.

16. *How good is your health?* The interviewer is treading on thin ice with this question (see the section on legal and illegal questions below). You can answer it by saying that there is nothing about your health that will prevent you from doing the job for which you are applying.

17. *I don't believe you have enough experience for this position.* Now is the best time to sell your functional skills, and if it is possible for you to do so, offer to begin at a little lower salary with the opportunity to prove yourself in a given period of time. You might want to ask for more information about the job: "What would a typical day in this position require? What would I be doing?" Get specifics and then use this information to show that your skills are appropriate. Most important, do not be defensive or argumentative; be agreeable, but sell yourself *with other qualities*. The objective is to persuade the interviewer that you can do the job and that you are able to learn quickly. If you've just graduated from college, stress the fact that in school you had hands-on or practical experience in the skills, if your college did provide you with a self-paced, work-simulated environment to prepare you for the actual workplace. You can add that since you just came from a learning environment, you can be trained quickly, thereby saving the company time and money. Point out that you are perfectly capable of learning from a manual if one is available.

18. *I see you've been out of the job market for several years; do you believe your skills are still up to date?* This question is usually directed to people returning from parental leaves, schooling, or sabbaticals. Focus on the knowledge and experience you gained through home study or research, volunteer work, schooling, and home projects. Inform the interviewer that although you were not employed for a salary, you have been continually learning and improving your skills. Stress that you learn quickly and that you would be willing to take whatever courses or training is needed to upgrade your skills. As with the previous question, suggest that you are capable of learning from an instruction manual or tutorial, which saves time and money.

19. *Have you met your military obligations? Are you currently serving in the National Guard?* The first question is illegal and is not relevant unless a draft is in place.

The second one is legal, and if you are in the National Guard, just assure the interviewer that your service is not going to interfere with your ability to perform the job.

20. *Of all the jobs you've held, which one did you like the most? The least? Why?* Interviewers ask questions like this to determine if the work environment is suitable for you. Be careful not to mention reasons that would conflict with the environment or the duties of the job. Formulate your answer around general work-related responsibilities and avoid specifics.

21. *If you are hired, how long do you plan to stay with our company?* I've heard a lot of career counselors tell job seekers to answer "Forever." Now, both you and the interviewer know that this is very unlikely to be true, so don't say it. An appropriate and honest answer is simply to say that you will stay as long as it's mutually beneficial. According to research by Walker Information Global Network, a workplace consulting firm, and Hudson, a think tank, the average employee has 12 to 15 jobs during his or her lifetime and stays with a job an average of 3.6 years.[8]

22. *Can you work under pressure or deadlines?* If you can and are willing to do so, give examples from your background that demonstrate your ability to handle stress, pressure, etc. Be sure to include *how* you handled it.

23. *How do you feel about working for a female (male) boss?* Caution! This is a loaded question and could put a noose around your neck. The only correct answer is to say that either would be fine, that gender is not an issue but that it is the management or supervisory ability of the person that matters.

24. *What immediate contribution can you make to our company?* The keyword in this question is "immediate"; very few employees make an immediate contribution to any company. New employees always have some "down time": time to train and just to get familiar with the company. So, be honest and say this, but add that after this period, you will contribute to the company by being an industrious and reliable employee. Illustrate this with one of your benefit statements.

25. *Do you have any questions?* This is usually the last question of the interview, and unless the interviewer had completely covered everything, you should have some relevant questions to ask. Remember, *don't ask about salary, benefits, or things of this nature*. You're probably dying to know so you can decide if this job is for you, right? But, unless you have been made an offer, you don't have a decision to make at this time.

26. *Are you interviewing with anyone else?* This is not exactly a professional question because the interviewer is asking for information that he really has no right to. However, since you don't want to ignore it or not answer, you could say, "Yes, I am. I realized when I began my job search that I should market my skills to as many companies as I could. This would enable me to choose the one that is best suited to my job goals."

Behavioral Screening Questions

Over the past few years, behavioral interviewing has become a popular method with many companies for selecting candidates. The idea behind behavioral interviewing is that the candidate's past performance is the most accurate for determining future performance. Some interviewers use a method called

behavioral screening—asking questions that deal with actual past experiences in specific situations. When an interviewer asks this kind of question, she is looking for a brief description of a specific problem or situation, what you did about it, and what were the results. The interviewer does not want to hear your opinion or how you deal with things in general. Do not respond to the questions in the future tense, that is, what you *would do* if faced with a particular situation. Before you respond to this kind of question, take your time to think about your answer. You don't have to answer immediately. This kind of question gives you the opportunity to sell yourself, so take advantage of it. Consider preparing some answers in advance about previous experiences when you, for example, dealt effectively with stress, showed initiative in your job, worked cooperatively and successfully in a team, or demonstrated proficient customer service skills. A few examples of behavioral screening questions are:

1. Give me an example of a time when you needed to adjust to a situation quickly. What did you do, and how did it turn out?

2. Tell me about a situation when you had to stand up for a decision you made even though it was unpopular.

3. What has been your experience in working with conflicting, delayed, or ambiguous information? What did you do to make the most of the situation?

4. Solving a problem often necessitates evaluation of alternate solutions. Give me an example of a time when you actively defined several solutions to a single problem. Did you use any tools such as research or brainstorming?

5. The correct understanding of differences in personality can affect work decisions such as work assignments, employee motivation, and conflict management. Tell how your knowledge of personality differences has benefited your effectiveness.

Dealing with Difficult Questions

Sometimes in an interview, you are asked questions for which you may not feel you have an answer. To deal with these, first be sure that you clearly understand what the question is. Ask the interviewer to repeat or rephrase it for you, or ask for examples. Encourage the interviewer to tell you more by asking specific questions. If you still are not sure how to answer, ask for a few minutes to think it over, or ask if you can come back to it. If you simply do not know the answer, say so. It is far better to admit not knowing than to give an answer that makes a fool of you. Some interviewers will ask questions that they are pretty certain you would not know the answer to in order to see if you will try to bluff your way through them. This could indicate to them that you would do the same on the job, which could cause accidents, poor-quality workmanship, and unhappy customers. Remember, no one has all the answers.

Additional Interview Questions

Following are more questions you might encounter during interviews. To prepare, think about how you would answer them.

1. How do you feel about your present job?

2. How many hours do you feel a person should devote to a job?

3. What are some of the things about which you and your former supervisor(s) have disagreed?

4. What kind of people do you like working with? What kind do you find difficult to work with?

5. What are some of the things you would like to avoid in a job? Why?

6. How would you describe a good supervisor?

7. Which one of your accomplishments has given you the most satisfaction?

8. Do you have reliable transportation to and from work?

9. What one thing do others need to know about you in order to work effectively with you?

10. How do you define success?

11. What was your most rewarding experience in college?

12. Why did you choose this career?

13. What have you learned from your mistakes?

14. Are you planning to continue your education?

15. Are you willing to spend three to six months as a trainee?

16. Do you work better in a team or by yourself?

17. Have you changed careers in the past year?

18. If you were hiring a person for this position, what skills and abilities would you look for?

Your Turn to Question

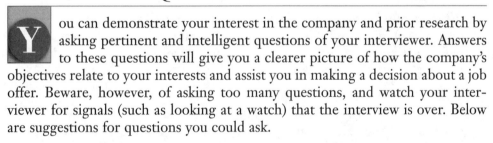 ou can demonstrate your interest in the company and prior research by asking pertinent and intelligent questions of your interviewer. Answers to these questions will give you a clearer picture of how the company's objectives relate to your interests and assist you in making a decision about a job offer. Beware, however, of asking too many questions, and watch your interviewer for signals (such as looking at a watch) that the interview is over. Below are suggestions for questions you could ask.

1. Can I answer any questions about my qualifications for this position?

2. Would you please describe the job duties for me? Do you have a copy of the job description I could see?

3. Do you have a formal training program? How long is it? Please describe it.

4. Is this a newly created position?

5. What type of education and experience do you most like to find in persons filling this position?

6. Was the person who previously held this job promoted?

7. Will I be responsible for supervising other staff? If so, how many?

8. How do you evaluate your employees? How often?

9. Could you describe a typical career pathway in your organization for an employee in this position?

10. How does today's economic environment affect your organization?

11. Do you have plans for expansion in terms of product development, services, new branch offices, etc.?

12. From your experience, what would you say are the company's greatest strengths?

13. How do you rate your competition?

14. What is your employee turnover rate?

15. Would you say that your company follows a chain-of-command-type management policy or one of a less structured, participative nature similar to MacGregor's Theory Y? (You may not want to use this question unless you have some basic understanding of management theories.)

16. How much involvement do your employees have in making decisions or setting policies and procedures?

17. How long have you been with this company, and what about it do you like best?

18. Will there be any further testing?

19. Will I be required to take a physical examination?

20. When will you be making your decision as to whom you're going to hire? May I call you on _____?

Questions Not to Ask

1. *Is this a union shop?* You should already know this from your research. It can also be a very threatening question to the interviewer if the company is not. You might be suspected of being a union organizer.

2. *What happened to the person who had this job before?* You are asking for personal information, and the question could sound antagonizing. Instead, rephrase it. See questions 4 and 6 in the list above.

3. *Will I have to work much overtime?* The interviewer will see you as a time-clock puncher.

4. *How much job security do you offer?* Job security is a myth—don't even mention it. Helen Keller said, "Security is mostly a superstition. It does not exist in nature, nor do the children of men, as a whole, experience it." This has never been more true than it is today with mergers, takeovers, outsourcing, and the total reorganization of many companies. Your security comes from within you.

5. *When will I get my first salary raise?* This question is totally inappropriate until you have been offered the position and have accepted.

6. *What is it that you people do at this company?* Believe it or not, applicants actually ask this question. Obviously, if you have to ask this, you are not in the running for the position. Do your homework so you know this before the interview.

7. *Can you afford me?* This question conveys a message of arrogance and over-confidence. It could be very insulting to the interviewer.

8. *What kind of benefits do you offer?* Any question related to salary or compensation, including benefits, is not appropriate until you have been made a job offer.

9. *If I'm asked to relocate, will the company pay for it?* You're assuming that you're going to get the job, so it is a premature question.

10. *How many people are you interviewing?* The answer to this question should really not be of concern to you. It might lead the interviewer to think that you are insecure or just plain "nosey."

Legal and Illegal Pre-Employment Questions

T he Equal Employment Opportunity Commission and two federal laws, the Civil Rights Act of 1991 and the employment provisions of the Americans with Disabilities Act of 1990, govern the questions that may be asked on application forms and in interviews. Employers who ask questions of an illegal nature leave themselves open to charges of bias and lawsuits. Read the following list to be aware of questions you do not have to answer.

- *Name:* It is legal to ask, for access purposes, whether the applicant's work records are under another name. It's illegal to ask if a woman is Miss, Ms., or Mrs. and to request the applicant to give a maiden name or any other name he or she has used. (Legislation: Title VII as amended by Equal Employment Opportunity Title IX.)

- *Address/housing:* It's legal to request a current address and phone number and how the applicant can be contacted if a phone number is not available. It is illegal to ask for past residences, length of residence at a particular address, and whether applicant owns or rents. (Legislation: Title VII.)

- *Age:* It is legal to ask age *only* if it is needed to show that applicant is old enough to work or serve alcohol. It's illegal to request a birth certificate or similar records showing age. (Legislation: Age Discrimination Act of 1967.)

- *Race/color:* Any inquiry about color or race is illegal unless it is done under the Affirmative Action program. (Legislation: Title VII.)

- *Sex:* Again, inquiries may be made only under an Affirmative Action program. The question is legal when it is job related, e.g., when hiring locker room or restroom attendants. (Legislation: Title VII and IX.)

- *Religion/creed:* There are no legal questions about religion or creed, religious customs, or holidays. (Legislation: Title VII.)

- *Marital/parental status:* Employers may ask these questions only after hiring and only for insurance purposes. It is illegal to ask questions of any nature regarding children, who cares for them, or if the applicant plans to have them. (Legislation: Title IX and VII.)

- *Relatives:* After hiring, employers may ask for the name, relationship, and address or phone number of a person to be notified in case of an emergency. Nepotism policies that have a disparate impact on one sex are illegal. (Legislation: Title IX.)

- *Military service:* It is legal to inquire about job-related experience in the U.S. Armed Forces, but illegal to request information on the type of discharge or for military service records.

- *Education:* Employers can ask about job-related education and English language skills only if they are required for the work to be performed.

Questions about nationality, racial, or religious affiliation of schools attended are illegal, as are inquiries as to how a foreign language ability was acquired. (Legislation: Title VII.)

- *Criminal records:* It is illegal to ask for arrest records involving no subsequent conviction. (Legislation: Title VII.)
- *Organizations:* It is legal to ask about organizational and professional affiliations that are job related so long as the information is not used to discriminate on the basis of race, color, etc. (Legislation: Title VII.)
- *Photographs:* After hiring, it is legal to request photos for identification or security purposes. (Legislation: Title VII.)
- *Work schedules:* It is legal to ask about willingness to work required schedules, but not to work specific religious holiday(s). (Legislation: Title VII.)
- *Physical data:* It is illegal to require applicants to give height and weight or other non-specified, non-job-related physical data. It is legal to ask applicants to prove their ability to do manual labor, lifting, and other physical requirements for the safe performance of the job. (Legislation: Title VII.)
- *Handicap(s):* It is legal to inquire about physical handicaps for the purpose of determining the applicant's capability to perform the job. (The burden of proof lies with the employer for non-discrimination.) It is illegal to exclude handicapped applicants on the basis of their type of handicap. (Each case must be determined on an individual basis by law.) (Legislation: Americans with Disabilities Act, Handicap Discrimination Guidelines of the Revised Code, Chapter 4112.)
- *National origin/citizenship:* All employers are required to have applicants (after hiring) complete the Employment Eligibility Verification (Form I-9), which is proof of citizenship or "intending citizen" (an alien who has been lawfully admitted to the United States). (Legislation: IRCA of 1986, EEOC, Title VII.)

Other questions that employers are advised to avoid are:

- Graduation date from grade school, high school, or college.
- Diseases or major illnesses for which the applicant has been treated.
- Hospitalization history, including mental health treatment.
- Prescription drugs being taken.
- Past treatment for drug addiction or alcoholism.
- Workers' compensation history.
- Whether applicant has ever filed for bankruptcy.
- Past garnishment of wages.

How to Close the Interview

 hen you are being interviewed, you let the person doing the interview take charge—up until the close, that is. During the interview, you do not interrupt, disagree with, or contradict your interviewer (even if it appears that he is inexperienced and is handling the interview rather badly). You can, however, influence how you are judged by the way you answer the questions, by being aware of your body language, and by the questions you ask. At the close of the interview, it is especially important that you get the information you need, so you should subtly and professionally exercise some control.

When you are asked if you have any questions, that's a signal that the interview is winding down. After you have asked your questions, you have the opportunity to make some important points. First, be sure to reiterate your strong points for the position; then ask if the interviewer has any questions about your qualifications. Finally, ask: When will a decision be made? Will you be contacted, or would it be appropriate for you to contact the interviewer? When would be the best time to call? Will there be second or third interviews? Will you be tested? The interviewer may not remember to tell you all these things, so ask now.

Always end the interview by asking for the job and thanking the interviewer for taking the time to consider you for the position. Many employers say that they hire the person who asks for the job. Reaffirm your interest in the company and the position.

Follow-Up After the Interview

When the interview is over, you wipe your brow, breathe a sigh of relief, and head for the nearest bar for a beer, right? Of course not! One of the first things you do is to find a quiet place and make some notes about the interview. How did you feel during the interview? Did you promise to provide more information if it was needed? If so, when? Did you forget to tell them something you felt would reinforce your credibility to do the job? Make a reminder to include it in your thank-you letter. Did you forget to ask something? Make yourself a note to ask when you call. Keeping records of and evaluating all interviews will help you to remember what took place, and later, to be able to make a sound decision as to an offer if one is made. You should also evaluate your performance. Take the time to reexamine your qualifications and your weak points. This time to recap is so important because after many interviews, the facts and your feelings will tend to blur. Don't trust your memory; jot it down.

After you've made your notes and done your evaluation, the last but most important follow-up to all interviews is to send a thank-you letter. A thank-you letter is a brief, well-written reminder that you are the best person for the job. Whether you want the job or not, and regardless of how the interview went, you should always send a thank-you to your interviewer(s). Send separate ones to each of your interviewers if there were more than one. As mentioned in Chapter 2, some hiring decisions have been made on this point alone.

One final note about follow-up: Even if you don't get the job, you should follow the rejection with a response. You can either call or write a short letter expressing your appreciation for the time spent with you and asking that you be considered for future openings when they arise. Sending a letter is best because job seekers do not often do it, so it sets you apart from your competition. Applicants who were turned down for the first position have often been called for a second one. In addition, if you were offered the job but turned it down, you should write a polite letter thanking the company for offering you the position and give valid reasons for declining. You want to keep your options open for future opportunities. Note: Go back and review the instructions for follow-up letters in Chapter 2.

What to Do Between Interviews

When you are looking for employment, you need to devote as much time to it as is possible. If you are unemployed, you should treat job hunting as though it were your job, giving it eight hours a day and no less than five days a week. If you are looking while you are holding a full-time job, you need to use all available time you have before and after work, during lunch hours, and on Saturdays. Many employers will meet with you on their lunch hour, after work, or on Saturday if you've given them good reason to do so—that is, if you've created a desire in them to consider you for a position they have open. The only way to acquire the job you want is to pursue it with all the energy, commitment, and determination you can muster. That means that you continue to search out job leads and openings and to arrange for interviews when you are between interviews. You do not sit by the phone waiting to hear from an interviewer who "almost promised" you the job.

Job seekers very often come back from an interview absolutely *positive* that they had the job because "the interviewer just the same as said so." Well, many times they didn't have it. Most interviewers are very positive during the interview and will give you strong indications that you are "the one." This may be because they do have an interest in you, and they want you to hold your options open for them *in case* they decide to offer you the job. Interviewers are also sometimes very inept at rejecting applicants face to face. Or it may be that at the time you were interviewed, you were the best applicant, but a subsequent interview may have produced another applicant who was better qualified.

So don't sit around waiting for a call. If you don't get the job, you are back to square one. You will have to get your momentum and morale up and your feelings of rejection down. So don't waste time sitting by the phone and checking the mailbox when you could be generating new job leads and interviews. The strongest argument in favor of keeping busy with your job search while you wait to hear is that your feelings of rejection will be minimized if you have another interview or offer pending when you get the "Sorry" call or letter.

Dealing with Rejection

Realistically, you usually do not get the first job for which you interview. You need to prepare yourself to accept the fact that you will have to deal with some rejection. Everyone has difficulty dealing with rejection. We often assume that there is something wrong with us, when in fact, there isn't. Ninety-nine percent of the time, rejection says nothing about you but more about the person who is doing the rejecting. In a job search, being rejected can be devastating unless you prepare yourself to handle it in a constructive manner. Here are some tips to help you.

Above all, don't take it personally.   Rejection has nothing to do with you as a person. The chances are, you didn't get the job because you didn't "fit" with the company because of some minor detail. If the employer didn't feel that you would fit in with the other employees, you probably *wouldn't* have. This can be a blessing in disguise because had you gotten the job, the possibility is very strong that you would not have felt comfortable and would have quit soon after taking it. That just wasn't the right job for you; yours is still out there waiting for you.

Find others who are job searching.   Either join a job search support group or establish one of your own. The employment section of your local newspaper publishes lists of activities, workshops, and support groups for all kinds of people looking for work. There is a lot to be gained from getting and giving help and support to others who are facing the same situation as you. You can give each other moral support and encouragement and exchange ideas about what works or doesn't work. You may even get job leads—all job seekers, when they are searching, uncover positions that do not apply to them.

Don't get sidetracked.   This is not the time to clean the garage or the hall closet, or to change the oil in your car. Devote your energy to finding a job.

Do your own footwork.   Don't sign up with an agency unless you have exhausted all possibilities. Even then, be very cautious because you are very vulnerable at this time and may be tempted to take a job that is not right for you. Besides, you have all the techniques right in this book that agencies use to find jobs, and maybe even more. Make more cold calls and get more information on what you are qualified to do and for which companies. The more you know about what employers are looking for in your field, the better you can sell yourself to them. Also, you could reap a double reward from this: In the process of getting information, you could acquire viable job leads.

Don't turn down any interview.   Even if the job looks like one that you wouldn't be particularly interested in, you just never know what might turn up. Also, the more you interview, the better you become at selling yourself.

Look at your job search as a positive, learning experience.   Every time you interview, get turned down, or talk to an employer about a job, you learn more about yourself and your capabilities.

Job searching is sometimes simply a "numbers game."   According to the law of averages, after so many calls, interviews, and "no's," you are bound to get a "yes." So just keep going!

Evaluating the Job Offer and Negotiating Salary

I received a phone call one day from a former student I had placed in an excellent position with a prestigious company. Julie said that it was a very good job, the employer was very good to her, and she was making more than an adequate salary, but she just wasn't happy. She said, "Carolyn, I need to come talk to you; this job is just not what I want. There is no challenge, and I'm not using the talents that I know I have. I guess I just didn't look at the job closely enough before I took it." Sound familiar?

This happens to many people. If you don't take the time to evaluate the job and the company in relation to your abilities and goals, you may become like the workers that Fredrick Herzberg, noted psychologist and professor at Case Western Reserve University, speaks of in his book *Work and the Nature of Man*. He says that most workers are in a sort of neutral world, neither satisfied nor dissatisfied. Do you doubt this? I challenge you—survey offices in any city in the

United States and observe how many workers display signs, posters, or pictures that say "Hang in there, it's only Monday," "I'd rather be fishing/camping/skiing," or "T.G.I.F. (Thank God It's Friday!)." Robert G. Allen, author of *Creating Wealth*, echoes the bumper sticker that reads "I owe, I owe, so it's off to work I go!" when he says that 20 million people go off to work each day to jobs they can't stand because they value security more than satisfaction.

How can you avoid being one of those 20 million? By taking the time to seriously consider the self-assessments you completed in Chapter 1 and comparing them to the job *before* you accept it. Evaluating a job offer is the final step in successful job searching and the key to job satisfaction. Many applicants accept jobs that are not right for them. After all, you've worked hard at doing all the "right" things to get interviews, and now you finally have an offer. Shouldn't you eagerly accept it? You can usually think of a thousand reasons why you should take it, but unfortunately, you probably haven't considered the reasons why perhaps you shouldn't. Often the only thing job searchers consider when given a job offer is the salary, and even then they usually accept less than what they are worth.

Only when you have matched the job offer to your self-assessment can you be certain that it is the right job for you. The "ideal job" is a match of several factors, not just the salary and benefits. If those factors are present, *then* it's appropriate to examine the salary and benefits.

Negotiating Your Salary

Before you attempt to negotiate with an employer for a salary, you must be certain that a solid job offer has been made. Once this has been established and you've decided you want the job, the next step—*before* you speak with the employer—is to learn as much as you can about how companies set salaries. Many factors determine the salary a company offers a prospective employee. A company may use the Job Worth system (sometimes called the Factor Comparison Method), the Market Worth system, the salaries of other employees within the company, the company's ability to pay, market demand, and sometimes, your last or current salary.

In the Job Worth system, each job in the company is assigned a point value. Points are awarded on the basis of the following criteria:

- Job responsibilities
- Minimum experience and training required
- Mental skill and knowledge
- Physical requirements
- Problem-solving skills
- Accountability

Everyone who fills this position will be paid exactly the same; in other words, the job has a certain salary value, and anyone occupying that position draws that salary.

If a Market Worth system is used, the salary will be commensurate with what the competition (the market) is paying, based on industry standards. Small- to medium-sized companies generally use this system. The market, and therefore the salary, will differ in different geographical areas, because it costs a lot more to live in cities such as New York City and Los Angeles than to live in, say, a small town in central Kansas.

The company's ability to pay is, of course, also a crucial factor in salary determination. Small and brand-new companies may not have the revenue of larger, more established companies so will offer non-monetary benefits instead of higher salaries. These benefits could vary from a free parking space to days off to flextime scheduling.

The company may use your last or current salary as a factor in their offer, but it is not always a fair judge of how much you're worth. You may have added educational and skill levels that were not required in that job.

Demand (as in market demand) is another possible factor. If the demand is high, meaning that there are too few qualified applicants to fill available positions, employers are more likely to offer higher salaries. The opposite may be true when the market is saturated with applicants.

You're probably wondering what to do with all this information. How is this going to help you with negotiating when you receive an offer? Now that you know the factors that determine salary, you can personalize your package for negotiation. To do this, you need information on the range of salaries in your geographical area, the skills required for the position, the market demand, and the "scoop" on the company. Guess what? You are going to do more research. Where? Here are a few places you can obtain salary surveys that contain comparative information on average wages across different occupations, regions of the country, and levels of experience:

- Annual State Occupational Guides.
- Publications such as your local newspapers and news and trade magazines (*U.S. News & World Report* is excellent).
- College placement offices.
- Peers and people you know who are in the field.
- *Are You Paid What You're Worth?* by Michael O'Malley, Broadway Books, New York.
- Recruiters and headhunters.

The Internet offers salary surveys at the following websites:

- www.careers.wsj.com
- www.bis.gov
- www.yahoo.com/society and www.yahoo.com/culture/organizations/professional
- www.yahoo.com/business and www.yahoo.com/economy/organizations/trade associations
- www.careersoncommand.com
- www.salary.com
- www.wageweb.com
- www.newslink.org
- www.dbm.com/jobguide
- www.careerbuilder.com (advice and resources)

When you know the salary ranges for your area, the skills required, the market demand, and the "scoop" on the company that has made you an offer, you're ready to assess your market value: what *you* are worth. Complete the forms on the next three pages and use them as a guide to help you determine the wage you can ask for.

DETERMINING YOUR PRICE TAG

Position Being Considered: _____

What are the skills and qualifications for this position? _____

_____

_____

_____

_____

_____

_____

_____

_____

_____

What did I find is the average salary for this type of job? _____

What are my skills and qualifications as compared to the average worker in this position? ___

_____

_____

_____

_____

_____

_____

_____

_____

_____

_____

_____

Based on the information above, I believe that I am worth $_____ in annual

(monthly, hourly) salary; therefore, I will request wages in the range of $_____ to

$_____.

YOUR BOTTOM LINE

What do you think you are worth? What is the job worth?
In Chapter 1, you evaluated the things that you value. Now is the time to determine if the job really offers the things you value—or the salary level you require. In the Needs/Interest area in Chapter 1 you answered some questions titled "What Do I Want?" You can now evaluate the job offer to see if the job offer provides those things.

YOUR BOTTOM LINE   _____ !

SALARY

_____ Hourly Wage

_____ Monthly Salary

_____ Annual Salary

QUALITY OF WORK LIFE

_____ Respect

_____ Scope of Responsibilities

_____ Professional Environment

_____ Coworker Compatibility

_____ Management Compatibility

_____ Advancement Opportunity or Career Path

_____ Time Off (Leisure Time)

_____ _____

_____ _____

_____ _____

_____ _____

_____ _____

_____ _____

_____ _____

BENEFITS

_____ Full Medical—Employer Paid

_____ Full Medical—with Copay

_____ Family Medical—Employer Paid

_____ Family Medical—with Copay

_____ Dental

_____ Vision

_____ Prescriptions

_____ Uniform Allowance

_____ Travel Allowance

_____ Cafeteria Plan

_____ Life Insurance

_____ Disability Insurance

_____ Pay for Time Not Worked/Overtime

_____ Retirement Plan

_____ Tuition Reimbursement

_____ Higher Salary if Some Benefits Waived

_____ _____

_____ _____

_____ _____

_____ _____

_____ _____

_____ _____

YOUR NEGOTIATING LINE

What will make you very happy? (Realistically)

Negotiating Line _____!

SALARY

_____   Hourly Wage

_____   Monthly Salary

_____   Annual Salary

QUALITY OF WORK LIFE

_____ _____

_____ _____

_____ _____

_____ _____

_____ _____

_____ _____

_____ _____

_____ _____

_____ _____

_____ _____

BENEFITS

_____ _____

_____ _____

_____ _____

_____ _____

_____ _____

_____ _____

_____ _____

_____ _____

_____ _____

_____ _____

Negotiating Your Benefits

Your compensation package includes benefits as well as salary. These, too, can be negotiated, so you should be prepared and not always accept what is offered if the benefits do not meet your needs. When deciding whether to reject or accept an offer, remember that money isn't everything, and that you can sometimes actually make *more* money with things like bonuses and stock options—anywhere from 30 to 60 percent of your base salary—than by receiving a higher salary. Some benefits, such as Social Security, unemployment, and workers' compensation, are mandated (all employers must offer them by law) and some are voluntary. Employers are realizing that in this day and age, they must change their thinking about what constitutes a benefits package. According to James E. Challenger, "companies are offering 'soft benefits' that are designed to give employees more time to work and enjoy life."[9] Employees now enjoy perks such as car washes at lunch and in-house dry cleaning. Some companies even adjust work schedules to allow early quitting times on Fridays during the summer. Other benefits that could be offered are relocation assistance, vacation time, stock options, club memberships, commissions, or even company cars. So before you negotiate with an employer for a benefit package, be aware of what you need and what is available to you. To begin, use the Benefit Checklist on pages 168 and 169. Your objective is to negotiate the maximum benefit package possible. Keep in mind that benefits can cost the employer anywhere from 15 to 40 percent of your salary, so it is in the company's best interest to keep those costs to a minimum.

Negotiating the Offer

Once you've established your worth and have the compensation package that you believe you deserve firmly in mind, the next step is negotiating with the employer. This step requires that you know what benefits you can bring to the company and are prepared to sell them. Why should an employer agree to give you the compensation for which you are asking? What are *you* offering in return? Why are you worth the figure you're asking? If you've done your research, you will know what the company's needs are and how you can help to fill those needs. Your job is to convince *them* you can fill their needs. Assure the employer that you are as interested in meeting the company's goals as well as your own. Keep your negotiation focused, and don't get sidetracked into talking only about your needs. You are paid a salary, not because you need a new computer, car, or house or because your kid needs braces, but because of your worth to the company. Do not under any circumstances let the negotiation become an adversarial (me against you) relationship by becoming argumentative or emotional. Your objective is a win/win solution.

Negotiating Tips

Ask for what you want (and negotiate if your request is declined).   If you don't ask, you may never get what you want, and more likely, you will get your bottom line (or lower). Be comfortable with silence. The person with the least tolerance of silence will attempt to fill the void by speaking—many times by offering to compromise.

If the proposed salary is too low, try to negotiate other ways to achieve both your goals and those of the prospective employer.   Be flexible: Introduce ways besides salary that will achieve both your goals and those of the prospective employer. You might want to negotiate the benefit package. For example, if you don't need the medical insurance and it costs the company $200 per month, decline coverage and ask for half of the premium to be added to your salary—a $100 increase for you and a $100 savings for the company. You might propose that the employer enlarge the job to give you more latitude in salary range. If you are going to do more than the current job description, a higher salary is appropriate.

Don't let the employer negotiate your salary down with non-monetary perks. Accept this only if the perks are ones that you place a high value on and would be happy with.

Avoid providing a specific salary figure, if possible, until the full negotiation of the position and other factors have been resolved.   Don't be the first to give a definitive figure; ask for the salary range of that position. If pressed, say that you believe your qualifications probably place you somewhere between the midpoint and maximum salary range and resell your best features again at this time. Understanding that there is a "going rate" range for similar personnel in the workforce and knowing what that range is lets you state a figure at the midpoint or higher level.

If asked, discuss your current salary honestly.   Sometime during the negotiating process, you may be asked a question about your current or most recent salary. How you answer this question could be a strong deciding factor in the salary offered you by the interviewer. Be truthful when you give them a figure, of course, and be sure to include your non-monetary compensation in addition to your base salary.

Know the benefits available in the workplace.   For example, some companies offer six paid holidays a year, and others may offer eight or more. Some offer one week of vacation with pay after one year, others may offer two weeks after a year. Some offer only a maximum of two weeks of vacation no matter how long you work for the company, while others allow you to take additional weeks of paid vacation per year after a certain number of years of employment. Not all health plans cover what you need. For example, some require you to use the plan's doctors, others allow you to use the plan's doctors at one rate (plan pays 100 percent) or to use doctors outside the plan at another rate (60/40—the plan pays 60 percent, you pay 40 percent). Keep in mind the benefits you want, including what kind of flexibility you want in a medical plan.

Read about employee benefits at the library. I recommend *The Handbook of Employee Benefits* by Jerry S. Rosenbloom. While you're there, also see Michael O'Malley's book *Are You Paid What You're Worth?* for some excellent tips on negotiating salaries, benefits, bonuses, and raises.

Negotiate from a position of strength and with enthusiasm.   How do you do this? Simple: Sell the employer on the idea that you are the best solution to the company's problems. If the employer has offered you the job, it has made the decision that you are the number one choice. Having selected you as number one, the employer will negotiate, to a point, to hire you rather than settle for their second or third choice. This gives you an advantage and a strong negotiating position. If you express your enthusiasm for the position and resell your abilities to meet the employer's needs, you will indeed be negotiating from a position of some power.

Have your completed Bottom Line and Negotiating Line checklists available when negotiating.   With this information readily available to you, you can usually make an immediate decision to accept the position or not. If you are not completely sure, the alternative is to say "I very much appreciate this offer, I believe it is an exciting opportunity for me, and I would like to think it over. If it's acceptable to you, may I call you tomorrow with my answer?" If the offer is too low, you can renegotiate by saying something such as "I am really thrilled with your offer and am highly motivated to work for your company; I know I can do an excellent job for you. However, I would have difficulty meeting my financial needs at the proposed salary. With school loans and other financial obligations, I need a salary of around $_____$. Would it be possible to meet again and take another look at the salary to see if we can somehow reach a position where I could help you to meet your needs and, at the same time, still meet my financial obligations?"

Be gracious.   Allow the employer to feel that he or she has won some compromises. "You've got to live with these people after you join them," says Scott Kingdom, managing director of the Chicago office of Korn/Ferry, the nation's biggest headhunting firm.[10]

Additional Considerations

In addition to the salary and benefits, a few other things warrant your attention. Are the company itself, the physical environment, and the personnel what you are looking for in a job?

- *The company:* Is it large or small, new to the community or an older, respected and reliable organization? Is the company progressive? Is the industry that it's in expanding or receding? Does the company have a policy manual (or written statements) regarding its policies on employee vacations, terminations, and working conditions?

- *The physical environment:* Where is the company located? Is it in a "better" part of town or in an inconvenient or even dangerous area? What do the buildings, furnishings, and equipment reflect: pride or indifference? Where will you be working: in the back of the building away from everyone, or up front where the action is? Where would you like to be?

- *The people:* What kind of people work for this company? Are they primarily of one age group, and is it yours? Who is going to be your immediate supervisor? Have you met this person and does your intuition tell you that you could work comfortably with him or her? In your interactions with this company during pre-interview and interview visits, how were you treated? Were you made to feel at ease and welcome? How did the employees interact with each other? How would you describe the company and the people, and will you be happy and productive working with these people?

- *The job:* How is this job going to affect your personal life? Is it going to require that you be away from home frequently, possibly on weekends, limiting your time with your family and friends? Do you know exactly what you will be doing during the day? Where does this position lead? What are your chances for promotion, transferring to other departments, and learning new skills?

Make the decision to accept or not accept a job offer based on all of the forgoing items. This decision is a vital one that will affect your life, your happiness, and your well-being. You should not make it hastily without carefully considering all the ramifications. If you've prepared an error-free resume and cover letter, have studied the tips on how to interview effectively, and have matched the job to your personal assessment of values and needs, you are well on your way to getting your ideal job with an ideal compensation package. The bottom line is, only *you* can decide whether or not the job is right for you.

EMPLOYEE BENEFIT CHECKLIST

- ○ Health Plan
  - _____ Employee Only—Company Paid
  - _____ Copay Premium for Employee
  - _____ Family
  - _____ Type _____ PPO _____ HMO _____ Other
  - _____ Dental
  - _____ Vision
  - _____ Rx Plan
  - _____ Wellness (Physical Exams)
- ○ Life Insurance
  - _____ Times _____ Year's Salary
  - _____ Additional Coverage Available
- ○ Disability Income Plan
- ○ Dependent Card—Child Care Assistance
- ○ Employee Assistance Programs (EAPs)
- ○ Payment for Time Not Worked/Overtime
  - _____ Vacation Policy
  - _____ Paid Holidays
  - _____ Comp Time
  - _____ Overtime Compensation
  - _____ Personal Leave of Absence (w/o pay)
  - _____ Funeral Leave
  - _____ Jury Duty
  - _____ Military Leave
  - _____ Inclement Weather Absences (office closed down)
  - _____ Sick Leave
- ○ Retirement Plans
  - _____ Profit Sharing Plans
    - _____ 401(k) Plans

(continued)

EMPLOYEE BENEFIT CHECKLIST Continued

_____ SEP (Simplified Employee Pension)

_____ Keogh Plans

_____ Employee Stock Option Plans (ESOPs)

- Pay Raises _____ Annual _____ Other _____ Merit _____ Negotiated

- Cafeteria Plan

  _____ Pretax Savings of Medical Premiums/Child Care/Adult Care

- Pay Status

  _____ Exempt Only basis for exemption from being paid overtime is if you are classified as:

    _____ Executive (Managers)

    _____ Administrative (for those who carry out the policies of the company)

    _____ Outside Sales

    _____ Computer Related (primarily programmers and systems analysts)

    _____ Professional (requires advanced degrees—teachers, lawyers, artistic endeavors)

- Pay Periods

  _____ Monthly

  _____ Biweekly

  _____ Twice a Month

- Salary/Wages

  $_____ Hourly

  $_____ Biweekly/Twice a Month

  $_____ Monthly

  $_____ Annually

- Travel

  _____ If you have to travel on behalf of your employer, are you compensated for using your car? (approximately 36 cents per mile)

- Tuition Assistance (for job-related courses)

- Other Benefits

  _____ _____

  _____ _____

  _____ _____

NOTES

1. Todd E. Van Hoosear, April 14, 1995, [online]. Available e-mail: vanhoose@gdl.msu.edu.

2. Mary B. Nemnich and Fred E. Jandt, *Cyberspace Job Search Kit 2001–2002 Edition, The Complete Guide to Online Job Seeking and Career Information* (Indianapolis, IN: JIST Publishing, 2001), 74–76. Reprinted by permission.

3. Kim Johnson Gross, *Work Clothes: Casual Dress for Serious Work* (New York: Knopf, 1996).

4. Nemnich and Jandt, p. 215.

5. Clinton T. Greenleaf III and Stefani Schaefer, *Attention to Detail: A Woman's Guide to Professional Appearance and Conduct* (Chesterland, OH: Greenleaf Enterprises, 2000), p. 12.

6. Caroline Hsu, The Testing of America, *U.S. News & World Report* (September 20, 2004): 67.

7. Caroline Hsu, Science & Society, *U.S. News & World Report* (September 20, 2004): 68.

8. Charting Your Own Course, *U.S. News & World Report*, Career Guide 2001 (November 6, 2000): 56.

9. James E. Challenger, Job Decision Isn't Just About the Money, January 16, 2000 [online]. Available: www.suntimes.com/output/challenger/chat.

10. How to Negotiate, *U.S. News & World Report* (November 1, 1999): 92.

Appendix

Postal Service Guidelines

The U.S. Postal Service offers these guidelines to ensure that your mail gets delivered quickly and accurately.

Write or type envelopes in all capital letters using no commas.

Always use your return address.

Attention line always goes above the firm name.

The delivery address line includes either the street address, the P.O. box number, rural route number, or the highway contract route number.

Indicate whether or not it's N, S, E, or W.

Include the RM (room), STE (suite) or APT (apartment) number.

The last line is reserved solely for the city, state, and ZIP code.

Use the ZIP code, and if you know the ZIP + 4 code, use that.

STATE ABBREVIATIONS

Alabama AL	Louisiana LA	Ohio OH
Alaska AK	Maine ME	Oklahoma OK
Arizona AZ	Maryland MD	Oregon OR
Arkansas AR	Massachusetts MA	Pennsylvania PA
California CA	Michigan MI	Puerto Rico PR
Colorado CO	Minnesota MN	Rhode Island RI
Connecticut CT	Mississippi MS	South Carolina SC
Delaware DE	Missouri MO	South Dakota SD
District of Columbia DC	Montana MT	Tennessee TN
Florida FL	Nebraska NE	Texas TX
Georgia GA	Nevada NV	Utah UT
Hawaii HI	New Hampshire NH	Vermont VT
Idaho ID	New Jersey NJ	Virginia VA
Illinois IL	New Mexico NM	Washington WA
Indiana IN	New York NY	West Virginia WV
Iowa IA	North Carolina NC	Wisconsin WI
Kansas KS	North Dakota ND	Wyoming WY
Kentucky KY		

STANDARD ABBREVIATIONS

Avenue AVE	Expressway EXPY	Road RD
Boulevard BLVD	Freeway FWY	Square SQ
Circle CIR	Lane LN	Street ST
Court CT	Parkway PKY	Turnpike TPKE

Figuring Monthly Income and Expenses

Before you speak with an employer about a salary, you should be fully aware of how much it costs you to live each month. Most people have very little idea how much they spend each month or why they run out of money before they run out of month. Rather than having a budget plan for paying bills first and then paying for entertainment and non-necessities, people often do the reverse. In order to meet your financial obligations, you must know what your income and expenses are and budget accordingly.

Using the Income and Expense form provided, or one that you prefer, figure out the salary you need to be able to live comfortably and to pay your bills. In the section for non-fixed expenses, inflate your figures rather than using a minimum amount. Allow for more rather than fewer expenses, so that if you do incur extra expenses, you'll have the money to pay for them. If extra is left over at the end of the month, put it in your savings account or buy something you've been wanting. It's better to have a nice surprise at the end of the month rather than a rude awakening when you discover that you need to fix your car or buy school supplies for your child—and you've already spent the money.

TIPS FOR MANAGING YOUR BUDGET

- *Keep track of everything you spend.* This is the area where most people get into trouble; they simply do not realize how much they're spending on trivial, unnecessary items. Ask for receipts for everything you buy. It is also the area over which you have the most control. If you keep track, you'll be able to honestly see your spending trends and where you can cut down if need be.

- *Set goals for extras.* If you want new clothes, DVDs, and so on, plan their purchase. Look ahead to a bonus, commission, or tax refund and earmark the extra money for your purchases. Don't fool yourself into thinking you'll manage by working overtime, cutting down on food, or going without your fun money. You won't!

- *Save money through wise shopping, do-it-yourself projects, and finding free events for entertainment.* Check local libraries and community centers for free shows, musicals, workshops, and holiday events. When you see something you want, before buying it, stall. Walk around the store or mall for 20 minutes, get a cup of coffee, do anything that will give you time to think about it and to check your budget (which you should carry with you when you shop). Do you really need it? Can you afford it? Is it really a bargain? Learn how to do your own hair, change the oil in your car, upholster your frayed couch or chair, or fix that broken door, etc.

- *Examine your thinking.* How you feel about money affects how and what you buy or save. Where do you want to be six months or a year from now? Develop a money consciousness. If you are not truly serious about changing your spending habits, paying your bills on time, and getting the things you know you deserve when you can afford them, all the tips in the world won't help you. If you are serious and committed to living responsibly, go to the next page and complete your Income and Expense sheet.

MONTHLY INCOME AND EXPENSE FORM

MONTHLY INCOME

Wages, salary, tips $ _____

Alimony, child support   _____

Dividends from stocks, mutual funds, etc.   _____

Interest on savings accounts, bonds, CDs, etc.   _____

Social Security benefits   _____

Pensions   _____

Other income   _____

TOTAL MONTHLY INCOME $ _____

FIXED EXPENSES

Savings $ _____

Rent/mortgage payment   _____

Utilities   _____

Telephone, Internet, cable, etc.   _____

Insurance (health, home, life, auto)   _____

Taxes (income, real estate)   _____

Installment payments (credit cards, car,
    department store accounts, etc.)   _____

Other installment loans (school, etc.)   _____

Subscriptions/memberships   _____

Medical (doctors, medicines, etc.)   _____

Child care   _____

Other   _____

TOTAL FIXED EXPENSES $ _____

(continued)

MONTHLY INCOME AND EXPENSE FORM Continued

NON-FIXED (FLUCTUATING) EXPENSES

Food $ _____

Household services/expenses _____

Transportation/car maintenance _____

Clothing _____

Furnishings/equipment _____

Personal care (grooming, cosmetics) _____

Recreation/entertainment _____

Gifts/contributions _____

Other _____

TOTAL NON-FIXED EXPENSES $ _____

TOTAL MONTHLY EXPENSES $ _____

TOTAL MONTHLY DISCRETIONARY INCOME*

Total monthly income $ _____

Minus total monthly expenses _____

Equals your NET CASH FLOW $ _____

*This amount reflects the amount of money you have available to put in savings or to spend on extras.

POST-INTERVIEW SELF-EVALUATION

1. Was I punctual, even early, for my interview? If not, why not?

_____
_____
_____
_____

2. Was my appearance appropriate and above reproach? Are there any areas that need improvement?

_____
_____
_____
_____

3. How would I rate my handshake?

_____
_____
_____
_____

4. What questions were asked of me that I feel I didn't answer adequately? How could I improve on them?

_____
_____
_____
_____

5. Was I relaxed, self-confident, and friendly?

_____

6. Did I sell myself with marketable skills applicable to the job for which I was applying? If not, should I rewrite my marketing appraisal?

_____
_____
_____
_____

(continued)

POST-INTERVIEW SELF-EVALUATION Continued

7. How would I rate my communication (oral and written) before and during the interview? If it needs improvement, how am I going to correct this?

_____

_____

_____

_____

8. What kind of body language did I convey to the interviewer? Was it open and friendly?

_____

_____

_____

_____

9. Were there things I forgot to tell the interviewer or to ask the interviewer? (Include them in your thank-you letter or follow-up call.)

_____

_____

_____

_____

_____

_____

_____

_____

_____

10. Am I scheduled for a second interview? (If so, write the date, time, location, and the name of the interviewer.)

_____

_____

_____

_____

ATTIRE/GROOMING TIPS

FOR MEN

1. Wear a long-sleeved shirt.
2. Make sure your tie is the current fashion. Don't wear a tie with funny sayings or cutesy pictures on it, or a bow tie. Best choices are solid colors, polka dots, foulard, or paisley. Patterned ties should be worn with solid-colored shirts.
3. Tuck in your shirttail and make sure your tie is not showing below the back of your collar.
4. Don't have things bulging in your pockets or keys dangling from a chain on your belt.
5. Don't wear a pocket handkerchief.
6. Do wear a belt in either brown, cordovan, or black.
7. If you wear an overcoat or hat, leave it in the outer office.
8. If you have facial hair, have it cut in an acceptable style. Make sure it is well trimmed and groomed.
9. Wear a watch.
10. Coordinate the colors of your suit, tie, shirt, socks, and shoes.
11. Beware of wearing too much aftershave, but do be certain you have good personal hygiene.

FOR WOMEN

1. Choose a hairstyle that will convey moderation and confidence; it should be modern and stylish.
2. If you carry a briefcase, don't carry a purse. If you carry a purse, clean it out before the interview.
3. Always wear a slip and be sure that it comes to above your skirt hemline.
4. Don't wear open-toed sandals or very high-heeled shoes.
5. Wear a skirt or dress with the hemline at or below the knees, even if the current rage is short skirts.
6. Always wear stockings, and they must be run-free. Bring an extra pair in case of an accident.
7. Don't wear pants: Even though they may be acceptable for work, it's risky to wear them to an interview. Research shows that women are viewed more favorably when dressed in a skirt or dress.
8. Wear a watch.
9. Don't wear any flirtatious or overly feminine clothes, and choose accessories that accentuate your clothing.
10. Check the heels of your shoes for scuff marks, and polish them if necessary.
11. Don't overdue fragrances (perfume), but make certain you have good personal hygiene.

HOW TO TIE A TIE

THE WINDSOR KNOT

Wide and triangular—for widespread shirt collar

 1 Start with wide end of tie on your right and extending a foot below narrow end.

 2 Cross wide end over narrow and bring up through loop.

 3 Bring wide end down, around behind narrow, and up on your right.

 4 Then put down through loop and around across narrow as shown.

 5 Turn and pass up through loop and . . .

 6 Complete by slipping down through the knot in front. Tighten and draw up snug to collar.

THE FOUR-IN-HAND KNOT

Long and straight—to complement a standard shirt collar

 1 Start with wide end of tie on your right and extending a foot below narrow end.

 2 Cross wide end over narrow, and back underneath.

 3 Continue around, passing wide end across front of narrow once more.

 4 Pass wide end up through loop.

 5 Holding front of knot loose with index finger, pass wide end down through loop in front.

 6 Remove finger and tighten knot carefully. Draw up tight to collar by holding narrow end and sliding knot up snug.

(continued)

HOW TO TIE A TIE Continued

THE HALF-WINDSOR KNOT

Medium symmetrical triangle—for standard shirt collars

1 Start with wide end of tie on your right and extending a foot below narrow end.

2 Cross wide end over narrow part and turn back underneath.

3 Bring up and turn down through loop.

4 Pass wide end around front from left to right.

5 Then, up through loop.

6 And down through knot in front. Tighten carefully and draw up to collar.

THE BOW TIE

Long and straight—to complement a standard shirt collar, but not recommended for interviews

1 Start with end in left hand extending 1-1/2" below that in right hand.

2 Cross longer end over shorter end and pass up through loop.

3 Form front loop of bow by doubling up shorter end (hanging) and placing across collar points.

4 Hold this front loop with thumb and forefinger of left hand. Drop long end down over front.

5 Place right forefinger, pointing up, on bottom half of hanging part. Pass up behind front loop and . . .

6 Push resulting loop through knot behind front loop (see illustration). Even ends and tighten.

U.S. Department of Justice
Immigration and Naturalization Service

OMB No. 1115-0136
Employment Eligibility Verification

Please read instructions carefully before completing this form. The instructions must be available during completion of this form. ANTI-DISCRIMINATION NOTICE. It is illegal to discriminate against work eligible individuals. Employers CANNOT specify which document(s) they will accept from an employee. The refusal to hire an individual because of a future expiration date may also constitute illegal discrimination.

Section 1. Employee Information and Verification. To be completed and signed by employee at the time employment begins

Print Name:	Last	First	Middle Initial	Maiden Name

Address	*(Street Name and Number)*		Apt. #	Date of Birth *(month/day/year)*

City		State	Zip Code	Social Security #

I am aware that federal law provides for imprisonment and/or fines for false statements or use of false documents in connection with the completion of this form.

I attest, under penalty of perjury, that I am (check one of the following):
☐ A citizen or national of the United States
☐ A Lawful Permanent Resident (Alien # A _____)
☐ An alien authorized to work until _____ /_____ /_____
  (Alien # or Admission # _____)

Employee's Signature	Date *(month/day/year)*

Preparer and/or Translator Certification. *(To be completed and signed if Section 1 is prepared by a person other than the employee.) I attest, under penalty of perjury, that I have assisted in the completion of this form and that to the best of my knowledge the information is true and correct.*

Preparer's/Translator's Signature	Print Name

Address *(Street Name and Number, City, State, Zip Code)*	Date *(month/day/year)*

Section 2. Employer Review and Verification. To be completed and signed by employer. Examine one document from list A OR examine one document from List B and one from List C as listed on the reverse of this form and record the title, number and expiration date, if any, of the document(s)

	List A	OR	List B	AND	List C
Document title:					
Issuing authority:					
Document #:					
Expiration Date *(if any)*:	__ / __ / __		__ / __ / __		__ / __ / __
Document #:					
Expiration Date *(if any)*:	__ / __ / __				

CERTIFICATION—I attest, under penalty of perjury, that I have examined the document(s) presented by the above-named employee, that the above-listed document(s) appear to be genuine and to relate to the employee named, that the employee began employment on *(month/day/year)* **____ / ____ / ____ and that to the best of my knowledge the employee is eligible to work in the United States. (State employment agencies may omit the date the employee began employment).**

Signature of Employer or Authorized Representative	Print Name	Title

Business or Organization Name Address *(Street Name and Number, City, State, Zip Code)*	Date *(month/day/year)*

Section 3. Updating and Reverification. To be completed and signed by employer

A. New Name *(if applicable)*	B. Date of rehire *(month/day/year)* *(if applicable)*

C. If employee's previous grant of work authorization has expired, provide the information below for the document that establishes current employment eligibility.

Document Title: _____   Document #: _____   Expiration Date (if any): ____ / ____ / ____

I attest, under penalty of perjury, that to the best of my knowledge, this employee is eligible to work in the United States, and if the employee presented document(s), the document(s) I have examined appear to be genuine and to relate to the individual.

Signature of Employer or Authorized Representative	Date *(month/day/year)*

Form I-9 (Rev. 11-21-91) N

All employers are required by the U.S. Department of Justice's Immigration and Naturalization Service to verify their employees' eligibility for employment by having the employees complete an I-9 form. If the employers do not submit this information within two weeks after the hire date, they can be fined a substantial amount of money. If you are working in the United States on a green card, work visa, or under any special circumstance, you need to be prepared to submit the necessary documents to prove your eligibility.

U.S. Department of Justice
Immigration and Naturalization Service

OMB No. 1115-0136
Employment Eligibility Verification

INSTRUCTIONS
PLEASE READ ALL INSTRUCTIONS CAREFULLY BEFORE COMPLETING THIS FORM

Anti-Discrimination Notice. It is illegal to discriminate against any individual (other than an alien not authorized to work in the U.S.) in hiring, discharging, or recruiting or referring for a fee because of that individual's national origin or citizenship status. It is illegal to discriminate against work eligible individuals. Employers **CANNOT** specify which document(s) they will accept from an employee. The refusal to hire an individual because of a future expiration date may also constitute illegal discrimination.

Section 1—Employee. All employees, citizens and noncitizens, hired after November 6, 1986, must complete Section 1 of this form at the time of hire, which is the actual beginning of employment. **The employer is responsible for ensuring that Section 1 is timely and properly completed.**

Preparer/Translator Certification. The Preparer/Translator Certification must be completed if Section 1 is prepared by a person other than the employee. A preparer/translator may be used only when the employee is unable to complete Section 1 on his/her own. However, the employee must still sign Section 1 personally.

Section 2—Employer. For the purpose of completing this form, the term "employer" includes those recruiters and referrers for a fee who are agricultural associations, agricultural employers, or farm labor contractors.

Employers must complete Section 2 by examining evidence of identity and employment eligibility with three (3) business days of the date employment begins. If employees are authorized to work, but are unable to present the required document(s) with three business days, they must present a receipt for the application of the document(s) within three business days and the actual document(s) within ninety (90) days. However, if employers hire individuals for a duration of less than three business days, Section 2 must be completed at the time employment begins. **Employers must record:** 1) document title; 2) issuing authority; 3) document number; 4) expiration date, if any; and 5) the date employment begins. Employers must sign and date the certification. Employees must present original documents. Employers may, but are not required to, photocopy the document(s) presented. These photocopies may only be used for the verification process and must be retained with the I-9. **However, employers are still responsible for completing the I-9.**

Section 3—Updating and Reverification. Employers must complete Section 3 when updating and/or reverifying the I-9. Employers must reverify employment eligibility of their employees on or before the expiration date recorded in Section 1. Employers **CANNOT** specify which document(s) they will accept from an employee.

- If an employee's name has changed at the time this form is being updated/reverified, complete Block A.

- If an employee is rehired within three (3) years of the date this form was originally completed and the employee is still to be employed on the same basis as previously indicated on this form (updating), complete Block B and the signature block.

- If an employee is rehired within three (3) years of the date this form was originally completed and the employee's work authorization has expired or if a current employee's work authorization is about to expire (reverification), complete Block B and:
  - examine any document that reflects that the employee is authorized to work in the U.S. (see List A or C),
  - record the document title, document number and expiration date (if any) in Block C, and
  - complete the signature block.

Photocopying and Retaining Form I-9. A blank I-9 may be reproduced provided both sides are copied. The instructions must be available to all employees completing this form. Employers must retain completed I-9s for three (3) years after the date of hire or one (1) year after the date employment ends, whichever is later.

For more detailed information, you may refer to the INS Handbook for Employers, (Form M-274). You may obtain the handbook at your local INS office.

Privacy Act Notice. The authority for collecting this information is the Immigration Reform and Control Act of 1986, Pub. L. 99-603 (8 U.S.C. 1324a).

This information is for employers to verify the eligibility of individuals for employment to preclude the unlawful hiring, or recruiting or referring for a fee, of aliens who are not authorized to work in the United States.

This information will be used by employers as a record of their basis for determining eligibility of an employee to work in the United States. The form will be kept by the employer and made available for inspection by officials of the U.S. Immigration and Naturalization Service, the Department of Labor, and the Office of Special Counsel for Immigration Related Unfair Employment Practices.

Submission of the information required in this form is voluntary. However, an individual may not begin employment unless this form is completed since employers are subject to civil or criminal penalties if they do not comply with the Immigration Reform and Control Act of 1986.

Reporting Burden. We try to create forms and instructions that are accurate, can be easily understood, and which impose the least possible burden on you to provide us with information. Often this is difficult because some immigration laws are very complex. Accordingly, the reporting burden for this collection of information is computed as follows: 1) learning about this form, 5 minutes; 2) completing the form, 5 minutes; and 3) assembling and filing (recordkeeping) the form, 5 minutes, for an average of 15 minutes per response. If you have comments regarding the accuracy of this burden estimate, or suggestions for making this form simpler, you can write to both the Immigration and Naturalization Service, 425 I Street, N.W., Room 5304, Washington, D.C. 20538; and the Office of Management and Budget, Paperwork Reduction Project, OMB No. 1115-0136, Washington, D.C. 20503.

Form I-9 (Rev. 11-21-91) N

EMPLOYERS MUST RETAIN COMPLETED I-9
PLEASE DO NOT MAIL COMPLETED I-9 TO INS

LISTS OF ACCEPTABLE DOCUMENTS

LIST A		LIST B		LIST C
Documents that Establish Both Identity and Employment Eligibility	**OR**	**Documents that Establish Identity**	**AND**	**Documents that Establish Employment Eligibility**

LIST A — Documents that Establish Both Identity and Employment Eligibility

1. U.S. Passport (unexpired or expired)

2. Certificate of U.S. Citizenship (INS Form N-560 or N-561)

3. Certificate of Naturalization (INS Form N-550 or N-570)

4. Unexpired foreign passport, with I-551 stamp or attached INS Form I-94 indicating unexpired employment authorization

5. Alien Registration Receipt Card with photograph (INS Form I-151 or I-551)

6. Unexpired Temporary Resident Card (INS Form I-688)

7. Unexpired Employment Authorization Card (INS Form I-688A)

8. Unexpired Reentry Permit (INS Form I-327)

9. Unexpired Refugee Travel Document (INS Form I-571)

10. Unexpired Employment Authorization Document issued by the INS which contains a photography (INS Form I-688B)

LIST B — Documents that Establish Identity

1. Driver's license or ID card issued by a state or outlying possession of the United States provided it contains a photograph or information such as name, date of birth, sex, height, eye color, and address

2. ID card issued by federal, state, or local government agencies or entities provided it contains a photograph or information such as name, date of birth, sex, height, eye color, and address

3. School ID card with a photograph

4. Voter's registration card

5. U.S. Military card or draft record

6. Military dependent's ID card

7. U.S. Coast Guard Merchant Mariner Card

8. Native American tribal document

9. Driver's license issued by a Canadian government authority

For persons under age 18 who are unable to present a document listed above:

10. School record or report card

11. Clinic, doctor, or hospital record

12. Day-care or nursery school record

LIST C — Documents that Establish Employment Eligibility

1. U.S. social security card issued by the Social Security Administration (other than a card stating it is not valid for employment)

2. Certification of Birth Abroad issued by the Department of State (Form FS-545 or Form DS-1350)

3. Original or certified copy of a birth certificate issued by a state, county, municipal authority or outlying possession of the United States bearing an official seal

4. Native American tribal document

5. U.S. Citizen ID Card (INS Form I-197)

6. ID Card for use of Resident Citizen in the United States (INS Form I-179)

7. Unexpired employment authorization document issued by the INS (other than those listed under List A)

Illustrations of many of these documents appear in Part 8 of the Handbook for Employers (M-274)

Form I-9 (Rev. 11-21-91) N

Works Consulted

AARP Bulletin. 601 E St. N.W., Washington, DC 20049: various volumes.

AARP The Magazine. 601 St. N.W., Washington, DC 20049, various volumes.

Allen, Robert G. *Creating Wealth.* 2nd ed. New York: Simon & Schuster, 1983.

Baldrige, Letitia. *Letitia Baldrige's Complete Guide to Executive Manners.* New York: Rawson Associates, 1985.

Brandt, Rhonda, and Barry L. Reece. *Effective Human Relations in Organizations.* 4th ed. Boston: Houghton Mifflin Company, 1990.

Challenger, James E. Job Decision Isn't Just About the Money [online]. Available: www.suntimes.com/output/challenger/chat, January 16, 2000.

Cicione, Maryellen. Creating a resume for the computer age. *Computer Edge*, Vol. 5, No. 14, April 5, 1999.

Cohen, Herb. *You Can Negotiate Anything.* New York: Bantam Books, 1980.

Denver Post, The. Jobs and Careers, Classified section. Denver: various editions.

Dikel, Margaret Riley. *The Guide to Internet Job Searching.* NTC/Contemporary Publishing Co., 1998–1999.

Graber, Steven. *The Everything Get-a-Job Book.* Avon, MA: Adams Media Corp., 2000.

Gray, James, Jr. *The Winning Image.* New York: American Management Association, 1982.

Greenleaf III, Clinton T., and Stefani Schaefer. *Attention to Detail: A Woman's Guide to Professional Appearance and Conduct.* Chesterland, OH: Greenleaf Enterprises, 2000.

Herzberg, Frederick. *Work and the Nature of Man.* Cleveland: World Publishing Co., 1966.

Holley, William H., and Kenneth M. Jennings. *Personnel Management, Functions and Issues.* New York: CBS College Publishers, 1983.

Lynch, Richard L., Herbert L. Ross, Ralph D. Wray, and Robert J. Welch. *Introduction to Marketing.* New York: McGraw-Hill, Inc., 1984.

MSN Careers, http://msn.careerbuilder.com. Various articles, July 2004.

MSN Money, http://moneycentral.msn.com. Various articles, July 2004.

Nemnich, Mary B., and Fred E. Jandt. *Cyberspace Job Search Kit 2001–2002, The Complete Guide to Online Job Seeking and Career Information.* Indianapolis, IN: JIST Works, 2001.

Occupational Outlook Handbook, U.S. Department of Labor, Bureau of Labor Statistics. Washington, DC: Government Printing Office, 2000.

O'Malley, Michael. *Are You Paid What You're Worth?* New York: Broadway Books, 1998.

Reader's Digest, Box 100, Pleasantville, NY 10572–0100, April 2004.

Reiss, Steven. www.osu.edu/units/research/archive/goals.htm.

Rocky Mountain News. Careers, Classified section, Denver: various editions.

Rosenbloom, Jerry. *The Handbook of Employee Benefits.* Vol. 1, 3rd ed. Homewood, IL: Dow Jones–Irwin, 1984.

Sinetar, Marsha. *Do What You Love and the Money Will Follow.* New York: Dell Publishers, 1987.

Straits, Don. CEO and Dragon Slayer, Corporate Warriors [online]. Available e-mail: don@corporatewarriors.com.

U.S. News & World Report. New York: various editions.

Welcome to Brand You: Creating and Delivering Career Value

How is the workplace changing?

Is Brand You a cool idea or a necessary innovation?

How can marketing strategies benefit my career?

Is my career choice compatible with my personal values?

5

Coca-Cola.   Nike.   The Gap.

Each of these companies has a strong brand name. Even if you haven't sipped the cola, worn the shoe, or bought the jeans, you probably have a clear image of each of these companies and their products.

In your Marketing course, you're learning about the importance of brands and how they're created. This supplement uses the same marketing principles to create Brand You—your own personal brand. This will help you to present yourself to employers as you seek internships and jobs during college, and later to differentiate you from all the other new college grads seeking work.

As CEO of Brand You, you'll discover not only your talents, but also the benefit of those talents and the ways you can add value for your customer—your employer. When you create Brand You, you'll see the workplace from a different perspective, one that allows you to see more clearly the importance of how you perform and present yourself.

Many people create brands for themselves. Rock stars and athletes, for example, create personal brands. We like stars we think we know, so their branding increases the popularity (and sales) of their team or musical group. If you think about political candidates, you'll realize they do it too. Many candidates seem to come out of nowhere. We know little about them or which issues they support. When candidates develop their brand, they create slogans and issue messages so we'll know something about their political views. Then they develop marketing strategies targeted toward their constituents so we'll take action and vote for them. CEOs create personal brands too. When we hear the names Jack Welsh (GE's power broker), Andy Grove (Intel's innovator), Bill Gates (Microsoft's entrepreneur), and Carly Fiona (HP's partnership builder), their reputation enhances our image of the company brand. These unique personal brands attract employees and investors, and even help in high-level negotiations.

You may not aspire to being famous, or even a CEO, yet the same strategies can help you build your career. Creating your brand now will clarify what you can do to prepare for the world of work. It can help you find courses that teach needed skills, as well as other steps to increase your value to employers—like landing an internship or finding a mentor. And, of course, marketing strategies will help you succeed whenever you search for work—you'll be able to communicate your value in dynamic ways.

The importance of branding doesn't stop with your first professional job. By maintaining and refining your brand over your lifetime, you will thrive no matter what the future holds. As CEO of Brand You, you'll be in charge of your career, always looking for special projects and experiences that will increase your value in the marketplace.

The Changing Workplace

Brand You is more than a cool idea. It's a necessity in today's workplace. Welcome to TempWorld—a constantly shifting arena where there's no guarantee of employment, where jobs change faster than the click of a mouse. It's a world where new markets, new technology, and new business models will frequently alter the way you work. Your work will be fast and fluid as you adapt to new challenges. You'll need to master new subjects, establish effective working relationships with a rapidly changing cast of players, and communicate with team members from different disciplines, often without the benefit of face-to-face interaction. This new work environment requires flexibility, continuous learning, and self-management to ensure your employability. In the new workplace, you can expect:

- Increased pressure for innovative products and services.
- A global economy and worldwide opportunities.
- A networked world where work flows from one member of a virtual team to the next, sometimes spanning the globe every twenty-four hours.
- More work options. At times you may have a so-called full-time job, but just as likely there will be times when you'll be an entrepreneur, contract worker, free agent, or job sharer.
- More alternative working arrangements like working from home or working from "third places."
- To retire later than age 65 or not at all. As we live longer, healthier lives, people will be willing to work longer, provided they can have alternative work options.

Fun Fact:
Some economists predict an overall labor shortfall in the United States of 6.6% in the year 2010, growing to 13% by 2020.

In this changing work world, you'll need a twenty-first century mindset, one that's in tune with the new economy. You're at risk if you're expecting a permanent job that will last a lifetime. Instead, re-invent your goal—strive for continuous employability. In TempWorld, you'll have to constantly re-earn your right to employment. You will need to prove and reprove continually that you have the right skills and know-how to be the "best person" for the job. Sounds like the same challenges marketers face to keep their products moving, doesn't it? The contemporary work world will require continuous marketing of your brand. You'll always be on the lookout for the next assignment, and finding ways to prepare for it.

The good news is this is an exciting landscape, where new job titles are created everyday. Just as jobs like Webmaster, Chief Learning Officer, game designer, and fish farmer were unheard of just a few years ago, we can't even imagine the new jobs that will appear in the next decade. Although you can't make any assumptions about job retention, you will still have security—the security that comes from being a career activist, security you create by constantly scanning the horizon for new opportunities to add value.

Whether you are self-employed or working for an organization, you are in charge of your career. The days of corporate career paths are over. It's just as well, for your can adapt to changes in the workplace much more rapidly than a corporation can. People who count on a company to tell them what skills they need usually discover they've become obsolete when the cyber economy takes a new turn. Besides, you wouldn't want to put someone else in charge of your happiness would you?

How Does Branding Increase Success?

Fundamentally, a brand is an identity that sets the product apart from the competition. We usually associate a brand with its logo (like Target's red bull's eye), or with a slogan (like Nike's "Just do it"). In fact, some brands are so powerful that advertisers need few words to describe their products—all we see is the brand name and pictures that evoke an ideal lifestyle. Now we're not suggesting that the hot new interviewing attire is a T-shirt with your personal

Brand:
A name, a term, or a symbol that identifies one firm's products and sets them apart from the competition.

Brand You:
A unique identity and coherent message that sets you apart from the competition.

logo emblazoned on it. Nor are we suggesting you hire a skywriter to stream your message over the stadium at game time. But figuring out the identity you want to communicate to your customers (potential employers) makes a lot of sense. You are a complex human being, with many talents, interests, and viewpoints. Discovering which ones you want to bring to the world of work, and which ones are important to employers are concrete benefits you'll achieve when you develop Brand You.

To develop a brand, marketers study the product to find out what the product can do. They ask, "Why would I want it?" They find the answers in the product's features. What you can do depends on your skills and knowledge. These are your "features." In building your brand, you'll want to answer the following questions: Why would an employer want your skills? What problems can you solve? Next, marketers explore the benefits of the product. They ask, "What will this product do for me?" and "What can I get from this product that's better than the others on the market?" To develop your brand, think about questions like these: What value can you add to an organization? What results will your skills achieve? What is the benefit of the problems you solve?

When your brand is clear to you, just like a marketing expert, you'll know what to communicate to your customer. Because you will have discovered your customer's needs, you'll have confidence that your messages, whether delivered in a cover letter, resume, or interview, will hit the mark. You'll have an effective, coherent message that will entice hiring managers to take action and hire you.

Benefits of Brand You

- A strong identity that you communicate to advance your career
- A focus on your customers' (that is, potential employers') needs
- An understanding of the benefits of your skills, knowledge, and experience
- The development of effective strategies to reach targeted employers
- A new attitude that puts you in charge of your career, able to adapt to change and maintain lifetime employability

Applying Marketing Concepts to Brand You

f course, developing a brand identity is only the first step. Once a brand has been created, it needs to be marketed. Here are three ways marketing concepts apply to Brand You:

1. **Marketing is about meeting needs.** Jobs exist because employers need people who accomplish tasks and solve problems. Your first step in creating Brand You is to discover what kind of employer you want to work for and what kinds of skills and knowledge are needed to accomplish the goals of the position.

2. **Marketing is about creating utility.** Utility creates value. The goal of Brand You is communicating that your skills and knowledge will be useful (that is, meet the needs) to the employer. A person is hired when an employer believes the value of their skills is greater than the cost of their salary. Your challenge is to uncover the benefits that employers look for in

job candidates and then develop the skills that will deliver those benefits. That's why creating Brand You is important to do now. The more you know now about the needs of employers in your target market, the more useful you will be when you graduate. To communicate utility, marketers develop a *value proposition*—a statement that sums up the value the customer will realize if he or she buys the product. This handbook will guide you in developing your own personal value proposition to sum up the value an employer will realize if he or she hires you.

3. **Marketing is about exchange relationships.** Work is the ultimate exchange relationship—you exchange your skills for learning opportunities and compatible work arrangements as well as financial rewards. In an exchange relationship, it's important for both the buyer (your employer) and the seller (you) to be satisfied. Job seekers sometimes make the mistake of taking the first job offered to them. You won't do your best if your don't like the work, the environment, and your boss. You'll spend at least 2,000 hours per year exchanging your skills for pay—that's a very long time if it doesn't fit *your* needs!

Stepping Through the Marketing Process

Creating and marketing Brand You is a decision process, just like any other type of marketing endeavor. In the *Brand You Survival Kit* you will work through the steps of this process. Here's a thumbnail sketch of what to expect:

Step 1 Making Marketing Value Decisions
When company executives develop strategic plans, they look at both the external environment and their internal strengths to evaluate their market position and product plans. For the career planner, recognizing your strengths and deciding which skills you want to use create the building blocks for your plan. In this step you'll get to know your product—you—and how you can apply your skills and knowledge in the workplace. You'll examine ten industry sectors to locate the work environments that fit your interests. You'll learn to search out trends for new opportunities and find employers who will value your skills.

Step 2 Understanding Consumers' Value Needs
In this step, the focus is on your customer, the person who has the power to hire you. You'll discover the general characteristics employers seek in new hires. In addition, you'll examine job descriptions to uncover the specific benefits your customers are looking for.

Step 3 Creating the Value Proposition
In this critical step, you'll develop a statement that summarizes the value you add to an organization. You'll learn techniques for using your value proposition during your search for work and to promote the advancement of your career.

Step 4 Communicating the Value Proposition
Your value proposition becomes the basis for writing dynamic resumes and standing out in job interviews. There are plenty of samples and Do's and Don'ts to make this easy. Finally, you'll develop a marketing plan to reach the employers you've targeted.

Getting to Know Your Product

W hat makes you unique? This question may seem startling, but each of us is quite unique. Your individuality is based on your particular constellation of characteristics, that is, your skills, interests, and personality. In the next few chapters, you'll have an opportunity to discover what makes you unique. Armed with this information, you'll be able to present yourself to employers in a compelling way. After cataloging your talents, you'll be able to describe the types of problems you can solve and the value you bring to an organization. This is an important step in creating your brand.

"If I hear one more person say, 'I'm good with people', I think I'll scream!"

HR Recruiter

There's another important reason to discover your talents. You may know precisely what you want to do upon graduation, but many college students have only a vague idea of their career goal, such as, "I want to go into business." But what exactly do you want to do in the business world? Do you want to manage a brand, train employees, or supervise a production team? Employers expect you to know what work you want to do, and they're likely to ask you why this career field interests you. So whether your career goal is quite definite or you're not sure at all, completing these activities will increase your confidence in your goal or help you discover a goal to pursue.

We've talked about the exchange relationship between you and an employer. People find satisfaction in their work when they know what they want from the exchange. Many people want more than "just a job." They want work that feels important, that makes a difference, and even work that is meaningful or provides a sense of calling. Your work will matter to you if it is aligned with your personal values. Values describe the things you want to get from work—the assets on your side of the exchange ledger. So, the first activity, which follows on the next page, gives you an opportunity to consider what you value.

EXPLORING VALUES

Meiko and Richard have different values and they are reflected in their work environments.

Meiko is part of an organization that is structured around teams rather than a typical organizational hierarchy. Work is distributed to more than 100 self-managed teams. People come together to work creatively and solve problems. Team roles are defined by each person's expertise. Meiko's team operates with very few rules. The ability to get resources and results depends on her ability to persuade others to support her. Meiko enjoys the variety of projects, her role as team leader, and developing leading-edge skills.

Richard's work centers on the belief that the world and its inhabitants deserve respect and care. He's constantly on the move, working in different places around the globe. His knowledge and education assist people with improving their environments and communities. His organization promotes international goodwill. Richard's work is filled with unexpected events requiring mental flexibility. He is free from routine activities and predictable work schedules. To Richard, success means following the direction of your heart.

ACTIVITY 5.1 SPEAKING OF VALUES . . .

Instructions: Read the values and descriptions listed below. Circle the **ten** that are most important to you.

VALUE	DESCRIPTION	VALUE	DESCRIPTION
Achievement	To accomplish important things	**Helpful**	To be of service to others; to contribute to the well-being of others
Advancement	To reach the top in an organization or profession	**High Income**	To be financially successful
Adventure	To take risks; to discover new things	**Influence**	To have influence over decisions; to influence people through my work
Autonomy	To set my own schedule and priorities	**Integrity**	To stand up for my beliefs; to be honest
Balance	To be able to balance my work life with my other interests	**Leadership**	To motivate others to achieve goals
Challenge	To be involved in interesting work; to solve a variety of problems	**Passion**	To care deeply about my work; commitment to a cause
Community	To be a part of a group; to support community activities	**Recognition**	To earn the respect and recognition of others
Contribution	To contribute to society; to have an impact on people's lives	**Security**	To achieve a stable work and financial situation
Creativity	To be original; to express myself	**Self-expression**	To be able to act in a way consistent with my values and beliefs; to be able to express my ideas
Expertise	To be respected for my competence; to be known as an expert in my field	**Spirituality**	To be at peace with myself; to achieve inner harmony
Friendship	To develop friendships at work; to have time for friends	**Structure**	To have order and a predictable work environment
Fun	To have fun; to enjoy my life and work	**Teamwork**	To accomplish goals as a member of a team
Growth	To develop personally and professionally	**Trust**	To work in an environment where people trust each other
Health/Wellness	To be physically and emotionally healthy	**Work independently**	To be responsible for my own accomplishments

(continued)

ACTIVITY 5.1 SPEAKING OF VALUES . . . . Continued

Instructions: In the left hand column, place your top ten values, ranking them from most to least important. Place the value most important to you in the top cell and move down the column in order of preference. Then think about the industry or profession you are considering. How well do you think this value will be satisfied in that work? For example, if you think there is strong compatibility between them, place a check mark in the circle labeled High.*

VALUE	HIGH	MED	LOW
1			
2			
3			
4			
5			
6			
7			
8			
9			
10			

*If you need information about the career you're considering, check out these Web sites:
   www.bls.gov/oco
   http://online.onetcenter.org
   www.collegegrad.com
   www.webfeet.com

Planning Your Career: The Advantage Is Undeniable

How do I develop a career plan?

What are my career strengths?

How can I find career opportunities in trends?

Are you actively planning your career, or are you among the "hang out and hope" category of college students? Students in the hang out and hope group avoid thinking about their future and hope that by graduation day they'll be inspired by a job title that grabs them. Things rarely work out that way. Leaving your career decisions until your senior year is risky. Without a clear sense of direction, you'll miss important opportunities to find mentors among your professors, internships with companies who might hire you, or contacts that could lead to job offers.

As you learned from your *Marketing: Real People, Real Choices* text, "Careful planning enables a firm to speak in a clear voice in the marketplace so that customers understand what the firm is and what it has to offer . . . " As CEO of Brand You, you also want to speak in a clear voice so that employers (your customers) understand who you are and what you have to offer. Actually, this is the whole point of developing Brand You.

Planning crystallizes your dreams. Your career ideas are transformed from a blurred image of vague possibilities to a clear vision of what you intend to accomplish. You'll drill down from the big picture of your strategic career plan to the details—the actions you'll need to take to make your plan a reality. With each step in the process, your career choice will take shape and become clearer. As you work out the details, you'll get a good view of what it will be like to do the work. Then one of two things will happen. Either you'll be more confident about your choice, or you'll realize you need to research a different profession or industry. The latter outcome is frustrating—but better to find it out during the planning stages than after you've accepted the job!

Success is not just doing your job— it's caring about it, the people you work with, and the results you achieve. Success requires a large dose of self-discovery to find what you really care about.

Businesses deliberately choose a time frame of five years for their strategic plans. In today's rapidly changing world, longer views usually prove to be meaningless. The probability of accurately forecasting developments in technology, business processes, and customer expectations beyond five years is very low. A relatively short timeframe gives businesses the flexibility to adapt to changes as they occur.

A five-year plan for your career is about the right length of time, too. You also need a flexible plan agile enough to adapt to changes in the workplace. Beyond five years, it's hard to predict what may happen in your job, your company, your profession, or your industry. In addition, your own personal interests and needs are likely to change over your lifetime. There will be times when your career is front and center, and times when it may take a back seat to raising a family, getting an advanced degree, or some other interest.

The right question. Students often start their career planning by asking the question, *"What do I want to be when I grow up?"* A question that fits our turbulent times better is *"What do I want to do now?"* This keeps you open to exciting possibilities that will develop.

We often hear people ask, "What do I want to be when I grow up?" If they're changing careers, the question is modified slightly to "What do I want to be this time when I grow up?" Career planning isn't about being anything—you're already a real live human being. It's about doing. Rephrase the question to, "What do I want to do with my skills and knowledge now"? With this question in mind, you'll be able to create a flexible plan that allows you to adapt to changes in the workplace—and there will be many! While spending 30 years in the same job may have been OK for your grandparents, it's not likely to be the way your career will unfold. And, besides, many people today think spending 30 years in the same job sounds like a life sentence.

In this chapter, you'll begin working on your strategic career plan. Luckily, you only have one SBU (Strategic Business Unit) to worry about—you. We'll begin where businesses begin, with creating a mission statement. Just like a business deciding on its strategic direction, making career decisions requires both an internal and external analysis. Your internal analysis involves a large dose of self-discovery to uncover your strengths and preferences. In our busy lives governed by to-do lists, we rarely allow ourselves to look inside ourselves and discover our own wants and needs. But without this knowledge, how can you make informed decisions? How will you know what work is right for you? Your external analysis will uncover opportunities in the workplace and identify ways you can apply your skills to meet employer's needs. The information you gather from the internal and external analysis will form the basis of your personal SWOT analysis. Your SWOT will be a great tool to help you prepare for the future and to interview effectively. It will help you see what skills you want to develop as well as new opportunities in the marketplace.

Although businesses look at five-year time frames for their strategic plans, they actually review and revise them every year. After all, within one year, a new start-up can grab market share or a new technology can offer new opportunities. You should review your career plan every year too. That way you'll be able to make incremental changes to your plan. It's much easier to make minor adjustments than to discover too late that your skills are obsolete and you'll have to start in a new career direction.

STUDENT PROFILE—CHRIS

Chris is a sophomore majoring in business. When she entered college, she considered a career in IT. After taking a few computer courses, however, she decided this field wasn't for her. She wanted more interaction with people and a chance to be creative. Right now her career goal is to go into marketing. She thinks she'd like to get involved in Web based marketing, either for a company with a large Web presence or with a marketing consulting firm. Chris would like to be more positive about her career goal. She wants to see if it fits her, so she is completing the activities in Brand You. We'll follow her progress—you'll be able to see examples of someone going through the process.

Create Your Mission Statement

Like an organization's mission statement, your mission statement defines your purpose. It should be narrow enough to give you a sense of focus, but broad enough to adapt to future opportunities. A mission statement that expresses your overall purpose and what you hope to achieve will help guide your search for a career choice now and in the future.

These two different mission statements reflect the differences in Sheryl and Chris' personalities. Sheryl knew she wanted to do a variety of things, yet she liked the idea of having a mission statement to express her purpose. At this point in time, Chris thinks she will try a variety of marketing opportunities during her career, but thinks it will always be her focus. Each mission fits the person who created it.

Your top values will give you some clues about a mission that describes your purpose for working. For example, if your top value is Community, you might try a mission statement similar to this: "To support community activities that sustain our environment." That would give you many options, such as working for the Environmental Protection Agency (EPA); starting a community garden in a low-income neighborhood; promoting a new technology to reduce pollution; or implementing new forest management practices. As varied as these options are, each is aligned with the mission.

REAL LIFE PROFILE

Alberto wrote the following mission statement:
"To bring extraordinary things to ordinary people." His first job, which he found through his local Sister Cities Program, was to teach English to adults in Japan. He signed up for two years, but enjoyed it so much he stayed for four. Now he is back in the United States marketing to art galleries. Both jobs, although very different, fit his mission.

STUDENT PROFILE—CHRIS

Chris wrote this mission statement:
"To create innovative strategies for marketing products and services in unique ways."
This mission fits her current goal of e-marketing, but will it still fit when new technologies change the way products are marketed.

It's true that some people work in order to live (as compared to those who live to work), and you may be one of them. However, this mission statement should focus on your work purpose, not a goal like "To find a balance between work and family." Although aiming for balance is a healthy aspiration, it doesn't guide your career choices, which is what a mission statement should do.

Your Turn:
Write your mission statement below:

To take today's technology & find better solutions for a better tomorrow.

Your Internal Analysis

Your internal analysis begins with uncovering your skills and talents. Skills are the basic building blocks of work. Read a job description and you will see a list of roles, activities, and tasks to be performed. If you broke these down further, you would see that skills make the performance possible. You can break down a job into these components:

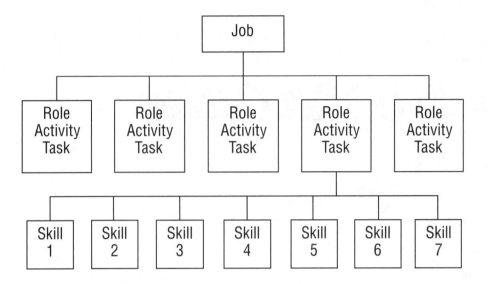

In the next exercise, you will determine your transferable skills. These are skills you can apply to a broad range of situations and settings—that's why they're called *transferable skills*. Consider a skill like resolving conflict. You can use this skill with customers, team members, or even your boss.

Your inventory of skills will help you in several ways. If you are looking for a career direction, research careers to find out which ones rely on the skill you've picked. If you have a career in mind, your skill inventory will increase your confidence that this is the right choice—provided the career is built on the skills you like to use. Finally, your inventory will help you clearly describe your skills so employers know what you have to offer.

Fun Facts:
Companies are starting to work hard to keep their talented employees. They define *talent* as people who have "learning agility."

Working with your preferred skills and talents is one of the key ingredients of career success. Everyone is more effective when they're using the skills they enjoy.

ACTIVITY 6.1 SKILLS INVENTORY

Instructions: To evaluate each skill, recall a time in which you demonstrated the skill, whether at work, in school, or any other area of your life. If you're not sure whether you have the skill, think about how others would describe you. Read each skill and *rate your enjoyment* of using the skill as follows:

V=Very High H=High M=Medium L=Low

Then rate *how effectively you use the skill* in the Degree of Skill column. If you could get paid for using the skill as part of your job, it deserves a score of Medium or higher.

SKILL	ENJOYMENT	DEGREE OF SKILL
Communication		
• Speaking persuasively	☐	☐
• Resolving conflicts, building consensus	☐	☐
• Giving effective presentations	☐	☐
• Developing compelling sales approaches	☐	☐
• Listening effectively	☐	☐
• Writing concisely and clearly	☐	☐
• Interviewing for information	☐	☐
• Giving advice or counseling	☐	☐
• Collaborating with team members	☐	☐
• Instructing, training people to perform new tasks	☐	☐
• Explaining complex ideas in everyday language	☐	☐
Using Information		
• Gathering information, doing research	☐	☐
• Synthesizing complex information	☐	☐
• Programming computers	☐	☐
• Classifying information, devising classification systems	☐	☐
• Evaluating data	☐	☐
• Observing and identifying data	☐	☐
• Solving problems using information	☐	☐
• Creating useful reports for information	☐	☐

(continued)

ACTIVITY 6.1 SKILLS INVENTORY Continued

SKILL	ENJOYMENT	DEGREE OF SKILL
Managing/Leading		
• Motivating, inspiring others to achieve goals	☐	☐
• Developing and communicating a compelling vision	☐	☐
• Managing multiple projects	☐	☐
• Coordinating, organizing work teams	☐	☐
• Mentoring	☐	☐
• Initiating and executing a plan, task, or idea	☐	☐
• Building trust	☐	☐
• Initiating change	☐	☐
• Coaching, developing employees' skills	☐	☐
• Leading individuals and groups to accomplish goals, objectives	☐	☐
Planning		
• Creating effective solutions to problems	☐	☐
• Developing strategies to achieve goals	☐	☐
• Estimating, reviewing project schedules	☐	☐
• Preparing budgets, computing costs	☐	☐
• Establishing cost controls	☐	☐
Creativity		
• Conceptualizing new or creative ideas, methods, structures	☐	☐
• Inventing/designing a new product, object, process, or art	☐	☐
• Generating innovate ideas	☐	☐
• Using intuition	☐	☐
• Visualizing concepts	☐	☐
• Using your imagination	☐	☐

List your strongest skills here:

List skills you want to develop here:

(continued)

A CTIVITY 6.1 SKILLS INVENTORY Continued

SKILL	ENJOYMENT	DEGREE OF SKILL
Customer Service		
• Focusing on customer, client needs	☐	☐
• Building and maintaining relationships	☐	☐
Business Development		
• Generating income	☐	☐
• Identifying and capitalizing on opportunities	☐	☐

List skills you want to develop here:

Your External Analysis

One reason businesses conduct an external analysis is to see how they stack up against the competition. Another reason they scan the external environment is to look for new opportunities. As the authors of *Marketing: Real People, Real Choices* point out, changes in the economy, regulations, consumers, competitors, and popular culture can have a profound impact on a firm's fortunes. Business leaders know it's imperative to identify these shifts and adapt to them.

Your career success will also depend on frequently scanning the external environment. Here are a few of the recent changes that have affected people's employability: technology that replaced human labor, the crash of the dot.coms, outsourcing of manufacturing and administrative functions, restructuring firms to reduce management layers, and off-shoring jobs to third world countries. People who didn't foresee these events were stranded and often spent long periods looking for comparable work.

At the same time, it's important to remember the world is full of new opportunities. Ever since breaking the genetic code, biotechnology has been growing exponentially. The advent of global terrorism has fueled the growth of security products and services. The retirement of baby boomers, the largest population in history, will create many jobs related to leisure activities and anti-aging products. New interconnected devices continue to find their way into the marketplace and affect the way we work and communicate. It's also comforting to note that it will be a long time before computers can replace jobs that require human interaction and creativity.

Savvy careerists scan the environment, searching for new opportunities to use their skills. They also stay up to date with trends in their industry and profession. They constantly develop networks outside their company and stay in touch. Industries and professions are more stable than individual jobs, and they change more gradually.

The next activity, *Finding Opportunities in Trends*, show one way to scratch below the surface of a trend and see how it might impact your career field and provide new work opportunities for you. You might just discover an opportunity on the cutting edge that excites you.

Top Technologies for the Next Ten Years

- Biogenetics
- Super materials
- High-definition energy sources
- Nanotechnology
- Smart manufacturing
- Anti-aging products
- Medical treatments
- Hybrid fuel vehicles
- Edutainment

Fun Fact:
In the United States, 10,000 people turn age 65 everyday, and the crest of the baby boom hasn't reached age 60 yet.

STUDENT PROFILE—CHRIS

When Chris completed the Skills Inventory, she learned her favorite skills were in the areas of Creativity, Communication, and Using Information. A nice fit for a marketing person!

ACTIVITY 6.2 FINDING OPPORTUNITIES IN TRENDS

Instructions: Choose four trends that could affect the career field you're considering. Then decide what the impact of each trend might be. Finally, brainstorm career opportunities that might result. This exercise is fun to do with friends or classmates, and it helps generate more ideas.

TREND	IMPACT	OPPORTUNITY
Males between the ages of 18–34 are watching less TV. They're spending more leisure time with TiVo and video games.	This prime marketing target is viewing fewer TV ads.	Create and sell advertising in new media; e.g., TiVo, video games, on-line games, on-line game sites.

Your Career SWOT

ow that you've identified your mission and your strengths (skills), and discovered some trends that may impact your career, you're ready to try out your personal SWOT analysis.

Chris' SWOT analysis is shown below. She used her Skills Inventory and work experiences to identify her strengths. She read several Web articles about marketing to identify threats and opportunities. In spite of the threats, she's even more excited about her career field.

STUDENT PROFILE—CHRIS

Strengths
- Great organizational skills—able to see the big picture and then figure out how the details relate.
- Leadership ability—often asked to lead study groups, also leader in two campus organizations.
- Good negotiator—solves interpersonal conflicts in study groups and at work.
- Persuader—often gets people to agree to her point of view.
- Enthusiastic, creative.
- Learning marketing theory, strategies.

Weaknesses
- Sometimes, impatient waiting for people to catch up to her ideas.
- Could be a better listener.
- Has so many interests, it's hard to focus on a goal.

Opportunities
- Large number of people retiring, most of whom are Web-savvy.
- Web-based marketing is growing.
- New devices, like handhelds, could be a new resource for marketing.
- More businesses realizing the value of marketing.

Threats
- Web-based marketing is a popular field—competition for jobs.

A CTIVITY 6.3 SWOT ANALYSIS

Instructions: Complete each section of the SWOT analysis. When describing your strengths, use your Skills Inventory and any personal characteristics that will be an asset in the workplace. You may need to do a little research into your career field to identify opportunities and threats.

Internal	*Strengths*	
	Weaknesses	
External	*Opportunities*	
	Threats	

Set Objectives for Brand You

J ust like a business, you're now ready to set objectives that broadly define what you hope to accomplish within the time frame of your career plan. A useful time line might be five years after your graduation. Your objectives should be a direct outgrowth of your mission.

To be effective, your objectives should be specific, measurable (so you'll know whether you've achieved them), and attainable. Attainability is especially important—otherwise you're setting yourself up for a feeling of defeat. Ask yourself, what can you realistically attain within five years?

Your objectives may relate to revenue, your esteem in your profession, types of work you'd like to do, where you might like to live, and so on.

STUDENT PROFILE—CHRIS

Chris wrote the following career goals:

- To obtain a position responsible for developing Web-based marketing strategies.
- To obtain a level of responsibility that fully utilizes my knowledge and skills.
- To work for an organization with annual sales in excess of $10 million.
- To be fairly compensated for my work.
- To be recognized by peers as an expert in Web-based marketing.

Your Turn:
Write your objectives in the box below:

MY CAREER OBJECTIVES

Creating the Product—You: Identifying Your Benefits

How can product layering help you define your strengths?

How can you uncover the benefits you have to offer?

How can you present a professional package?

CHAPTER 7

If you've held part-time jobs during the school year or summer vacations, you may think job hunting is no big deal. If your jobs have been in retail as a part-time clerk, or in the service industry as a server of some kind, your view is pretty accurate. You may have seen a sign in the window, gone in without an appointment, and filled out a job application. A few days later, you were called for an interview, answered a few questions, and were offered the job. It may even have seemed like they'd hire anyone, as long as the person was breathing! In these kinds of low-wage jobs, where turnover is high, that experience is often typical. Getting your first professional job as a college graduate will be a different experience, however.

During your post-college work search, you'll be competing with other new grads and experienced pros. To be successful, new grads must compete at the same level as the pros do. You will need a professional image, a spotless resume, and dynamic responses to interview questions. Seeing yourself as a tangible product can help you prepare for each step of the job search process. Using the concept of product layers can help you break down your preparations so they seem less overwhelming.

The marketing adage cited in *Marketing, Real People, Real Choices* that states, "A marketer may make and sell a 1/2" drill bit, but a customer buys a 1/2" hole" is a good metaphor to keep in mind as you develop your brand. Your skills, knowledge, and experience are your tools—the drill that enables you to perform various tasks. The results you achieve are the benefits of those features—the 1/2" hole. You have many skills and a great deal of knowledge, but an employer buys results—the value you can add to their organization.

The work you'll be doing in this chapter includes essential steps for developing your value proposition. In this chapter, you'll learn exactly how to identify and describe the benefits an employer can expect from you and your work.

You already have most of the information you need. You've evaluated your talents, strengths, and skills on the key dimensions employers seek. You've researched industry sectors and companies within those sectors to gain insider knowledge about the characteristics for success. With this information, you'll be able to develop your unique value proposition.

Defining Your Product Layers

Think of yourself as a bundle of attributes that includes the core features, benefits, packaging, and supporting features of your product. In developing a compelling brand, you want to consider your total package—everything an employer will receive when she hires you. The three product layers are a helpful way to see yourself. Defining each of these layers, as they relate to your job performance, will help you develop your value proposition.

Figure 7.1 shows how a marketing major could adapt the concept of marketing layers to describe himself. No matter what field you plan to enter, you can design a similar graphic. One benefit of this illustration is that you can see the salient features and benefits you want to emphasize during your search for work. Once you've completed the diagram, you can check the items you've included against the information you've gathered about what employers in your industry sector are seeking in job candidates. If you've missed something, add it to your illustration.

Figure 7.1 Sample Product Layers for a Marketing Major

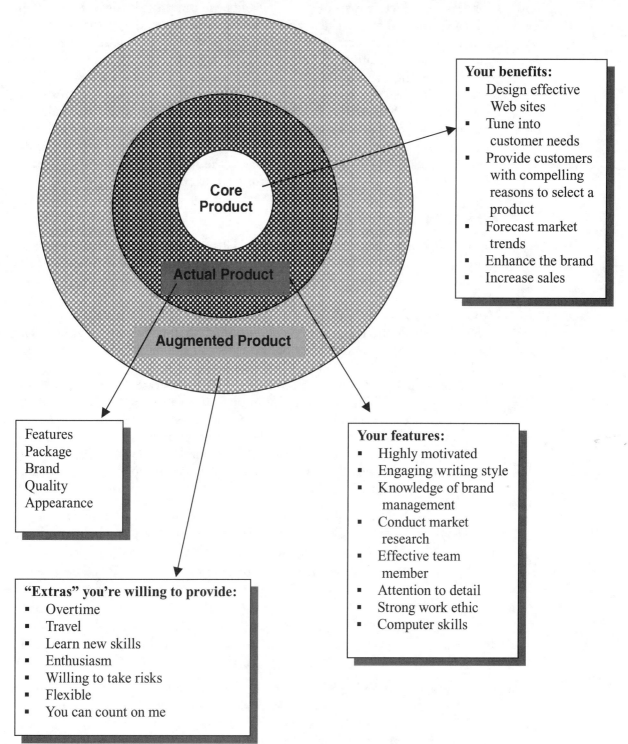

Core Product

Actual Product

Augmented Product

Your benefits:
- Design effective Web sites
- Tune into customer needs
- Provide customers with compelling reasons to select a product
- Forecast market trends
- Enhance the brand
- Increase sales

Features
Package
Brand
Quality
Appearance

Your features:
- Highly motivated
- Engaging writing style
- Knowledge of brand management
- Conduct market research
- Effective team member
- Attention to detail
- Strong work ethic
- Computer skills

"Extras" you're willing to provide:
- Overtime
- Travel
- Learn new skills
- Enthusiasm
- Willing to take risks
- Flexible
- You can count on me

The Core Product

The core product consists of all the benefits you can provide for your customer. Because you have many skills, a wealth of knowledge, and a history of diverse experiences, you can provide many benefits to employers. But as we've said all along, the key to exciting your customers is to zoom in on those benefits that will add value to their enterprise.

Defining benefits is a little more difficult than identifying features (your skills and knowledge). The NAB (Need, Action, Benefit) process will help you pinpoint the benefits you can provide that focus on an employer's needs. These benefits will become critical elements of your value proposition. Knowing the key benefits of your skills and knowledge is the secret to communicating effectively, whether you want to interview for a job or write a dynamic resume.

The NAB Process

Employers want proof that you have the skills you say you do. Many people go into job interviews with a ready list of adjectives. They say something like, "I'm hard working, good with people, and can work in a team environment." Anyone can say these things, but by themselves, they aren't convincing. Being able to talk about how you've demonstrated these skills in the past assures employers that you can deliver the goods. *Employers believe that past performance predicts future performance.* So, if you can describe the skills and the results you achieved, you will convince employers that you'll use them in the future.

The NAB process shows you how you can demonstrate that you've used the skills you're describing. You'll notice in our example that past jobs are not the only reference you can use. For instance, you've used some skills to complete class assignments. If you've been active in campus activities, you've also used skills employers seek. Past jobs, even if they're unrelated to your career field, are also examples that you can use. Of course, if you've completed an internship, you'll have even better examples.

> **Step 1—Need.** What does the employer need or want? Identify an employer's needs and the problems you can solve. Look at job descriptions, talk to employers, read trade journals, and visit Web sites.
>
> **Step 2—Action.** How have you demonstrated each skill? Write down a time when you used each skill or knowledge. Include who, what, where, and why.
>
> **Step 3—Benefit.** What was the result of your action? Describe the results you achieved—the benefit of your skills in the situation. Use numbers, dollars, and percentages whenever you can.

Chris, the marketing student we've been following, used a job description to list the skills important to an employer she has targeted. She added some characteristics she knew from her research were important to hiring managers in marketing departments. After completing this activity, Chris realized she had more experience related to marketing than she thought she had. She was much more confident about her chances to land the kind of job she wanted. You'll be happily surprised too!

MARKETING ASSISTANT

We're Optibiz Corporation, a leading supplier of optics, photonics instruments and components, optomechanical components, positioning equipment, and vibration control. We are currently seeking a detail-oriented and highly motivated marketing assistant. Selected candidate will assist in the development and implementation of promotional marketing activities in our vibration control group. This will include: forecasting marketing trends of new/existing products; developing catalogs, brochures, and other collateral material; tracking and reporting advertising/collateral budget expenditures; implementing trade show efforts; and supporting product management processes. Requires a bachelor's degree in marketing or 3+ years applicable marketing experience. Knowledge of MS Excel is essential. We offer an excellent compensation and benefits package, a leading-edge work environment, and opportunities for professional growth. We invite qualified candidates to send or fax a resume to. . . .

NEED What does the employer need?	ACTION How have you demonstrated each skill?	BENEFIT What was the result?
Detail-oriented	Accounting clerk	Accurately maintained accounts receivable; reduced delinquent accounts by 20 percent
Highly motivated	Worked while maintaining high grade point average	3.8 GPA
Forecast market trends	Marketing class—wrote paper forecasting market trends in publishing	Learned how to research and forecast trends
Develop brochure	Fundraiser	Helped write fund-raising flyer, raised $1,800 for local candidates
Track budget	Treasurer, Young Republicans	We raised 20 percent more money in one year than ever before
Trade show	Canvassed local residents for reelection campaign	Learned to be comfortable informing and persuading public
Excel	Designed new format for reporting accounts receivable	Streamlined reporting and facilitated collections
Develop collateral materials	Term papers	Excellent comments on PowerPoint visuals; writing skills
Communication skills	Speech class, club treasurer	Received an A in speech class; treasurer's reports helped us set goals
Teamwork	Study group	Kept group on track by facilitating discussions—received an A on project
Creative	State Republican Party Web site	Posted articles geared to young people; increased voter registrations by 20 percent

ACTIVITY 7.1 USE NAB TO COMMUNICATE YOUR VALUE

Instructions: Complete the worksheet below using a job description and other information about skills, knowledge, and characteristics that employers in your field seek in job candidates. Write these in the "Need" column. Use your experiences in school, work, internships, or volunteer activities to fill in the "Action" column. Describe the benefits of the results you achieved in the last column.

NEED What does the employer need?	ACTION How have you demonstrated each skill?	BENEFIT What was the result?

The Actual Product

Your actual product is the work you deliver that supplies the desired benefits. In the NAB activity, you identified the features—your skills—that employers in your career field look for in job candidates. Recruiters also evaluate your attitudes toward work. One attitude employers seek is a person who is committed to their career and quality job performance. If you've done your "homework" by researching the company, its products, mission, and culture, you'll be able to convey that you're a determined candidate who takes their job search seriously. You can do this by discussing what you've learned about the company and how your skills match their needs.

Put yourself in the shoes of the employer. If you were recruiting someone for this position, what attitudes do you think would be important? For instance, many employers focus a good deal of attention on customer service. You could discuss ways in which you'll put the customer first. Other attitudes that might be important: self-confidence, a willingness to take on new tasks, a desire to produce top-quality work, and a desire to continue learning. After you've identified important attitudes, think of things you've done—actions you've taken—that demonstrate those attitudes. There's a place for these characteristics on your resume and in the job interview.

Remember, however, your brand will have little meaning if you can't deliver the goods you promised in your interview. This is a key reason why you shouldn't over-promise or exaggerate your abilities.

You are a total package, not just the work you perform. Another major aspect of your package is how you present yourself when job hunting and meeting people. Your transition from student to careerist requires more than trading in your backpack for a briefcase. Your first real impression will likely be made in the first few seconds—right about the time you say, "My name is. . ."

Looking professional takes preparation. Here's the scoop.

- Dress appropriately for the position you are seeking. For a traditional company—established manufacturer, bank, accounting firm—lean toward the formal side by wearing a suit. If, however, you're applying for jobs in a more creative field—design, entertainment, public relations, or advertising—you can show a bit more individuality and flare.

- When in doubt, choose a conservative look. You can't go wrong with neutral colors such as gray, black, or navy. Your clothes don't have to be expensive, but they should fit well.

- Pay attention to details. Scuffed shoes won't cut it.

- Women should avoid too much makeup. Bright over-outlined lips and dark-lined eyes should definitely be avoided.

- Body piercings are better left at home.

- Leave cell phones and pagers turned off and out of sight.

- The perfect accessory is a smile.

The Augmented Product

If you think about it, the "extras" are often the very things that convince you to buy one product over another. If you've purchased a car, for instance, it may have been the warranty or the interest rate that clinched the deal for you.

What are the "extras" you can offer an employer? If you're willing to travel or work overtime, that might be the offer that tips the scale in your favor. However, don't promise what you're not prepared to deliver.

Other extras may relate specifically to the position being discussed. Perhaps you have a solution to a problem that other candidates aren't likely to have. Some successful candidates offer to take classes or attend training to pick up a skill that would be useful to the employer.

Sometimes giving an employer the opportunity to size up your potential sweetens the deal. You might offer to work on contract, or work as a temp through an employment agency. Working arrangements like these involve less risk on the part of the employer, and give both of you an opportunity to test the match between you and the position. Other successful candidates have offered to work as an intern. This is another effective way for the employer to test-drive your abilities. Strategies such as these are useful during a tight job market, of if you really want to work for a particular employer. They aren't always necessary.

ACTIVITY 7.2 MY PRODUCT LAYERS

Instructions: Fill in the boxes below with descriptions of your product layers. This information will come in handy when you write your resume and prepare for networking and interviews.

The benefits I have to offer:

Core Product-- Benefits

My features, etc:

Actual Product

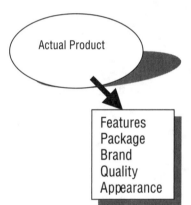

Features
Package
Brand
Quality
Appearance

Extras I'm willing to provide:

Augmented Product

What to Know and Do

That first day on the new job finally arrived. You finished your orientation with the Human Resources Department, met with your manager, and were introduced to some of your colleagues. You were shown your office or workstation and are now ready to get down to business. You are hopeful, excited, stimulated, determined, and maybe just a little nervous. All of these feelings are very typical when starting a new job. This chapter discusses what you must know and do as a new employee to start yourself off on the right foot and continue to travel down your personal path to success.

8

Maximizing Job Performance

The biggest mistake we could ever make in our lives is to think we work for anybody but ourselves.

—Brian Tracy

Chapter Objectives

After completing this chapter, you will be able to:

- Realize the importance of answering the question "Why do I work?"
- Understand how to perform during your probationary period.
- Keep a log of personal accomplishments to use in your formal self-assessment.
- Understand the importance of the annual review to your career advancement.
- Understand what employees should not do while working.
- Apply the New Employees Tips to your personal employment situation.

Fitting In

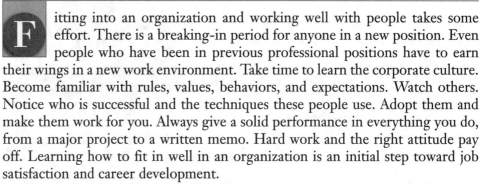

itting into an organization and working well with people takes some effort. There is a breaking-in period for anyone in a new position. Even people who have been in previous professional positions have to earn their wings in a new work environment. Take time to learn the corporate culture. Become familiar with rules, values, behaviors, and expectations. Watch others. Notice who is successful and the techniques these people use. Adopt them and make them work for you. Always give a solid performance in everything you do, from a major project to a written memo. Hard work and the right attitude pay off. Learning how to fit in well in an organization is an initial step toward job satisfaction and career development.

What you should know and do as you begin your new job includes some ideas on what's important to you, how you will be assessed or evaluated, the value of a mentor, good things to do and some things you should not do, and tips for new (and not so new) employees.

What's Important

irst, let's explore what is important to you and how you define success. For most of us, it is important to be employed—to be working. However, different people take different things from their work. Ask yourself, "Why do I work?" "What benefits do I get from what I do on the job?" What is your personal definition of success in your work and your life? Is it having a high salary and good benefits that provide for you and your family? Is it the professional pride you get from being respected for your work? Would you call success your ability to advance into higher positions of responsibility and compensation? How you see your reason for working and how you define your personal success have a lot to do with how you will approach your work and prepare for your future.

Assessment

ne important thing to know about your job is how you will be assessed or evaluated. As a new employee, you may have a probationary period when you first start working.

Probationary Period

What is this probationary period? In many companies, this is the first few months or so when you may be learning the ropes of your job and establishing your typical work behaviors and practices. During this probationary time, you may be given some special assistance or help. Typically, you and your work are looked at more closely than after you become a seasoned employee.

Don't let this idea scare you. It is a very typical procedure. A probationary period is not a problem if an employee is working hard and doing his best to be a productive part of the department or company. However, if a new employee is not completing tasks on time, is spending work time on personal matters, is tardy or has excessive absenteeism, the firm may re-evaluate his position in the company. So, during your first several months of employment in particular, show them the best you've got. Be a model citizen of the organization.

Performance Review

Probationary period or not, you will have a formal evaluation of your work from time to time. In most organizations, this happens once a year and may be called a performance review. If you have had these reviews before, you already have an idea of how they work and the role they play in receiving raises and promotions. If you are not familiar with this assessment tool, a performance review is a written assessment of your work that is used to determine future pay raises and promotions.

Because this assessment usually happens only once a year, keep a record of the projects you did, the kudos you received, and the specific ways you contributed to the department and the company overall. Keep a log of these efforts and save samples of any notable written work you created or to which you contributed. This type of personal file is extremely valuable later on, particularly if you are asked to do any type of self-assessment or self-evaluation. These self-assessments are routinely asked for by managers to help them prepare their employees' annual performance reviews. So, as you begin performing in your new work environment, remember that you will eventually be evaluated. Be as prepared as possible to help your manager give you the glowing performance evaluation that you deserve!

The Value of a Mentor

nother idea to consider as you begin your new employment is to seek out a mentor in the organization. A mentor is someone who can assist you when you have questions, guide you along in your new work environment, and serve as a type of role model. A mentor can be someone you admire and wish to emulate. A mentor can be someone who has achieved success in the organization and can teach you some of the ways to be successful in that particular environment or field. Observe the people around you. Who seems to be successful and admirable? Who would you like to seek out for advice? Selecting and using a mentor in your career can bring you many great benefits.

Either through your immediate manager or perhaps your mentor, find out about your career path in the organization. What is the next position you could aspire to? What is a typical career path for someone in your position, and how long does it usually take to get to the next level? What type of training or education is necessary to get promoted? Who can help you prepare your career path? This is all very worthwhile information to gather.

Good Things to Do in a New Job

ollowing are some good things to do in a new job.

- Understand your probationary period.
- Keep a log of your accomplishments and activities in preparation for your annual review.
- Find a mentor.
- Find out about your career path and how it can be achieved.

Things to Avoid Doing in a New Job

t may seem strange to discuss some things you should not do. However, sometimes what seems to be common sense to us may not be quite that common. The qualities discussed below are surefire ways not to impress a new employer and can lead to serious problems.

Dishonesty and lying.   If an employee lacks integrity, most all other qualities are meaningless.

Irresponsibility, goofing off, attending to personal business on company time.   One who wastes the company's resources and is unreliable may not be trustworthy.

Arrogance, egotism, and excessive aggressiveness.   There is nothing redeeming about someone who spends more time bragging or boasting than working, or one who feels she deserves special treatment or privileges.

Absenteeism and lateness.   If employees are chronically late or absent, most employers feel they don't deserve to be paid for time they did not work and work they did not do.

Other undesirable traits include not following instructions, ignoring company policies, laziness, lack of enthusiasm, making ill-informed decisions, and taking credit for work done by others.

Closing Advice

The box on the following page offers tips for new (and not so new) employees. To some of you, this advice may seem like common sense. However, most of us can benefit from it.

In addition to these tips, there are some additional considerations: Set your own personal work goals, be willing to put in long days, make sure your dress is appropriate for your office and the dress code, limit personal calls and other communications, observe proper business meeting etiquette, learn how to handle stress and work overloads, foster positive business relationships, and seek a balance in your life. This advice is useful for all of us to keep in mind, whether we are new employees or experienced professionals!

Obviously, there is a lot more to know and do as a new employee, but, hopefully, this chapter touches on some important considerations. Your work ethic, your personal and professional standards, and your treatment of others all combine to make you who you are on and off the job. You are working for a variety of reasons. Your work is a major part of your life. Work hard and enjoy the benefits. Work is an essential ingredient to success. In the words of Mark Twain, "The dictionary is the only place where success comes before work."

TIPS FOR NEW EMPLOYEES

- Watch how things are done in the company. Observe the business culture and how people interact personally.

- Be sensitive to a diverse work culture. Because you will be working with people from different ethnic and cultural backgrounds, you must understand the different ways others think, communicate, and act.

- Be respectful of others' time. Use it wisely and don't assume it is owed to you. Time is precious to everyone, especially in today's face-paced and demanding business world.

- Be careful with the way you use communication technology. It can be your best friend or your enemy. Electronic business communications should be professional, clear, concise, and correct.

- Understand that you will make mistakes, but realize that's how you learn. A wise person once said that mistakes are just lessons you haven't learned yet.

MY FOCUS

Following are ways you can implement some of the suggestions found in this chapter.

Make a list of traits you feel a good employee must have. You may use traits from the chapter and include your own original ones. After each trait, indicate the level (on a scale of 1 to 10, with 10 being the best or highest) that best reflects your level of that trait. If you rank a trait low for yourself, write a suggestion of how you could make that trait stronger in yourself.

Join a professional organization that relates to your field. (Many employers will pay for professional memberships for employees.) Get to know individuals in that organization who may serve as mentors or guides for your own career. Ask your potential mentor if you could shadow him or her sometime to see how he or she performs on the job.

The night before you start your new job, create a folder to bring to your office. This folder can have a descriptive title such as "Brag Folder" or "My Best Stuff" or even "What I've Done All Year." Place the folder in a convenient but discreet spot and remind yourself to place material in it when appropriate.

FINDING YOUR FOCUS

1. What is your personal definition of success and how will it guide you in your new job?

2. What is your impression of a probationary period for employees? Is it warranted? Unfair? Why?

3. If you have experienced performance reviews before, what is your opinion of them? How are they useful? How can they be damaging?

4. Review the Tips for New Employees in this chapter. Which do you consider to be the top two to keep in mind?

Career Success Skills

You finally made it through the process. You successfully assessed and marketed yourself, and assembled and used marketing tools to get the job you wanted. You interviewed well and convinced the employer that you were the best person for the job. You have a good idea of what to do on the job to maximize job performance. There is just one more thing to keep in mind: career success skills. These skills don't pertain just to new employees. They are relevant for new, experienced, and even senior-level employees. They are called career success skills because they are extremely important in the work setting. They can be considered life success skills as well.

So, what are some of these career success skills? There has been much written about the skills and traits that employers want today. Although no two lists of desirable skills or traits are the same, many share similar qualities. A couple of these lists appear later in this chapter, but for now let's examine some of the basic skills that are desirable in any work environment.

9

BEING THE BEST YOU CAN BE

Let us realize that the privilege to work is a gift, that power to work is a blessing, that love of work is success.

—David O. McKay

Chapter Objectives

After completing this chapter, you will be able to:

- List the basic career success skills necessary for top job performance and career success.
- Apply the top 10 traits employers seek to your personal profile of traits.
- Recognize the difference between employee skills and personal values and characteristics.

Basic Skills

I f you saw a list of the most basic career success skills the list would look something like this: reading, writing, speaking, listening, teamwork, and problem solving or creativity. You may have expected to see the first four skills, but might have been a little surprised by the last two. Let's take a look at each individually.

Reading

This seems pretty basic, doesn't it? Actually, this refers not only to the reading skills one uses on the job, but also the ability to read and learn in general. With all of the information at our fingertips in today's technological world, how does one stay ahead? Employees must be able to read, skim, summarize, synthesize, and manipulate what they read. They must have a strong vocabulary, not only in their own field, but in business, industry, technology, and even in science. Reading is essential to learning.

Writing

Writing has always been essential to conveying ideas or informing, persuading, and communicating on a personal basis. In today's culture of electronic written communications such as e-mail, writing has continued to be an important skill. From creating basic business correspondence (memos, letters, proposals, reports) to creating and sending electronic information, employees must have good writing skills. Of course, clear writing reflects clear thinking, so these two skills go hand in hand.

The three key features critical to successful writing on the job are clarity, conciseness, and correctness. Successful writers present their ideas clearly. They know how to communicate ideas carefully and accurately. Good writers are also concise. No one has time to read through unnecessary words or ideas. Although conciseness in writing has always been important, in today's fast-paced world, being able to communicate ideas in a streamlined yet complete manner is essential. Correctness is another factor of successful communication skills. Our image is reflected in how we communicate. If our writing is full of mechanical errors and awkward wording, our readers will not think much of our message or us.

Speaking

This skill goes beyond public speaking. Although public speaking can be key to your future career success in some instances, your general interpersonal communication skills are on display all the time. In addition to being able to compose and deliver a good speech to an audience, you must be skilled and confident when addressing smaller groups of people during a business meeting, business luncheon, or professional conference. Just as you may be judged by the clothes you wear, you are always being evaluated by your speech.

Listening

Not much is said or taught about the skill of listening. But consider this: you probably spend a large part of your day on the job listening to people—in meetings, personal conversations, on the telephone, and talking to clients. Listening is a skill—and an important one. Successful listeners give their complete attention to the speaker. At the same time, they mentally summarize what the speaker is saying, analyze the information, and formulate a clear response to the message. The ability to listen is a critical skill that all employees must have. Miscommunication in the workplace can be very costly on many levels.

Teamwork

Some time ago, the average worker was able to do her job alone. No one else was needed. The individual worker knew all that was necessary to get the job done. Fast forward to today. The world, and particularly the business world, is full of complexities and rapidly evolving innovation. One person alone doesn't have all of the knowledge and skills to get the job done. Increasingly, grouping workers into teams has been necessary to share knowledge and information as the team moves toward a common goal.

What does it take to work well in teams? It takes an understanding of different communication styles, particularly those of people from diverse cultures. It takes a willingness to share responsibility and accountability. It requires that you practice give and take and sometimes conflict resolution to solve problems and continue to move forward. Teamwork allows us to share one another's talents. Teamwork skills are highly sought after by today's employers.

Problem Solving and Creativity

In today's complex society and global marketplace, companies need employees who are equipped to solve problems efficiently and effectively. They need people who can take data/facts/information, draw conclusions, and make appropriate recommendations. They need people with fresh approaches to situations, people who can handle change and the challenges of a global marketplace. Thinking "outside of the box" is important in a society where creativity is required to solve challenging problems.

Specific Skill Sets

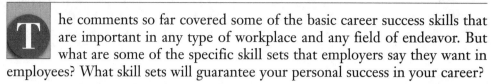 he comments so far covered some of the basic career success skills that are important in any type of workplace and any field of endeavor. But what are some of the specific skill sets that employers say they want in employees? What skill sets will guarantee your personal success in your career?

Skills Needed to Get Ahead

The first list of skills needed to get ahead in the current work culture was mentioned in a presentation given by Dr. Phillip D. Gardner, Research Director at the Collegiate Employment Research Institute at Michigan State Universities. Following are some of the conclusions from that presentation:

- In today's workplace, everyone has to be professional.
- Learning is now a job requirement, and employees must have agility.
- The linear thinking of yesterday will not work with the abstract systems of today.
- Employees must be aware of and learn from the gurus in their fields.
- Employees need organizational savvy in order to get things done.
- Employees need to go well beyond their typical job descriptions to be successful.
- The more you know and can do successfully on the job, the more freedom, flexibility, and autonomy you are given.

Finally, Dr. Gardner indicates that in the workplace of today and the future, with our culture stuck in fast-forward, the prize is not what you know, rather how quickly you can innovate.

Another list of employee traits was found in an article published by a U.S. university system. The article summarizes 10 capabilities looked for by corporations in their new employees.*

Top 10 Traits Employers Seek

Excellent verbal and written skills.   Employers emphasize the ability to communicate clearly to teammates, peers, superiors, and subordinates.

Ability to turn theory into practice.   Higher-level thinking is always desirable; however, companies need personnel who can put into practice what they know, people who can get results.

Working well in groups.   Companies want team players. Employers often want employees who can work well in teams of four to six people. Such teamwork also requires that team members be able to function well with those of different ethnic and social backgrounds.

Flexibility.   Rapid advances in technology and customer needs combine to make constant demands on companies and their employees. Employees must be able

Adapted from pamphlet "Survival of the Fittest," published originally by DeVry University.

to adapt to and use new structures, programs, and procedures. They should be flexible and willing to change as needed.

Problem solving. Critical-thinking skills and good communication skills are essential for today's employees. They must be able to recognize, define, and solve work-related problems efficiently and effectively.

Creativity. Employers value those who can go beyond currently accepted models to find original solutions. Realizing that each challenge requires a unique answer, individuals must have the confidence needed to take risks and try new and different ideas.

Living a balanced life. Today's world is full of stresses. How you deal with these stresses helps to determine who and what you are. Those who lead lives balanced with outside recreational and social activities are better adjusted and more productive workers.

Time management. Managing time and meeting schedules and deadlines are important. Competing responsibilities and multiple work tasks can often be challenging. Effective employees are those who handle their responsibilities dependably and in an efficient manner.

Fearlessness. Although employers do not want reckless behavior in their employees, they do find that breakthrough successes require professionals who are not afraid of failure. Also, employees who do fail must learn from those failures, adapt, and try again.

Commitment. Being committed and dedicated to corporate or group goals is crucial. Loyalty and goal orientation are key traits. Employees possessing these traits are seen as cornerstones of the corporation. These are the individuals who are responsible for the company's long-range success.

Skills and Values Prized by Employers

A final list of skills and values prized by employers is presented in an article entitled "What Do Employers *Really* Want? Top Skills and Values Employers Seek from Job-Seekers" by Randall S. Hansen and Katharine Hansen.* Their discussion of skills and values prized by employers is summarized here.

Skills Mentioned Most Frequently

According to the Hansens, studies have identified several important employee skills, sometimes called soft skills due to their nontechnical nature. The following list includes those skills mentioned most frequently by employers.

1. *Communication skills (listening, verbal, written).* This was the one skill mentioned most often.
2. *Analytical/research skills.* Individuals must assess situations, seek different perspectives, and identify key issues.

*Copyright by Quintessential Careers and found at QuinCareers.com, an online career development Webpage. Used with permission.

3. *Computer/technical literacy.* A basic understanding of software and hardware, such as word processing, spreadsheets, and e-mail, is required.

4. *Flexibility/adaptability/managing multiple priorities.* This is the ability to handle multiple assignments, set priorities, and adapt to change.

5. *Interpersonal abilities.* The ability to relate to coworkers, inspire others, and manage conflict.

6. *Leadership/management skills.* This includes taking charge and managing workers.

7. *Multicultural sensitivity/awareness.* Some feel that there is no bigger issue in the workplace than diversity. Employees must show an awareness and sensitivity to other people and cultures.

8. *Planning/organizing.* The ability to design, plan, organize, and implement projects; includes goal setting.

9. *Problem solving/reasoning/creativity.* Solving problems with powers of creativity, reasoning, and past experiences in combination with available information and resources.

10. *Teamwork.* The ability to work with others in a professional manner while working toward a common goal.

Personal Values Employers Seek

In their article, the Hansens also present a list of personal values employers want in their employees. Although the specific skills already mentioned are critical to career success, what the employee is or values is as important as what he can do. Values, personality traits, and personal characteristics are also critically important to career success and satisfaction. Following are some values mentioned in the Hansens' article.

1. *Honesty/integrity/morality.* Employers probably respect personal integrity more than any other value.

2. *Adaptability/flexibility.* Being open to new ideas, working in teams or alone, multitasking.

3. *Dedication/hard working/work ethic/tenacity.* Employers want and value employees who love what they do and will stick with the job until it's done.

4. *Dependability/reliability/responsibility.* Punctual employees who have a keen sense of responsibility.

5. *Loyalty.* Devotion to the company under a variety of conditions.

6. *Positive attitude/motivation/energy/passion.* These are people with drive and passion, who show enthusiasm with their words and actions.

7. *Professionalism.* Acting in a responsible and fair way, signs of maturity and self-confidence, lack of pettiness.

8. *Self-confidence.* Obvious belief in what you can do and in your mix of skills, education, and abilities.

9. *Self-motivated/ability to work with little or no supervision.* Although teamwork is a coveted ability, so is the ability to work independently with minimal direction.

10. *Willingness to learn.* No matter the employee's age or experience, an open attitude to learn new skills or techniques is vital.

Being the best you can be on the job requires much of you. You must cultivate the skills and traits most prized by employers and personify the values and attitudes that lead to success on the job. With the right combination of these skills, traits, and personal values and attitudes, you will be successful in achieving long-term career growth and personal satisfaction.

MY FOCUS

Several lists of desirable skills and traits have been discussed in this chapter. Review the lists, and make your own list of the ones that were mentioned the most.

Next, circle the ones you feel you currently possess to a high degree. Next, take a look at the other skills and think about how you may work at developing these.

A variation on this activity is to involve a peer or coworker who knows you and your work well. Ask this person to write down a list of your most prominent work traits, skills, and attitudes. Compare this list to the lists in this chapter and see which ones others believe you possess. Note which ones you still could use some work on.

FINDING YOUR FOCUS

1. Using the following skills discussed at the beginning of the chapter, rank them in order of importance according to your personal experience. Be able to justify your ranking.

    _____ Reading

    _____ Writing

    _____ Speaking

    _____ Listening

    _____ Teamwork

    _____ Problem solving/creativity

2. According to the Hansens' article, a fact in today's workplace is that "everyone has to be professional." What does it mean to you to be professional? Ask others and see if their definitions agree with yours.

3. Define agility. Why is that a necessary skill for today's employees?

4. Commitment to the company is a skill that is desired by employers today. Does this desire seem realistic considering the tendency of many employees to change jobs and companies rather frequently? Do you feel the value of commitment to a company is important? Why or why not?

Index